# Dr Brian Iddon

# SCIENCE & POLITICS:
## AN UNLIKELY MIXTURE

AUTOBIOGRAPHY, 1940-2010 (VOLUME 1)

# Dr Brian Iddon

# SCIENCE & POLITICS:
## AN UNLIKELY MIXTURE

AUTOBIOGRAPHY, 1940-2010 (VOLUME 1)

**MEMOIRS**
Cirencester

# OTHER BOOKS AND SELECTED CONTRIBUTIONS IN JOURNALS AND BOOKS BY THE SAME AUTHOR

*James Lawrence Isherwood* (1917-1989), a biography,
Memoirs Publishing, Cirencester, 20 December 2013.

"Science in Parliament", *Memoirs and Proceedings of the Manchester Literary & Philosophical Society*, 2012, **149**, pp. 24-37.

"Government Seeks More Impact from Its Research Investment", *Future Medicinal Chemistry*, 2009, **1**(3), pp. 427-430.

"Fizz, bang, whizz behind the magic show", B. Iddon, R. Lancaster and C. Stirling, *Chemistry in Britain*, 1993, **29**, 656-657.

*Bromine Compounds: Chemistry and Applications*, (D. Price, B. Iddon and B. J. Wakefield, eds.), Elsevier, Amsterdam, 1988, 181-251.

*The Magic of Chemistry*, published by B.D.H., Poole, Dorset, 1985 (a booklet based on a 90-minute demonstration lecture) (out of print but copies can be found for sale on the internet).

"Polychloroheterocyclic Compounds", B. Iddon and H. Suschitzky, in *Polychloroaromatic Compounds* (H. Suschitzky, ed.), Plenum Press, 1974, pp. 197-364.

**Mereo Books**

1A The Wool Market Dyer Street Cirencester Gloucestershire GL7 2PR
An imprint of Memoirs Publishing www.mereobooks.com

Science and Politics: An unlikely mixture: ISBN 978-1-86151-364-9

First published in Great Britain in 2015
by Mereo Books, an imprint of Memoirs Publishing

Copyright ©2015

Dr Brian Iddon has asserted his right under the Copyright Designs and Patents Act 1988 to be identified as the author of this work.

A CIP catalogue record for this book is available from the British Library.

This book is sold subject to the condition that it shall not by way of trade or otherwise be lent, resold, hired out or otherwise circulated without the publisher's prior consent in any form of binding or cover, other than that in which it is published and without a similar condition, including this condition being imposed on the subsequent purchaser.

Although the author has made every effort to ensure that the information in this book was correct when going to press, he does not assume and hereby disclaims any liability to any party for any loss, damage or disruption caused by errors or omissions, whether such errors or omissions result from negligence, accident, or any other cause. The views expressed in this book are purely the author's.

The address for Memoirs Publishing Group Limited can be found at www.memoirspublishing.com

The Memoirs Publishing Group Ltd Reg. No. 7834348

The Memoirs Publishing Group supports both The Forest Stewardship Council® (FSC®) and the PEFC® leading international forest-certification organisations. Our books carrying both the FSC label and the PEFC® and are printed on FSC®-certified paper. FSC® is the only forest-certification scheme supported by the leading environmental organisations including Greenpeace. Our paper procurement policy can be found at www.memoirspublishing.com/environment

Typeset in 11/16pt Plantin
by Wiltshire Associates Publisher Services Ltd. Printed and bound in Great Britain by Printondemand-Worldwide, Peterborough PE2 6XD

# CONTENTS

ACKNOWLEDGEMENTS
DEDICATION
ABOUT THE AUTHOR
PROLOGUE

## PART 1: EARLY LIFE AND EDUCATION

CHAPTER 1 - Early years on the West Lancashire Plain    P.1

CHAPTER 2 - Teenage years; a wake-up call    P.70

CHAPTER 3 - Hull University    P.114

## PART 2: A CAREER IN CHEMISTRY

CHAPTER 4 - Starting my career as a chemist    P.158

CHAPTER 5 - Continuing my career in Salford    P.177

CHAPTER 6 - Experiences as a Safety Officer    P.224

CHAPTER 7 - Opportunities to travel    P.236

CHAPTER 8 - The Magic of Chemistry    P.260

    Photographs and Illustrations    P.290

    Index    P.292

# ACKNOWLEDGEMENTS

∽

I want to thank all those who have shared my life with me, whether they are mentioned in this book or not, especially my close family and those who have inspired me in any way. I thank my wife Eileen, my daughters Sally and Sheena, Merrilyn Guest*, my brother Graham, my good friends John and Elaine Hartshorne, Dr Tom McC. Paterson, Dr Michael Rodgers, George Caswell and Cllrs Noel Spencer and Frank White for reading the manuscript and for spotting factual errors and suggesting improvements to the original manuscript. Any remaining errors of fact are entirely mine. I also thank Karen Lawrinson for her help in preparing the manuscript.

This book would not have been possible without the excellent professional help I received from Chris Newton, Tony Tingle and designer Ray Lipscombe at Memoirs Publishing, and I thank them also.

*Merrilyn, my first wife, sadly died at the age of 69 on 20 May 2014 in Ireland. Eileen, my second wife, and I attended her funeral at the Hop Kiln, Risbury Court, near Leominster, on 12 June.

This book is dedicated to my mother and father,
Violet Stazicker and John Iddon.

# ABOUT THE AUTHOR

Brian Iddon was born on the West Lancashire Plain in Tarleton and educated at Tarleton C of E Primary School, Christ Church Boys' Secondary Modern School and the Technical College in Southport, and at the University of Hull from where he graduated in 1961 with a BSc in Honours Chemistry. He was awarded a PhD by the university in 1964 and a DSc in 1981.

He was employed teaching and researching chemistry at the Universities of Durham (1964-1966) and Salford (1966-1997) and became well-known for presenting a demonstration lecture The Magic of Chemistry throughout Britain and in Europe.

Brian was elected to Bolton Metropolitan Borough Council in 1977 and held various positions and served several committees of the Council until 1997, when he was elected to Parliament in the safe Labour seat of Bolton South East, from which he retired in 2010. He was chairman of Bolton's Housing Committee from 1986 to 1996.

Brian's interests in Parliament covered a multitude of topics in the education, health and social services, housing, home affairs and science and technology policy areas. He grasped some controversial subjects such as the policy on illicit drugs, euthanasia, legislation surrounding health food products, the Middle East Peace Process and Kashmir. He helped to steer through three Acts of Parliament and was a member of the Science and Technology Select Committee.

Today, apart from his various writing projects, he holds a number of voluntary posts in the science policy area, in education and with a community charity.

# PROLOGUE

Why did I decide to write the story of my life? They say that there is a book in everyone; the problem is that the story has to be recorded in some way to be of any benefit to others. Many fascinating stories have passed away with the people who knew them best. In any case, I have a passion for writing and I have always been interested in local history.

I believe that I have had an interesting life which reflects the social and political history of my time, and I hope future generations will gain something from me telling 'My Story'. But, I write it mainly for my children and grandchildren and their children and grandchildren to read.

I have always regretted that I didn't find out more about my family from those who knew the facts before they passed away. Sadly, genealogical searches only reveal the bare facts of a life and not its intimate details. Here then is the story of 70 years (1940-2010) of my life.

'My Story' is divided into four parts. In Part 1 I describe my early years on the West Lancashire Plain, my primary and secondary school education and my decision to be a chemist, ending up with three degrees from Hull University (BSc in 1961, PhD in 1964 and DSc in 1981).

In Part 2 I write about my academic life, beginning at the University of Durham in 1964 and ending at the University of Salford in 1997. There are separate chapters on my role as the Safety Officer in what was at the time the largest department of chemistry in Britain and on presenting The Magic of Chemistry.

In Part 3, I discuss my involvement in politics in Bolton.

I always said that I had three careers before my election to Parliament in 1997. I was a Reader in Organic Chemistry at the University of

Salford, where I also ran a research group; I presented a 'stage show' entitled The Magic of Chemistry, which became quite famous; and I served on Bolton Council for 21 years (10 as chairman of the Housing Committee). As a result, Bolton made me an Honorary Alderman in 1998 for my services to the town.

I was privileged to be elected to Parliament in the Blair landslide General Election of 1 May 1997, with a huge majority, 25,211, and a significant turnout of 65.2% for a safe seat, which was an indication of how fed up the electorate were with the Tories under John Major's leadership. People had had enough of 'Thatcherism' and it was time for a change (a powerful political slogan). It was the first time that Bolton had returned three Labour Members of Parliament, the others being David Crausby (in the Bolton North East Constituency), previously a lathe operator and shop steward in the engineering industry, and Ruth Kelly (Bolton West), an economist and journalist. She was Head of the Bank of England's Inflation Report Division when she was selected. Being elected to Parliament was the high point in my political career. Life in Westminster is discussed in Part 4 of 'My Story'.

Because my autobiography might be of interest to two separate groups of readers, I have decided to divide it into two volumes; the first volume is about my early life, education and career in chemistry (1964-1997) and the second volume is about politics, both in Bolton and Westminster (1972-2010).

Brian Iddon | July 2014

SCIENCE AND POLITICS:
AN UNLIKELY MIXTURE

# PART 1

~

# EARLY LIFE & EDUCATION

# CHAPTER ONE

# EARLY YEARS ON THE WEST LANCASHIRE PLAIN

My father was one of five brothers and two sisters who I came to know as my close family. Grandma Iddon (her maiden name was Alice Miller), who I frequently visited, lived on Church Road, Tarleton, in the 'old school house' at the junction of Hesketh Lane and Church Road (113 Church Road is unrecognisable today; it is occupied by Express Instrument Hire). My paternal grandfather, Richard Iddon, who was a butcher, died before I was born.

The dominant feature of the living room of the 'old school house', which had an uneven stone-flagged floor, was a blacklead grate which my grandma used to prepare all her food. A large metal kettle was ready on a hob to be swung over the log fire to brew mugs of tea whenever visitors called. Fresh bread and pies were baked and the meat roasted in the large blacklead oven, heated by the fire. Bolted to one wall of this living room was a large iron ring which, I was frequently told, was used to tie up naughty schoolchildren when the building was used as a school house. Grandma Iddon usually sat in a large wooden rocking chair placed before the fireplace.

The 'old school house' had a stone-flagged pantry which dropped below ground level by a step or two to keep it cool. It had thick stone walls and beams along the ceiling on which cured hams and sides of bacon were hung, along with dried onions and herbs such as sage. There were large stone jars too, containing salt, which my father used to cure meat on the large stone slabs which were supported by the thick stone walls. I helped my dad break up the large blocks of salt that came from the Cheshire salt mines on the stone slabs. Fruit was kept cool in this pantry, and Dad kept his seed potatoes there over the winter so that they would sprout in time for the spring planting season. The fresh milk was stored there too; it came from Howard's farm across Church Road.

Behind the 'old school house' was a large orchard, where I picked apples, pears and plums with my father when autumn came. He kept geese and chickens in the orchard. I took a dislike to the geese, which were taller than I was, and charged me in an alarming way until my father knocked them away.

One of our family treasures is a photograph of the Iddon family, taken in 1913, sitting at the end of the drive of the 'old school house', with Howard's farmhouse in the background. It shows Robert (then aged 19), William (20), Ellen (22) and Henry (17) on the back row, John (my father, then only 11), mother Alice, father Richard, and Richard (13) on the middle row, and Alice (5) and Betty (9) on the front row.

Altogether, Alice Iddon gave birth to ten children. She lost Miriam, born after Alice, and James, born after Henry, when they were only six months old, and Betty died at the age of ten, not long after the photograph was taken. Alice and Richard

Iddon also adopted a nephew, John Iddon, at the age of nine, shortly after they were married in 1892. Tragically, John was killed in World War I on active service, on 26 February 1919.

My paternal grandparents are buried in St Mary's Church graveyard, on the A59 Preston to Liverpool road, in a grave marked with a military tombstone and carrying the inscription '84598 Private J. Iddon, The Kings Liverpool Regiment, 26 Feb 1919'. Miriam, James and Betty, as well as John, are probably also buried in this family grave.

With one exception, Henry Iddon, who is buried in the graveyard of Old Becconsall Church, overlooking the boatyard on the River Douglas at Hesketh (Bank), this generation of the Iddon family are buried in St Mary's Church graveyard in Tarleton. With the exception of Uncle Bob, who served in the navy, they lived and worked in Tarleton all their lives. St Mary's Church is a lovely Georgian building which today is only used in August on what the locals call 'old church Sunday'. The church has a small balcony. Downstairs there are private pews for the wealthier families near the altar and plain wooden benches at the back for the main congregation.

William Iddon (known as Bill) worked for Lancashire County Council's Water Board, Robert Iddon (known as Bob) was a stoker of boilers, initially in the navy then at the cotton mill in Tarleton, Henry Iddon was a blacksmith, Richard Iddon was a market gardener and coal merchant, Alice Iddon married a basket maker, John Thomas Thompson, and Ellen Iddon married Percy Lunt Johnson, who died in 1929 before I was born, and worked most of her life on the land until illness disabled her. These were my uncles and aunts on the Iddon side of our family. We were a close family.

Photograph of the Iddon family in 1913 taken in the drive of the 'old school house', Church Road, Tarleton: back row – Robert, William, Ellen and Henry; middle row – John, mother Alice, father Richard and Richard; front row – Alice and Betty.

The 'old school house' in Church Road, Tarleton; home of the Iddon family (the original house, now rendered, was built partly of stone and partly of handmade bricks).

## SCIENCE AND POLITICS: AN UNLIKELY MIXTURE

View of Howard's farm taken down the drive of the 'old school house' - from where the 1913 photograph was taken.

Saint Mary's Church and graveyard, Tarleton.

Becconsall Church and graveyard.

The Iddon family grave in St Mary's Church graveyard.

The five Iddon brothers (left to right): Dick, Harry, Bill, Bob, and Jack (my father), with Cousin Frank, Brother Graham and me on the front row.

Grandma Iddon and Cousin Richard Thompson

Grandma Iddon (seated), with Uncle Bob and Cousin Harry (standing)

Grandad Iddon

Grandad Iddon

Tarleton Women's Institute: front row – Aunt Alice Thompson (second left), Aunt Ellen Johnson (fourth left), Aunt Jane Ellen Iddon (second right); Grandma Iddon is in the second row under the clock, wearing a lapel pin.

The wedding of Uncle Dick and Aunt Ada; my father is seated on the extreme left and Aunt Alice is standing on the extreme right.

Wikipedia lists only five well-known people from Tarleton: David Ball, a sport shooter; myself; Richard Iddon (my Uncle Dick), listed as a forward, playing football for Tarleton FC, Preston North End FC, Leyland FC, Chorley FC and Manchester United FC (1925-1927); Dame Nancy Rothwell DBE, FRS, a physiologist, who became President and Vice-Chancellor of the University of Manchester in 2010; and Dave Sutton, another footballer, who played for Plymouth Argyle FC, Reading FC, Huddersfield Town FC, Bolton Wanderers FC and Rochdale FC.

In the 1940s and up to the time that I went to university in 1958, the Iddon name was almost unknown outside the villages of Hesketh Bank and Tarleton. I was aware of the journalist Don Iddon, but the most famous Iddon in my youth was Jack (born John) Iddon, who played cricket for Lancashire from 1926 to 1939 and for England in their 1934-35 tour of the West Indies. He was born in the Lancashire village of Mawdesley on 8 January 1902 and was tragically killed in a road accident in Manchester just before the start of the 1946 season, on 17 April of that year. My mother worked with his daughter in the mills of Preston, and I remember visiting their home in Leyland with my parents and admiring all Jack Iddon's cricket trophies that were on display there.

According to the website sofeminine.co.uk, 1,571 people shared the name Iddon in the UK in 2010, and it is the 6,880th most common name in this country, so it is in fact rather uncommon. The myth circulating about the origin of the name that I learned in my youth is that two Welshmen were washed out to sea off the coast of North Wales in a coracle (a small boat made from wickerwork covered in a waterproof material) and carried by the tides until the sea washed them up on the shore of the fishing village of Hesketh Bank, where they stayed and married into the local population. In more recent times I discovered using the internet that Iddon (born circa 468) was a King of Gwent and a major patron of Llandaff Cathedral. He ruled a small kingdom near the English border until he marched north and disappeared from the records. When I was Patron of the Society of Registration Officers (more about that in Volume 2), I addressed their Annual Conference at a venue in South Wales at which a woman registrar told me that the name Ithon was a common one in their registers, so, it is highly probable that there are drops of Welsh blood and some Welsh genes in all the Iddons.

The Iddon name will be extinguished shortly in my branch of the family. The five Iddon brothers of my dad's generation produced seven male heirs, who either didn't marry or produced only daughters. Charlotte, the wife of my nephew John Iddon, gave birth to a daughter, Lucy Jayne Iddon, on 1 September 2010. Our future is in their hands now; we can only hope that their second child is a boy.[1]

My father, John Iddon, aged 30, married Violet Stazicker, aged 28, at Rufford with Holmeswood St Mary the Virgin Church on 20 October 1934. John Iddon (known locally as 'Jack the butcher'), was a nurseryman - or market gardener - and part-time pig butcher, and my mother, Violet Stazicker, was a weaver, born in Rufford, separated from Tarleton only by the hamlet of Sollom, all straddling the A59 Preston to Liverpool road. The Stazicker family are related locally to the Chadwick and Lingard families. The Lingards owned the blacksmith's smithy in Rufford, which was situated at the heart of the village on the A59 road, close to the Hesketh Arms public house.

My mother Violet and her sister Margaret Stazicker (my Aunt Maggie), who never married, were born on 20 September 1906 and 17 January 1908 respectively in Holly Lane, Rufford. Their father William Hugh Stazicker died there of acute rheumatism and pneumonia at the very early age of 42 on 7 May 1916.

William Hugh Stazicker, a 21-year-old railway passenger clerk, married Elizabeth Chadwick, a 19-year-old labourer, at Rufford with Holmeswood St Mary the Virgin Church on 8 January 1896. They spent their short married life living with the Chadwick family in Holly Lane, Rufford. The house in Holly

Wedding of my father and mother: In the bottom photograph Aunt Alice Thompson is seated on the far left, George Fazackerley (my godfather) is to the right of my mother and her sister and my Aunt Maggie Stazicker is seated on the far right.

Lane is still there today. Later, my maternal grandma moved with her two daughters to Tootle Cottage, then a very humble abode built at the end of a track, off Tootle Lane, Rufford. When council houses were built round the corner in Tootle Lane the family moved to number 9, and I remember frequently visiting my maternal grandma Elizabeth Stazicker there, usually on Sundays.

When I visited 9 Tootle Lane to take a photograph of the house in August 2011 I met Robert West, who told me he had moved into the house on the day that my Aunt Maggie had moved into a new bungalow round the corner in The Grove. Amazingly, therefore, only two families have lived in this house during most of my lifetime.

Aunt Maggie worked most of her life at Rufford Hospital (Rufford 'New Hall', which had been a home of the Hesketh family) as a hospital domestic. The hall became a hospital for the recovery of the sick and injured of World War II and later a place of recuperation, when no longer required for that purpose. In quite recent times it was converted into executive housing.

Home of the Chadwick family in Holly Lane, Rufford in former times (Grandma Stazicker is the women on the left) and today.

The oldest surviving photograph of Margaret and Violet Stazicker.

Holmeswood with Rufford
St Mary the Virgin Church

Aunt Maggie Stazicker.

Grandma Stazicker at Tootle Cottage (on the left) and 9 Tootle Lane (on the right).

9 Tootle Lane, Rufford, home of the Stazicker family.

Attending the funeral of Grandma Stazicker, (from right to left): me, brother Graham and Dad at the front; my mum is the woman in the middle at the rear – she is with members of the Chadwick family.

Rufford Old Hall.

The council house in which the Stazicker family lived was sparsely furnished, as were most of the houses that working-class people lived in during the 1940s, but I remember one of their treasures - an HMV (His Master's Voice) gramophone, which had to be constantly wound up, and which belted out its sound from a large horn. Guess who did most of the winding up on Sundays. The needles had to be changed frequently, and the vinyl records became quite scratched with time.

Even today, Rufford is a Lancashire village that has remained largely unspoiled, unlike Tarleton, which is now a small town. The Leeds and Liverpool Canal (Burscough branch) runs close to the village centre on its way to Tarleton. A treasure of the village is Rufford Old Hall, once the ancestral home of the Hesketh family. Lord Hesketh presented the hall and its 11 acres of gardens to the National Trust in 1936. In the same year Philip Ashcroft, who was my mother's cousin and curator of Rufford Old Hall for a while (until he tragically drowned himself in the Leeds and Liverpool Canal), began a collection of early farm implements and other artefacts of rural life. It forms part of the National Trust's collection on display in the hall today. As a small boy I was often told that there was a tunnel between Rufford Old Hall and Holmeswood with Rufford St Mary the Virgin Church, but I never saw any evidence that it existed.

In 1936, my father and his brother Richard (my Uncle Dick) built a pair of semi-detached houses, 74 and 76 Hesketh Lane, Tarleton, on a large plot of land already in the ownership of the family. A local builder, Philip Barron, built both of them for less than £700, which was a small fortune at that time. My father and Uncle Dick made sure that the houses were built of Accrington brick. Our house was called 'Linsdale', although neither my brother nor I can remember why. Behind the properties the land was subdivided into two market gardens, one for each brother. Eventually they were each able to construct greenhouses on these plots of land. Later, my father rented more land from the local landowner, Lord Lilford.

A source of friction was the fact that the two brothers had agreed an access to both businesses down the side of 74 Hesketh Lane, in other words a right of way was established for my Uncle Dick and his family. This caused problems for years, when my father parked his car on our drive and my uncle wanted access to his market garden. Produce merchants, middlemen who collected the products of the market gardens to take the fruit and vegetables to the wholesale markets in nearby towns and cities, often needed access to pick up the day's freshly-picked produce.

I was born in the front bedroom of 74 Hesketh Lane, Tarleton on 5 July 1940. Tarleton was then a small village on the West Lancashire Plain with a population of about 2,500, situated midway between the towns of Ormskirk, where my birth is registered, Preston and Southport. I was born in the reign of King George VI with an all-party coalition governing the country in Westminster, led by Winston Churchill.

I was baptized by the Reverend L. N. Forse, Rector of Holy Trinity Church, Tarleton on 11 August 1940, and was confirmed there later. My three godparents were Henry Heyes, who lived at Lostock Hall, near Preston, George Fazackerley (see Page 11), a postman who lived opposite Rufford Old Hall on the A59 Preston to Liverpool Road, and my Aunt Alice (Thompson). In her youth my mother worked in the cotton mills in Lostock Hall, where she became very friendly with Milly Heyes. We were regular visitors at their terraced house in Lindley Street, Lostock Hall, and they regularly came to Tarleton. Milly and Henry didn't have children of their own, so they spoiled me and my brother instead.

My mother and her best friend Doris Pickervance travelled by bus the ten miles to Preston one week and Southport the next to shop because there were few shops in Tarleton, and I was taken with them. My father spent as many Saturdays as he could in the winter watching Preston North End FC (their star player in this era was Tom Finney) and in summer he was at the local cricket matches or bowling at the bowling club.

74 Hesketh Lane, Tarleton, with the secondary school built on fields that I played on in my early years on the extreme left of the picture.

# SCIENCE AND POLITICS: AN UNLIKELY MIXTURE

The earliest photograph of me, taken on 22 November 1941.

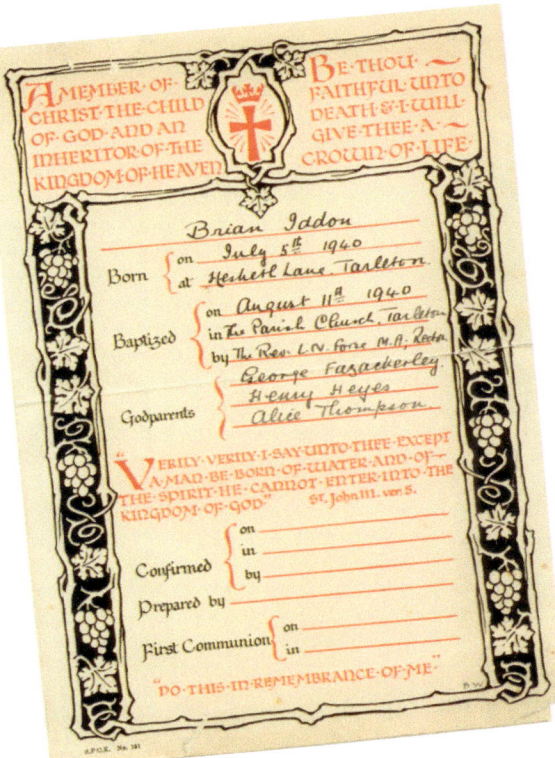

My Certificate of Baptism.

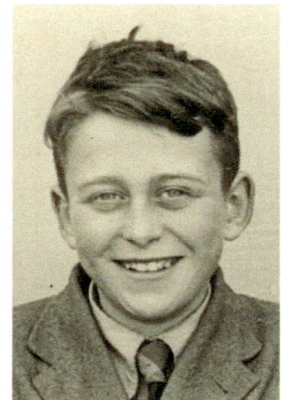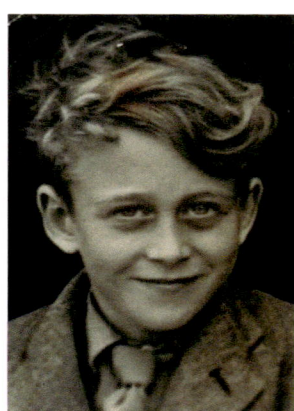

Photographs of me 'growing up'.

Henry (godfather) and Milly Heyes

# SCIENCE AND POLITICS: AN UNLIKELY MIXTURE

The wedding of Alice Iddon (godmother) and John Thomas Thompson.

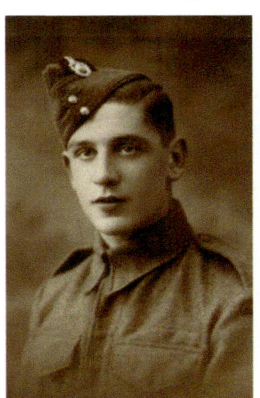

## COUSINS
Cousins (clockwise) Harry, Ronnie
(Brother Graham is presenting the horseshoe),
Celia and Richard.

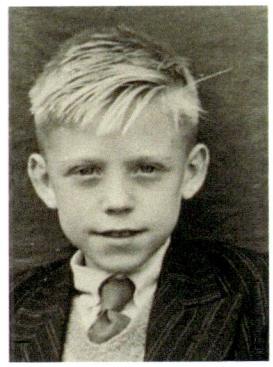

Cousin Frank and Bessie's wedding
(Uncle Dick and Aunt Ada are on the right of Bessie).

Cousin Betty Iddon Johnson and Enoch Johnson's wedding
(Cousin Janie is sat next to Uncle Bob on the far right).

I remember sitting on top of a board laid across the arms of a hairdresser's chair in Southport having my hair cut. I must have been doing quite a bit of wriggling, because the kindly hairdresser produced a paper bag from which he asked me to take a sweet, a 'dolly mixture'. I was fascinated; I had never seen such a coloured sweet in all my seven years of existence until that moment. Sugar was a very difficult commodity to buy during the war years and for several years afterwards. Of course, I was told how lucky I was to receive such a treasure, and it did the trick. I sat still until the hairdresser had completed his task.

By all accounts I was a 'bonny' baby, with very curly blonde hair which I kept for several years. In November 1941, when I was 17 months old, my mother dressed me up and off we went to Phil Wayne, a photographer at 56 Friargate in Preston, for a posed photograph. Toys, at least those bought from shops, were another very rare commodity at this time. To keep me still the photographer placed me on top of a carpet-covered piece of furniture with a very beautiful large tin car. I hope he kept it, because it would be worth a fortune today. I was full of admiration for it and kept still until the photographer produced just the picture that my mother wanted. I have it in my collection. She repeated this exercise to keep a record of me growing up.

We are often asked to describe our earliest memories. I know my mother used to put me out in all weathers and every season in a rather grand pram with a curved bottom, which sat on the top of four enormous wheels. Parents in those days believed that this was good for babies. Sometimes I imagine that I can remember lying in that pram. I can certainly remember being taken to the local 'clinic', which was a prefabricated hut on the site where Tarleton's fire station stands today. Babies were examined and weighed in the clinic and mothers given bottles of pure orange juice and cod liver oil.

There was a 'Green Goddess' fire engine in a shed on the adjacent site in those days. The Auxiliary Fire Service was set up in 1940 and disbanded in 1968, when the 'Green Goddess' was joined by a fire engine belonging to Lancashire County Fire Brigade.

The part of Lancashire where I was born is known locally as 'Little Holland'; the soil is black and extremely fertile.[2] It is the home of a significant market gardening industry, with acres upon acres of greenhouses, just as in Holland, growing mainly lettuce and tomatoes but many other crops too including peppers, watercress, cucumbers and a variety of flowers, all grown for the local wholesale markets in places like Preston, Liverpool and Manchester.

The area between the villages of Rufford and Tarleton and Southport on the west coast is known as Martin Mere and was largely under water until recent times. Because of its inaccessibility the farm houses in this region of Lancashire became hiding places for Jesuit priests during the years when Roman Catholics were persecuted. Rufford Old Hall and many of the other older buildings in the area have priest's hiding holes built into their structures.

Immediately to the east of Martin Mere was a main route from the south to the north carrying travellers heading for Hesketh Bank, then a fishing village, where they proceeded down Guide Road to be guided across the treacherous sands of the Ribble estuary at low tide to Guide House in Lytham (at Naze Mount) on the northern shore of the Ribble.

In the graveyard of Old Becconsall Church a gravestone shows evidence of the danger of crossing the sands of both the River Ribble and the River Astland, the former name of the

River Douglas. Its inscription reads:

> James Blundell, late of H. Bank,
> who unfortunately drowned on 6th July, 1844
> Often times I've crossed the sands
> And through the Ribble deep
> But I was found in Astlan drown'd
> It was God's will it should be so
> Some way or other all must go.

Rufford is on the edge of Martin Mere, and the soil in the area consists of fertile sand. Consequently, this is one of the best areas for growing root crops, especially carrots. Today, the area between the villages of Rufford and Tarleton and the coast at Southport, which is below sea level, is drained and the water is pumped into the sea at the coastal village of Crossens. The whole area has the feel of Holland about it, with long, deep, wide ditches criss-crossing it. The land in many places has sunk below the road levels as the underlying peat substructure has dried out and been drawn downwards. It is not unusual in this area for farm machinery to drag fossilised trees out of the peat.

Hundred End (named because it was the end of the Leyland 'hundred', a measure of land area), on the edge of the mere, is a place famous for growing celery. It was known in my youth as 'Celery Junction' (it was on the Preston to Southport railway line). Today, the part of Martin Mere that is still under water is a famous bird sanctuary.

I recall my life in Tarleton, despite the austerity and rationing of the war years, as a happy one. I enjoyed playing with my close friends, Stephen Melling, who lived next door at 72 Hesketh Lane, and Martin Ashcroft, who lived at 12

Hesketh Lane. Joan Melling, Stephen's sister, and David Barron, who lived directly across the road to us at 59 Hesketh Lane, were often part of 'our gang'. I also went to school and played in my early days with Thomas Alan Parkinson (who lived at 44 Carr Lane) and Derrick Pickervance (who lived at 62 Carr Lane) and, less frequently, with Kenneth Klee, who lived close to us on Hesketh Lane.

We played on the acres of open fields that surrounded our houses and in 'Carr Wood' (Carr Heys Plantation on the Ordnance Survey maps), off Carr Lane, where we built elaborate tree houses and played cowboys and Indians and, later, built rafts on the Burscough branch of the Leeds and Liverpool Canal that flows through locks into the River Douglas at Tarleton. We constructed our rafts from oil or paint drums with planks of wood lashed to them with ropes.

The canal was a big attraction. In my secondary school years we swam in it, fished in it (for perch and roach), played on the boats moored at the local boatyard, run by the Mayor family, and even tried hurtling down cobbled Plox Brow on old bicycles in an attempt to leap over the canal where it narrows and can be crossed using the Town End swing bridge at the bottom of the steep brow. Inevitably both bicycle and rider ended up in the canal. There was a cotton mill at the edge of the canal at the bottom of Plox Brow, and the warm water that was pumped into the canal from its boiler house was an attractive place to swim in colder weather. Some of the oldest houses in Tarleton are on Plox Brow.

The land in Tarleton falls quite steeply from Hesketh Lane, which runs along a ridge, into the River Douglas valley, and the brows provided ample opportunity for fun in the snow in winter. 'Our gang' built sledges as well as 'trolleys', which we constructed from wooden boxes and old pram wheels and their axles. We hurtled down these brows on old bicycles and in our homemade trolleys. We had several 'dens', in Carr Wood and in a disused air-raid shelter in Oakland Avenue.

Adjacent to the market garden owned by my father was Melling's mill, which ground the locally-produced grain into flour and imported, mainly from Liverpool, products for feeding the local poultry and cattle. My father helped them out from time to time, especially during the war years and immediately after, by driving wagons to collect the poultry and cattle food, delivered in bulk by the large cargo ships arriving in Liverpool, and prepared by Bibby's and the other firms lining the Liverpool dock road. The dock road was a hive of activity in those days. Tate and Lyle had a big sugar refinery there and the smells varied from oilseed cake to molasses.

I often accompanied my father on these journeys to Liverpool and was fascinated by life along the dock road. I was also disgusted by the sight of small children walking the cobbled streets, even in the winter months, without shoes or stockings and wearing very few clothes. I have always felt that it was the extreme poverty that I saw in Liverpool during my early years that later led to my interest in left-wing politics. The scenes of destruction in the dock area also created a big impression on my young mind at that time. It was his experience of working in Liverpool a decade earlier that converted Michael Foot from liberalism to socialism.

Dock workers queued for a job each morning and if their face didn't fit, they had no luck. It wasn't until the trade unions organised the labour force that conditions improved. Those were the days of formidable politicians such as Bessie Braddock, whose statue stands in Lime Street Station today.

She became a Member of Parliament of some stature – she told it as it was for her working class community - and her large family were well-known on the dock road in Liverpool.

I remember too Liverpool's overhead dock railway, which ran on tracks elevated to the height of a double-decker bus for the full distance of the dock road (it closed in 1956). Whilst my father waited for his wagon to be loaded up he would take me on journeys on the overhead railway so that we could observe the bustling activity along the dock road. At that time some of the largest cargo ships and liners called into the Liverpool docks, and the ships were moored bow towards land so that a traveller on the overhead railway could easily read their names and their ports of origin. I learned the names of some exotic far-away places. The Cunard liners and the ships of the P&O line were the most impressive of all the ships that called into Liverpool. The contrast between life in Tarleton and the deprivation that I saw in Liverpool in my early years was huge.

Tarleton's buildings were not damaged during the war years, although the Luftwaffe dropped a bomb in a field adjacent to Old Becconsall Church. The deep crater it created is still there for all to see today, and the church still carries the shrapnel marks it sustained on that night. When the air raid siren wailed on top of Tarleton fire station, we took refuge under the stairs in a small cupboard, where we stored all our junk and hung our coats and raincoats. That special sound of air raid sirens still makes my hair (what I have left) stand on end today. We were all supplied with our individual gas masks, which we also kept under the stairs in cardboard boxes. I hated putting one of those things on. I remember too the extreme precautions my parents had to take in the blackout at night.

Many of the men who lived in Tarleton were not expected to serve in the war because they were members of 'protected occupations', like my father. Mainly, they were producers of foodstuffs. A few men, such as Cousin Frank, became Bevin boys and worked down the Lancashire pits. But Tarleton lost 11 young men, and their names are inscribed on the village war memorial on Church Road. The adult males who were not required to join the forces, including my father, served in the local Home Guard ('Dad's Army').

My friend Alan Parkinson and his sister Molly never knew their father Thomas, who was killed whilst serving in the RAF, and they were brought up by their mother. The only person we lost in my own family was Cousin Dick, who I never knew. His full name was Richard Lunt Johnson and he was the son of Aunt Ellen, my father's sister. She married Percy Lunt Johnson, who died in 1929 aged 35. Aunt Ellen also gave birth to a daughter, Betty Iddon Johnson. They lived in a council house at 48 Carr Lane, Tarleton, before moving to a newly built bungalow, 'Westmead', at 194 Carr Lane.

Cousin Dick, Richard Lunt Johnson.

The locks at the bottom of Plox Brow on the Leeds and Liverpool Canal (showing the Town End swing bridge).

Tarleton Home Guard - my father is second from the right in the back row.

Dick was a joiner with a well-known Tarleton builder, Philip Barron, and joined the Royal Engineers 143 Field Park Squadron in 1939 as a volunteer. As Sapper 1902637, he survived Dunkirk. Whilst waiting to be evacuated from the beach there, he discovered two broken 'pot' fish in the sand and brought them home to present them (after repair) to his mother

Ellen and to his maternal grandma, Alice Iddon. They are now united in the ownership of my Cousin Richard Thompson.

After the horrors of Dunkirk, Dick became a 'Desert Rat' and fought his way across North Africa with Field Marshal Viscount Montgomery's army, from El Alamein to Tunis. The army then proceeded to drive Rommel's army out of the Mediterranean islands before beginning battles on the Italian mainland.

Dick died aged 25 on 30 January 1944 in 92 General Hospital in Naples. The cause of death is recorded as staphylococcal septicaemia. Ironically, he was not killed as a result of enemy fire but from a scratch, possibly from barbed wire on the island of Sicily, and became seriously ill as a result. When he became ill, Dick was on a ship in the Bay of Naples, which would have transported him home with his comrades. I have visited his grave, which is in the immaculately-kept Naples War Cemetery at Capodimonte.

There were rival 'gangs' in the village of Tarleton, but trespassing out of the village was perilous. From the locks at Tarleton boatyard, where the Leeds and Liverpool Canal (Burscough branch) joins the River Douglas, there was a path which ran along the banks of the river all the way to Hesketh Bank. It was a popular walk for local people, especially on Sundays. In fact, this path once carried a single track railway line that was abandoned before I was born.

Just below the hill on which sits Old Becconsall Church, almost where the River Douglas joins the River Ribble, was another boatyard on the River Douglas. However, to get to that boatyard, walkers had to pass under an iron bridge, which carried the Preston to Southport railway line over the river. That was a boundary beyond which Tarleton lads shouldn't pass without expecting retaliation from the lads of Hesketh Bank, who often gathered on the railway bridge to throw stones at the people below. The railway line was removed in 1964 and the bridge in October 1965, following the Beeching closures of hundreds of miles of railway lines in Britain.

Just beyond the bridge, Alty's brick works was an interesting place to explore and, close to Hesketh Bank station, my Uncle Henry (known as Harry) ran a blacksmith's business. It was fascinating to watch him bend and shape iron in his forge and shoe the many carthorses that the local farmers brought to his smithy. I enjoyed watching him use the bellows to get the fire red hot and seeing the sparks fly as he worked the metal on his anvil. As the demand for blacksmiths declined, my Uncle Harry and his two sons, Wilf and Arnold, turned their hand to fitting and maintaining industrial-scale central heating. They installed and repaired the iron pipes and coke-fired boilers used to heat the local greenhouses.

This was the land I was brought up in and grew to love, but the time came for me to stop playing all day and start school. I remember my first day, in the autumn of 1945. I didn't want to go to school; at the age of five I could see no point in it. Life had been good in the big outdoors. There were still things I wanted to discover, places farther afield that I wanted to explore. My father often referred jokingly to 'The Edge of Leet' - the village of Bretherton, which lies between Tarleton and Croston. It seemed like a fascinating place to visit at the age of five. But now my father chased me across his land and dumped me in an old Ford car, and off we went to Tarleton Holy Trinity Church of England Primary School, a mile away in the centre of the village of Tarleton and adjacent to Holy Trinity Parish Church, which has a rather grand spire.

# SCIENCE AND POLITICS: AN UNLIKELY MIXTURE

Holy Trinity Church and School, Tarleton (the school has been extended behind the original building since I was a pupil).

Tarleton Holy Trinity Church of England Primary School. Mrs Airey with my class – I am sitting squinting third from the right on the front row

# SCIENCE AND POLITICS: AN UNLIKELY MIXTURE

Here in physical education kit – I am fifth from the left on the middle row
(Derrick Pickervance is seated)

(from right to left) Headteacher Mr Corless, Mrs Airey and Mrs Aughton.

After ensuring that I had been secured by Mrs Aughton, my first teacher, my father left and I attempted to follow him. She grabbed me and lifted me off the floor, at which I scratched her face and she put me down to attend to her wound. I fled and ran all the way home, down Church Road and along Hesketh Lane to number 74. I didn't receive a very good welcome at home, as you might expect. My father was a strict disciplinarian, and I was afraid of him as a young boy but later grew to respect him. Occasionally, when I was really bad, he applied his belt to my tender parts. I was returned to school and decided never to repeat that exercise again.

In fact Mrs Aughton was a very kind woman. In my later life she was always interested in how I was getting on in life, and I had a feeling that she was very proud of me when I became the first boy from our village to be accepted by a university. Unfortunately, I left faint reminders of my scratches on her face for life, and I do remember her showing them to me several times as I grew up, although she always laughed at the thought of what had happened on my first day at school. Fortunately, she lived into her 80s, or even 90s, in the village of Hesketh Bank.

Mr Corless was the Head Teacher of my primary school, and another teacher whose name I still remember was Mrs Airey. My mixed class was very large, at least 30 of us, probably nearer to 40. I walked to school and back with my friends; traffic on the roads was very light in 1945-1951. Many of the children in the class came from very poor homes. Agricultural wages were some of the lowest in the country, and these were the post-war years of rationing and the black market.

Life at Tarleton Church of England Primary School provided me with a few lasting memories. Looking back on that time now it seems that the teachers were preparing us for a life on the land, either as farmers or market gardeners. After all, most of us came from these backgrounds. We went on an endless round of nature walks during which we were expected to be able to identify all the different trees, the wild flowers and the birds and insects. Flowers were brought back to the school, where we pressed them dry and stuck them in our scrap books.

Behind the school was a large garden in which I remember we also spent a lot of time, doing the things that the teachers expected us to be doing for the rest of our lives, growing and harvesting as many varieties of fruit and vegetables that the land could accommodate.

In May, we learned how to 'dress' the Maypole and I remember doing a lot of country dancing as a young boy. In my first years at primary school there were no school meals; I think I went home for lunch. Later my primary school provided meals at lunchtime. In the early days they were delivered from a central kitchen elsewhere.

We regularly visited the adjacent Holy Trinity Church. When people ask me today what is my religion, I say that I don't practise one, but I do tell them I was born half a Methodist (my father's religion) and half a member of the Church of England (my mother's religion). I was more often in a chapel than I was in a church. My mother and father were very insistent on me attending Sunday school every Sunday morning, and I missed very few lessons. I believed in God as much as any child does at that age.

Our Sunday school often arranged trips and picnics. A favourite destination was the small village of Barrow Bridge in Bolton, under a mile from where I now live, where there was a boating lake (now a car park) and a café.

When I was old enough, I joined the church choir. I was quite mischievous at that time and was a pretty good shot with a peashooter as well. At one choir practice the choirmaster caught me firing peas at the back of another boy's neck; he happened to be a good choral singer. His visit to our home ended my singing career. Mind you, I have never been able to sing, so it was perhaps as well that I didn't waste any more time in his choir. Nevertheless, it gave me a liking for organ music and hymn singing.

For its time the house I was born into was a substantial property, with tall gables at the front, which gave it character. The opening windows were made of iron and the front ones were lead glazed, with stained glass inserts, just like church windows, I thought. Downstairs we had a front room furnished with a leather suite, an extendable table with six chairs and a substantial 'dresser' in which was kept the best china and cutlery, along with the family's important papers. The room had a fireplace for burning wood or coal. Most of our furniture came from the local furniture store, Websters on Church Road, which was still an important business in Tarleton when I completed this book.

We only used our front room at the weekends, when my parents entertained their friends. They were very generous with their entertaining, although my mother wasn't the best of cooks. I remember that her custard pies, which I could never resist, sometimes turned upside down in the oven.

The front room was also the place where my mother and father were laid out in open coffins when they later died. Sleeping in the house on those occasions was a spooky experience. It was traditional in the village to bring the dead in through the front door and take them out the same way on the day of the funeral. The front curtains were kept drawn from the day of death to the day of the funeral, and friends and relatives came round to pay their respects to the departed. A local joiner, Bill Hull, was the family's undertaker.

The main living room in the house was the adjacent kitchen, which was fitted with a Belfast sink and a coal/wood-burning fireplace around which we all gathered in the cold weather. This fireplace had a 'back boiler', which provided hot water for a storage tank in the back upstairs bedroom. We were fortunate in also having an immersion heater, fitted to the storage tank. All the water pipes in the house were made of lead. In cold weather they could, and occasionally did, fracture as the water froze inside the soft lead pipes and split them open. My father would position paraffin-lit storm lanterns close to the most exposed of these pipes in winter to keep the frost at bay. Plaster in new houses dried out over many months and my parents 'stippled' the bare plaster walls with coloured emulsion paint to make them look more attractive.

It was in our 'kitchen' that I had a frightening experience at the age of about 13. My father was putting the electric kettle on when my mother realised that the electricity was going through him. She grabbed him and became part of the problem. I didn't know what to do at that age. Fortunately, in the nick of time, my mother had the presence of mind to knock the switch off, and they both collapsed onto chairs to recover. I have always been very careful with electrical equipment since that awful day.

Most of our living room floors were covered in linoleum. Fitted carpets were considered to be an unnecessary luxury and rugs covered parts of the floors. I got quite adept at making rag rugs and 'pegging' wool into what became peg wool rugs.

Going backwards in the house from the main road, the next room, which was in a single story extension, was the 'back kitchen'. Today we would call it the utility room. It had a concrete floor and it was here that my mother would do the washing. Mondays were washing days. I remember her using 'dolly blue' in a large electrically-heated tub, and using a wash board to 'scrub' the clothes with large pieces of Lever Brothers' soap, made at Port Sunlight. She then put the wet clothes through a hand-turned 'mangle' to squeeze out the water, and dried them in the kitchen, with the fire lit, on wooden hangers that could be lowered by rope from the ceiling ('clothes horses'). Later, an electric washing machine arrived, which had an electrically driven 'mangle' attached, which made life a lot easier for my mum. Whilst these mangles were running the operator had to make sure they did not get their fingers in between the rollers. The back kitchen was equipped with a large Belfast sink too and there was enough room in there to store bicycles and other equipment.

We had a small pantry, also equipped with a sink and draining board, where food was prepared. My mother did her cooking in the pantry with an electric cooker. There were no refrigerators; milk was delivered fresh from Howard's farm and was not sterilised - in summer it would not keep fresh more than a day. Bread had to be fetched from the local Co-operative shop at the end of Hesketh Lane.

The Co-op was the centre of village life. It had a wooden floor and very large serving counters. Customers' money was put inside a round tube which was blown by compressed air to the upstairs office, and the change and the 'divvy' slip returned in the same way. When my mum asked me to buy cheese I had to ask her, "Which one?" To her the stronger-tasting Lancashire cheese was 'cooking cheese', and the milder-tasting Cheshire cheese was 'eating cheese'.

I made a considerable fortune in my early years searching for jam jars and used pop bottles to return to the Co-op, where I received a halfpenny (0.5d; 240d = £1) for each one. A lot of items were sold loose. A large wooden spatula was used to cut up the butter, which was placed for weighing onto greaseproof paper. Large hams and sides of beef and pork were sliced on a huge bacon slicer which, to a young boy, was a fearsome-looking machine. The person serving the sliced meat could alter the setting to deliver thinner or thicker slices, which they caught on greaseproof paper held with one hand whilst driving the bacon slicer with the other.

In a small village, with all the middens scattered throughout the farms, there were an awful lot of flies and wasps about. We hung twisted sticky strips of paper from our ceilings to reduce their populations, and even enticed the wasps to enter jam jars containing a bit of jam and an awful lot of water.

Adjacent to our back door was a small room where the coalman tipped the coal – either soft Lancashire coal or the more expensive and harder Welsh anthracite. Uncle Dick was our coal merchant. His son Frank was a 'Bevin Boy' who worked down the Lancashire pits during the war years. After the war he was allowed to come home and run the market garden and deliver coal.

We were lucky – indoors we had a downstairs toilet. In the 1930s and 1940s Tarleton had no sewerage system, and all the sewerage was piped into a cesspit in the garden at the back of our house. The waste water was piped into a ditch. In the 1960s most houses in Tarleton were connected to a main sewer and a sewerage farm was built on the outskirts of the village.

We very seldom locked the back door when we left the house in the 1940s. When my parents locked themselves out, I was slim enough to be helped through the window of the downstairs toilet to open the back door. I was unaware of crime in the village as a young boy; most people only had the basics to steal. Everyone knew everyone else, so the 'bad uns' were easy to identify, but fortunately there were very few of them.

Upstairs at 74 Hesketh Lane we had a bathroom (a luxury in the early 1940s), two double bedrooms and a box room, which became my bedroom. Both the double bedrooms had fireplaces, but fires were only lit when someone was in bed ill. The back double bedroom was occupied by my brother Graham after he was born on 19 June 1947. He was also born at home with the help of the local midwife. That room had a degree of warmth, because it housed the hot water storage tank. However, going to bed was a cold experience most of the time, and hot water bottles were a must, preferably taken up earlier to get the bed clothes warm in advance of getting into the bed.

Most Sunday mornings in the warmer weather, when it wasn't raining, the five Iddon brothers sat on the garden wall fronting 74 and 76 Hesketh Lane to watch the world go by and exchange gossip (see page 7). Cousin Frank, who lived at number 76, and I would sometimes join them. My father often walked me up to Windygate Corner, at the junction of the A59 Preston to Liverpool Road and Southport New Road (the A585). It was there that I saw my first smartly-uniformed Automobile Association man, with his motorcycle and sidecar. They were very polite, saluting all the cars that they observed carrying the distinctive AA metal badge attached to their front metal bumper. Car bumpers in those days protruded out from the front and back of cars, and the name indicated their use.

We were suspicious of 'foreigners' - people not born and bred in the village. Tarleton is highly populated by 'foreigners' today, as it has become a commuter area for the surrounding towns. Indeed, I am told that the villagers prefer not to work on the farms or market gardens today, probably because agricultural wages are so low, and the managers or owners of these businesses have to attract real foreigners as employees, usually from other European Union countries.

Fortunately, we were never short of food during the war years, and my parents were generous to those who did run short. With commodities in short supply, such as sugar, everybody had to help each other. On many occasions my parents sent me out to borrow a cupful of sugar from a kind neighbour, and we did the same for them when they ran short of these rationed foodstuffs. My father's market garden provided us with an ample supply of fresh fruit and vegetables, and he was also the village pork butcher, which gave us an ample supply of fresh meat. Like everyone else, we received our share of food and clothes coupons. Those with plenty of money could get what they wanted from the 'spivs' who operated the black market.

In 1940-1948, the first eight years of my life, there was no National Health Service (NHS). All health care had to be paid for. My parents had retained my mother's general practitioner, Dr P. J. Rogan, whose surgery was some distance away at 3 School Lane, Burscough Bridge (known locally as 'camel town' because of its two bridges built close together, one over the railway and the other over the Leeds and Liverpool Canal), further along the A59 from Rufford in the Ormskirk direction.

It had a small, dark waiting room at the front, a consulting room in the middle of the building and a room at the back where Dr Rogan made up his prescriptions, which had to be paid for on the spot. I remember well the vile 'tonics' that he used to mix, essentially brightly coloured and tasting awful. Goodness only knows what they contained; I never found out. I never knew either whether they really made me better or whether I just got better out of fear because I didn't want to be prescribed another bottle.

The early sulphonamide antibiotics were introduced in 1938 (born out of a study on azo-dyes), two years before my birth, and penicillin was developed during the war years, so I suppose 1940 was a good year to be born. Years later, when I worked at the University of Salford, I was privileged to meet on several occasions Frank (actually Francis Leslie) Rose (1909-1988). He was Head of the Medicinal Chemicals Section of ICI Dyestuffs Division at Blackley, Manchester, which manufactured azo-dyes. Some highly successful pyrimidine sulphonamide antibacterial drugs were developed at Blackley by this group before they moved to establish ICI Pharmaceuticals Division at Alderley Park in Cheshire. It became AstraZeneca.

During my early years, many diseases were prominent which we hear far less about today. Obviously, hard labour on the land wore people out and heart disease struck many people down, including some from my own family. Ulcers were also dangerous, especially when they ruptured and bled internally. We lived ten miles from the nearest hospitals, which didn't make for speedy treatment either. Most of the males and many of the women smoked heavy tar cigarettes, such as Woodbines and Capstan Full Strength.

Pork, a staple food of village life, carried tapeworms that could be six feet long and I knew several children who suffered them, although fortunately I never had one. I did entertain a ringworm, just once, which wasn't pleasant, and boils were common. Diphtheria, scarlet fever, smallpox, chicken pox, whooping cough, mumps, meningitis and measles, tuberculosis, polio, typhoid, jaundice and yellow fever were potential killers and were quite common.

Before the birth of the NHS there were people in every village who had a good knowledge of the ancient healing techniques, mainly using extracts of plants. I had several bread poultices applied, goose grease rubbed on my chest and smelling salts held under my nose when I felt dizzy, and I consumed several herbal teas.

It seems hard to believe in the 21st Century that general practitioners carried out operations in their patients' homes in the mid-20th Century. My close friend Stephen Melling had his tonsils removed on the kitchen table by the legendary Tarleton GP Dr Croft. There were boils to lance, ears to syringe, even broken limbs to set before the long wait for an ambulance. And, doctors were on 24-hour call. In those days they earned their money, in my opinion.

The post-war Labour Government, which introduced the NHS in 1948, was elected by the General Election of 1945, held on my birthday (5 July), although the results were not known until 26 July because the votes of servicemen had to be collected and counted.

I was introduced to death very early in my young life. Derrick Pickervance, the son of my mother's best friends Bill and Doris Pickervance, who lived in Carr Lane (they gave birth to a daughter too, Muriel), was born with a hole in his heart and looked blue (born a 'blue baby') most of his short life. 'My gang' pushed him all over Tarleton in his wheelchair. He was great fun and enjoyed life as much as he could. I regularly visited his house to play with him. Like my father, his father was a market gardener.

Tragically, Derrick developed jaundice, and his frail heart couldn't cope with it. I remember visiting him and watching him become more and more ill as his skin turned a deeper shade of yellow. He died at the age of ten, on 10 January 1951, my final year in primary school. Today he could have had his heart repaired shortly after birth and would probably have lived to a ripe old age. I often visit his grave in St Mary's Church graveyard in Tarleton and remember the good times we had together.

Marbles was a popular game in my schooldays, as was 'conkers' in season. I hardened my conkers by soaking them in vinegar and baking them lightly in the oven. As a young boy I could climb any tree; I had no fear of heights. We made our own pleasures. Bows and arrows for cowboys and Indians were made from my father's bamboo canes and greenhouse string that he used to grow his tomatoes up. It is amazing how many different kinds of marbles we traded. Some were simply glass spheres; others were like the Crown Jewels.

One of the first 'toys' my parents ever bought for me was a wonderful hand-made wooden rocking horse. I won a lot of races on that horse. Several years later the first film I ever saw in a cinema was *Rocking Horse Winner*, which I found very frightening. Dad and Mum also bought me a little red metal pedal car in which I raced round the house.

Another prestigious present I received later from my parents was a miniature projector through which the celluloid film was wound by hand. I projected the early silent movies onto a bed sheet pinned to a wall for the entertainment of my close friends and relatives. One of the silent films showed the hunting of a magnificent stag with a pack of hounds. It was chased into a deep lake, where the hounds bayed at it until it froze to death. I always wondered why such a film was provided as a present for a young boy.

I had a good collection of lead soldiers, some on horseback, and my parents produced a fort as a present. Later, I was provided with the amazing Meccano sets,[3] which kept me happy for many long hours. After the war was over, I graduated to Hornby train sets[3] and eventually to building and flying model aircraft, which I spent many hours constructing from kits containing balsa wood, glue, tissue paper, 'dope' (which was applied to the tissue paper) and the plans and instructions. We also built and flew our own kites. Dinky toys[3] were also a passion. They were built of metal, unlike earlier toy cars and wagons.

A material that came to be known as Bakelite was introduced, and the early cheap toy cars and wagons were made out of it. Unfortunately, industry had not learned how to plasticise Bakelite properly; the toys were brittle and had short lives. Not many of them have survived to this day, unlike the early metal Dinky toys which are now highly collectable. The Danish firm Lego started to manufacture plastic toys in 1940, but it wasn't until 1949 that the now famous Lego bricks began to appear in the UK.

We collected and swopped cigarette cards too, endless varieties of them, and I had lots of jigsaws. The passion was to collect and swop cigarette cards until a complete set of famous footballers, or whatever, had been collected, then into the scrap book they would go. Collecting and swopping stamps was a passion of mine too for a while.

Another toy that fascinated me was a model steam boiler, complete with a methylated spirits burner to generate the steam; we enjoyed making its flywheel go as fast as we could make it turn.

We played a lot of games at Christmas time and at birthday parties – hide and seek, musical chairs, charades, pass the parcel, card games such as snap and board games such as snakes and ladders and draughts. Every household had a pack of playing cards and a set of dominoes and, later, Monopoly. I fancied myself as a budding magician and entertained my young friends with a variety of magic tricks. I enjoyed watching the faces of adults as I set fire to their £10 notes. Bank notes were so big in the 1940s and early 1950s that they had to be folded up to be put into a wallet.

I think I stopped believing in Father Christmas around the age of six or seven. Like all children, I tried to catch him coming into my bedroom, where I hung up a sock on the fireplace and left a mince pie and a glass of milk for him, sometimes carrots for his reindeer. I became curious about Father Christmas's existence when I saw my father constantly peeping round the bedroom door to see if I was asleep. Toys were a rare commodity during the war years and in the years shortly after, so the most enjoyable part of my early Christmases was to find out what my parents had filled my sock with, usually fruit and nuts and marbles.

There were always lots of people in our house at Christmas when I was a child. A happy memory I have of Christmas time is the sound of the Salvation Army Band coming down Hesketh Lane. They always stopped outside 74 and 76 and people gathered round them to listen to the carols and join in the singing. A group of villagers also toured the village singing Christmas Carols and collecting money for local charities. Once or twice I joined them, but as I have mentioned, I am not the best singer in the world.

Aunt Ada was one of the few in our family who made 'real' mince pies well into my teenage years and beyond. I remember watching her clamp the metal mincer to her kitchen table and mince the beef before proceeding to mix it with the other ingredients, mainly fruits of different kinds. She used to let me turn the handle of her mincer while she prepared the pastry. Although I wasn't keen on eating meat in those days, I have to admit that those mince pies were the best that I have ever tasted.

Years later my youngest daughter, Sheena, was offered one of Aunt Ada's mince pies. Although she knew there was something 'strange' about them, we were reluctant to make the obvious confession, at least not in the presence of Aunt Ada. Sheena is a vegetarian.

We also engaged in more exciting play. Behind Melling's flour mill the firm had built an open Dutch barn, where they kept bales of hay and straw, collected from local farmers and sold to other local farmers to feed their cattle through the winters. Melling's also left the doors of the mill open overnight and at the weekends. The mill and the barn were great places to play hide and seek. Although, I accept now, we trespassed, we never did any damage.

The barn provided the most exciting play space. There, we built dens using the bales of straw. It also became our 'circus' ring. I qualified at that time as a budding trapeze artist. We tied ropes to the top beams of the barn and swung from one rope to another along the length of the barn. Of course, we fell, but onto hay and straw without damaging ourselves seriously on the concrete floor of the barn. Nevertheless, these falls knocked the wind out of our lungs.

Hugh Melling had a poultry shed behind the mill and made nightly visits to feed his battery hens. When we played at night or at the weekends, we had to listen – we posted a 'lookout' – for this man coming through the mill to feed his hens. As the signal was given we either ran away or hid in our dens in the barn and kept very quiet. Occasionally we got caught and were duly scolded by Mr Melling.

Just once, 'my gang' decided to swim at low tide off a sandbank in the River Douglas, near the boatyard at Old Becconsall. Before people started to bathe at places like Southport and Blackpool they bathed in the River Douglas at this spot. This was my first (and last) experience with leeches. We came out of the water with them stuck to our flesh. Fortunately, one of my older mates was an early smoker and we removed them with a lit cigarette.

My parents were keen that I should learn to read, and I spent a lot of time on my father's knee looking at Rupert Bear stories (I got a Rupert Bear Album every Christmas) and a weekly comic - *Radio Fun*. I was given Enid Blyton books and read them all when I had mastered reading. Biggles was one of my heroes.

In Tarleton we had a small cinema (we called it the 'flea pit'), set back from the road at the junction of Church Road and Blackgate Lane. With my friends I spent a lot of time in there watching cowboys and Indians films on a Saturday morning. We left ready to enact the battles that we had seen on the big screen. Wild Bill Hickok, Roy Rogers (and his horse Trigger), Buffalo Bill, Gene Autry, Hopalong Cassidy and Tex Ritter were our heroes. Films featuring Lassie the dog and Tarzan and Jane were also popular. The good thing about going to the cinema in the 1950s and 1960s was that the programme included a 'B' film as well as the *Pathe News*.

One film, *Rock Around the Clock*, starring Bill Haley and the Comets, released in 1956, had a major impact on the lives of most teenagers who lived through the fifties and sixties. I saw it at the cinema in Tarleton, though some time after its release. The media were convinced, and so were our parents, that this film meant it was the end of the world as they had known it, and it was. Rock and roll was here to stay.

With Stephen Melling inside the steeple of Holy Trinity Church, Tarleton; a view from a stone window above the bells.

# SCIENCE AND POLITICS: AN UNLIKELY MIXTURE

With my brother Graham.  The barn at the rear of Melling's corn mill.

Leeds and Liverpool Canal, Burscough branch, at the locks where it joins the River Douglas.

The River Douglas at Becconsall boatyard

Actually, we in Britain were behind the times; Bill Haley released his record, the first to sell a million copies in Britain alone, on 12 April 1954. Whilst that was an exciting day for most teenagers of that time, the day before, Sunday 11 April 1954, still holds the record as the most boring day in history. Belgium had a General Election on that day, but that's about all that happened that the media felt like recording.

As November 5th approached my father always allowed me and my mates to build a huge bonfire on his land, but away from the greenhouses for obvious reasons. It provided him with an opportunity to burn all his waste wood and other rubbish. We spent weeks constructing the bonfires and putting together a Guy Fawkes.

There was a profusion of trees growing in the hedgerows of the fields surrounding our house and market garden, and we sawed off the lower branches to fuel our bonfires – without damaging the trees. It sounds unlikely, but one of my mates actually sawed himself off an oak tree with the branch. Fortunately, his fall was broken by the foliage of the sawn-off branch, as well as by the grass onto which everything fell. He was shocked by his experience, but we often laughed at what happened on that day.

My mother prepared the treacle toffees and parkin (cake), and friends and neighbours knew they could join us and enjoy themselves, and many did. When my dad had lit the fire it didn't matter whether or not it was raining; the heat of the fire kept us dry. We baked potatoes in the embers to fill ourselves up. These traditional bonfire nights gave me a liking for fireworks and firework displays which I still enjoy today. I can't remember anybody getting injured by a firework; we treated them with respect.

Another tradition we always celebrated was Shrove Tuesday or Pancake Day. If a young person was unable to eat all the pancakes prepared for them, they were loaded into a wheelbarrow and carted off to the nearest midden, on to which they were tipped.

Stephen Melling and I would climb anything; we were fearless. One day we decided we would climb Tarleton's Holy Trinity Church spire (from the inside!) When we got to the belfry, we decided to follow the steps up to the room in which the bells are hung to watch them chime and to listen to the din. We could see the people below through the open stone windows waiting for the Southport bus and keeping a check on their watches. When the bell was due to strike one o'clock on that day, it struck two o'clock. We didn't dare look out of the window again to see the reaction of the villagers below us.

We made our own catapults from Y-shaped pieces of wood that we obtained from the trees and thick pieces of rubber with a square cross-section. We used them mainly for target practice, usually firing at some old tin cans or other objects that could be knocked over. Unfortunately, some boys used catapults as weapons for gang warfare. For many years I carried a scar where I was hit by a stone accidentally fired at short range from a friendly boy's catapult.

One of the great moments of my early years was to be given a Raleigh bicycle. With my close friends I began to explore the surrounding countryside. We travelled as far as Parbold Hill, where we visited the Delph Tea Gardens, and to Ashurst Beacon, and visited the villages of Bretherton, Croston, Mawdesley, Rufford and many others. On the low, wet meadows along the road from Rufford to Mawdesley farmers grew willow for the local basket-making industry.

From the top of Parbold Hill and Ashurst Beacon the whole of the West Lancashire Plain was laid out at our feet and, on a particularly clear day, the far-away coastal places could be seen. We even cycled the 20 miles to Southport and back several times.

In my younger days I was fascinated by the bicycle lamps that were lit at the front by burning acetylene, generated by dropping water onto calcium carbide. Fortunately, our bicycles were fitted with dynamos that could be clamped onto the front tyre, which provided electricity for both front and back lights.

My earlier experiences of butchering kept me a vegetarian for the first 19 years of my life. It was only when I went to Hull University in 1958 that I began, out of necessity, to eat meat, because they would not provide meals for vegetarians unless you made a lot of fuss. I was a very poor eater in my early years, living on 'jam butties' and tins of Heinz vegetable soup. I did enjoy cakes and puddings when sugar became more plentiful after the war, and I still do. Consequently, most of my life I was as thin as a beanpole. I developed a liking for syrup and condensed milk but I hated the taste of Camp coffee.

From a very early age, when my father killed pigs on the local farms, I accompanied him. It was impossible to cut the throat of a pig on the wooden trestle unless four adults held the pig down, one holding each leg, until it was dead. If there were not enough helpers on the farm to perform this initial task, my father would engage my cousins and, later, myself. I have a vivid memory of the day - my Cousin Frank was helping my dad that day - when a very strong pig that had obviously decided its own fate leapt off the trestle and fled across the farmyard, with my father on its back trying to bring the pig down for a return match. The sound of squealing pigs and the sight of the blood pouring from the pig's throat into a bucket, where it was collected to make black puddings later, live with me until this day. My father hung the pigs up with hooks to slit and gut them, which was an equally appalling sight for me to behold.

Just as my grandfather had taught my father to butcher pigs, my father was trying to teach me the same tradition. Later, the Government brought in what was called 'humane killing' of pigs. My father regretted the day he was forced by law to start using a 'stun gun' because he could not bleed the pigs properly. He knew it would be more difficult to cure the meat in the traditional ways, and it was. At that time meat could not be kept in the large refrigerated rooms we have today; it had to be 'cured' with salt if it was going to be kept for any length of time. I wasn't aware of an abattoir anywhere near the village of Tarleton. They were built later, in the towns.

After every butchery job my father was paid in kind. He kept the blood to make black puddings, he kept the intestines to make sausages, he kept the pig's trotters and ears to give or sell to friends or family, and he even kept the pig's brains. I carried pig's brains in a dish to Jack Melling, who was keen on eating them, and I was allowed to keep the threepence or sixpence (3d or 6d; 6d = 2.5p) he gave me as pocket money. Is it any wonder that I was a vegetarian in my early days?

One of the good things about visiting the farms in Tarleton and the surrounding countryside was that the farmer and his wife always invited us into their farmhouse when the job was done. There, on their kitchen table, they laid out quite a spread of homemade cakes, scones, apple or damson pies and other delicious food. The milk was fresh from the cows and the cheese was freshly churned on the farm. My father was a well-known person who was well received wherever he went.

Another of my memories from those early days is of the profusion of wildlife I saw in the countryside surrounding my village. Once I found violets (my mother's name was Violet) growing under a hawthorn hedge, which was a great find. The water courses were populated with marigolds, and bluebells and celandines grew in the woods, red and white campions in the hedgerows, buttercups and daisies grew in the meadows and nearly every other wild flower you can think of could be found somewhere. It is not so today; the use of pesticides and herbicides and the different ways of working the land have seen off a lot of the wildlife I saw as a young boy.

My father's 'pit' (pond) from which he drew water to irrigate the plants in his greenhouses was surrounded by cuckoo flowers, and I was fascinated by the variety of newts and fish that lived in it and in the ponds of surrounding meadows. Water attracted a lot of dragonflies too.

My dad's pit almost ended my life in my early years. Both my mum and dad constantly warned me about playing near water – near the canal, the rivers and the many ponds that there were for the cattle to drink from in the meadows. They told me that if I fell into our pit, 'Ginny Greenteeth' would 'get me'. This was the green algae that grew all over the surface of the pit, especially in the summer months. I learned to swim only in my teenage years.

One day, when my father was engaged in starting the petrol-driven pump that pumped water from this pit into his greenhouse irrigation system, I was standing on the edge of it on wet earth – it was raining – when I suddenly felt my feet slipping from under me. Within seconds I was in the water and going under. It was a terrifying experience that I can remember vividly to this day. Fortunately, above the noise the running mechanical pump made, my father must have heard the splash and caught me before I slipped to the depths of that pit. I was saved from 'Ginny Greenteeth'.

There were far more hedges dividing the different arable fields from the meadows than there are today, and consequently there was a wide variety of bird life that we could observe. I am ashamed to say now that we collected birds' eggs and kept our collections, after 'blowing' the eggs, on layers of cotton wool in drawers at home.

I earned pocket money by picking hundreds of pounds of

rose hips in the hedgerows, and picked wild blackberries which my mother and aunts turned into pies. When I got older I discovered elderberry wine and likewise, there were a lot of those fruits to be picked too.

Behind 74 Hesketh Lane our family had a small piece of land on which we cultivated gooseberries, blackcurrants and strawberries, which I also spent many hours harvesting. On our trips to the Ribble marshes at the end of Guide Road, Hesketh Bank, we found large wild mushrooms in the meadows of Slinger's farm. My parents always prepared mushrooms in boiling milk.

In the 1940s, every town and village in Lancashire had a 'walking day', when the different churches and other organisations of the village walked in a parade, and dressed in their finest clothes, from one end of the village to the other and on to a free tea or entertainment on a field. The parade was usually led by a brass band, and some farmers or other businesses lent their carthorses and carts or a wagon, which were dressed up as 'floats' on which some people were fortunate enough to be able to ride. Sometimes the 'floats' represented a theme.

Tarleton still has its walking day, in July, when Silcock's funfair visits the village. Similarly, Croston has its 'coffee day'. I remember taking part in these parades. The people sat out in the streets to cheer us on. I remember passing Aunt Jane Ellen's house every year, when she would call me over to present me with an octagonal threepenny piece (3d) for spending on the fairground later. Aunt Jane Ellen introduced me to 'Biros' (ball-point pens) when she gave me a metal one as a present. On passing Webster's furniture store in the centre of the village, Mrs Webster would call some children over (their parents, like mine, were probably their customers) to give them a sixpence.

After the parade ended in the centre of the village, the children stormed the school, where a free tea was provided by our parents. The highlight of the day was to spend our pocket money on Silcock's fair, where the brass band would play again for the entertainment of the adults. There were coconuts and tin cans to be knocked over, air rifles to fire at targets, hoopla and roll-a-penny stalls, and all manner of rides provided to make sure the jelly and cream were firmly mixed with the sandwiches in our stomachs. The marvellous fairground organs blared out their music from the carousel and Wurlitzer rides.

Tarleton walking day – Thomas Alan Parkinson, me and my brother Graham are in the second row, and Martin Ashcroft and Stephen Melling are in the next to the back row.

Ruth Myers leading Tarleton Morris Dancers; Joan Melling is in the first row on the right of the picture.

In my youth, fairgrounds were magical places. In Parliament, many years later, I was very happy to support showmen by becoming Secretary to the All-Party Parliamentary Fairs and Show Grounds Group. They made me an Honorary Member of the Showman's Guild on 16 January 2008.

From a very early age I was taken to pantomimes, usually matinees in Blackpool when we were very young. A visit to the UCP restaurant behind the Tower was obligatory. They were famous for their tripe. Our family, often accompanied by the Pickervances, made annual pilgrimages in the summer to Blackpool Tower, which was a complete day out. We entered through a back door, which led into a large aquarium, and worked our way up the building. In those days the Tower housed a small zoo, exhibiting lions and tigers as well as monkeys, apes, baboons and other animals. I have always enjoyed listening to those who can recite Albert and the Lion (made famous by Stanley Holloway).

The Tower put on a show in the afternoons in the famous Tower Ballroom, performed by children and attended by other children like me and Derrick. It was always enjoyable. There were penny slot machines in the Tower and plenty of places to eat as well as drink. On rare occasions we were shot up in the lift to the very top of the Tower to admire the view of Blackpool and its hinterland. It was of course mandatory to listen to Reginald Dixon play the huge Wurlitzer organ that came up out of the floor by the stage in the Tower Ballroom. Then the adults would show us their ballroom dancing skills.

Perhaps even more exciting for me than Blackpool Tower were our regular outings to the Tower Circus. I saw some amazing acts there, but I was always astonished as a young boy to see acrobats performing on horses in such a small circus ring, and elephants there too. Of course, that would not be acceptable today but then was a different era with different values. Blackpool Tower Circus stopped using animal acts in 1990.

The clown Charlie Cairoli performed there every summer season for 40 years. He holds the record for the clown with the most performances at a single venue. Always, at the end of the circus the ring was flooded and the show turned into an aqua-spectacular. I became very fond of circuses and visited quite a few travelling circuses in my youth. For me circuses and fairgrounds go together. They represent a special way of life, entertainment on wheels.

Fortunately, my parents could afford to run a car, if only a second-hand one, for most of my life with them. The early cars had no indicators; the driver had to wind down the window and stick his (few women learned to drive) hand out of the window to indicate whether he was going to the left or the right at a junction. A straight arm meant a turn to the right, a rotating arm meant a turn to the left, an arm moving up and down meant that the driver was slowing down and an arm waving backwards and forwards meant that the driver behind should overtake.

Later, cars were produced with mechanical indicators that would lift out of the right hand or left hand central door pillar of the car and light up yellow. They had a habit of sticking when activated. Power steering was unheard of and there were no internal heating systems. I remember too that the windscreens were very small and were wiped with a single wiper blade. When my father's windscreen became dirty he had to get out of the car to clean it.

Starting these early cars was quite a performance, and could be hazardous too. After the ignition system had been switched on, the engine was cranked by inserting a starting handle at the front. If you weren't careful the engine could spin the handle in the opposite direction so that it would hit the operator's wrist or arm, sometimes breaking a bone.

Early cars were always breaking down, or so it seemed to me as a young boy. The fan belts broke, the carburettors became clogged up or the points failed to provide sparks for the ignition. Points had to be removed and reset after rubbing their pitted surfaces down with fine sandpaper, or even replaced. Spark plugs too had to be constantly removed, cleaned and reset, or replaced. And, there was no antifreeze available, so radiators constantly froze up and even fractured if the water wasn't drained out at night or the vehicle garaged. Rust was a constant problem, especially around the wheel arches.

## SCIENCE AND POLITICS: AN UNLIKELY MIXTURE

One of the biggest advances in my lifetime has been in the design and operation of motor cars and other vehicles. They are far less trouble to operate than they were in my youth and a joy to drive today. My Vauxhall Insignia has electric windows, an electronically controlled engine, adjustable seats, FM radio, a Bluetooth connection for my mobile telephone, a connection point for an iPod, and a CD player, not to mention its air bags and other safety devices.

The best car my father ever bought was a Rover 90, light grey with matching upholstery, which was his pride and joy. It was mine too, especially since he allowed me to drive it in my late teenage years and my early twenties. It had leather bench seats front and rear. The car was fitted with a gear lever on the driving column, and the handbrake came out of the car's front end instead of being fitted to the floor. It had power steering and a heating system too, which made it much easier to drive than my father's earlier cars. Henry Ford once said, "You can have any colour of car you like providing it is black", and most of my father's cars were black until he bought his Rover. Unfortunately, I was lucky if I got 20 miles to the gallon out of it, which made my evenings out quite expensive. On the positive side, my girlfriends enjoyed riding in it.

We had a lot of foggy weather in those days, probably partly as a result of burning coal as a fuel for domestic and industrial use. Wherever you looked there were factory chimneys belching out thick black smoke. The worst of the fogs were called 'pea soup fogs'. 'A Foggy Day in London Town' is a well-known line from a Sinatra song. These fogs made driving extremely hazardous, especially on unlit country lanes. My father praised 'cats' eyes', the studs fitted to roads which reflect back the light from a car's headlights. We take them for granted now. They were invented in 1933 by Percy Shaw, who lived in Boothtown, Halifax.

The snowstorms seemed worse too in the 1940s. Probably the most spectacular was that of 1947. I couldn't get out of our house until my father dug a trench, because the snow was deeper than my height at that time. The snowdrifts made the roads of our village impassable for a few days of every winter in the 1940s.

The winter of 1950-51 was an important turning point in my life. I became vaguely aware that the boys and girls in my class would be divided soon and that the determining factor would be an examination. At this stage in my life I knew very little. I was a good reader but I had not learned my multiplication tables, and nobody had bothered to detect my lack of general knowledge.

Too late in the day, the school sent me home with a book of examination papers to practise for the infamous 11-plus examination, which determined who should go to Hutton Grammar School for Boys or to Ormskirk Grammar School for Girls. Sadly, I never realised the gravity of my situation. The questions asked in the papers didn't seem to have any relevance to the life that I was leading at that time. I sat the examination in a cold classroom in January 1951, just a few days after Derrick Pickervance died. I failed.

Ann Mee, the daughter of a village butcher, and Mary Glover went off to Ormskirk Grammar School, and my friends Martin Ashcroft and Thomas Alan Parkinson, who I discovered later had been coached by the local vicar (Rev. L. N. Forse or 'Pa Forse', as we called him), went off to Hutton Grammar School. Alan was an altar boy in the church and one of his favourite boys. As far as I can remember today, they were the only children who passed the 11-plus examination in my primary school class of over 30 children.

I was destined for the local County Council Secondary School, which was situated just along Hesketh Lane from where we lived. The education I would have received would have been more of the same – preparation for a life on the land. That would have pleased my father, for his intention was for me to succeed him in the business. But my mother had other ideas. She was stunned by my failure and decided to do something about it.

I am often asked, "Who have been the most influential people in your life?" Undoubtedly, my mother was the first and probably the most important of them. Off she went to the offices of the Lancashire County Council's Education Department at County Hall, Preston, where she demanded that I be allowed to attend Christ Church Boys' Secondary Modern School in Southport. I never discovered what drove her to choose this school, but it had been equivalent to a grammar school before King Edward Grammar School was built on Scarisbrick Road, Southport.

Not surprisingly, the initial reaction from the officials was a strong 'NO'. Southport was a separate Local Education Authority and, at that time, pupils were not usually allowed to cross the county boundary unless there were exceptional circumstances, or parents were prepared to pay for private schools. My friends David Barron and Stephen Melling attended private schools in Southport. Nevertheless, my mother was determined. She told the officials that she would sit in their department until it closed that day or longer if necessary, until they agreed to her request. Much to her surprise, close to the time when the offices closed for the night, they agreed, and I became the first boy or girl from Tarleton to cross the county boundary to attend a state school in Southport.

Those officials must have deeply regretted that decision later because the flood gates had been opened, and the parents of Tarleton children soon cottoned on to the fact that there was better education to be had in Southport for their children. Seven years later my brother Graham attended the same secondary school as myself.

On 22 January 1953, my mother wrote to the Lancashire Education Committee (Divisional Executive, No. 4) demanding that they publish my 11-plus results, and requesting that I be allowed to retake the 11-plus examination. A letter came back from 5 Camden Place, Preston, dated 2 March 1953, which was signed by F. Gainer, the Divisional Education Officer. It read:

"Dear Madam

With reference to your letter of the 22nd January, 1953, I find that your son Brian did not sit the Examination for Selection for Secondary Education in 1952 but sat as an 11-plus candidate in 1951. An assessment of his performance at that Examination is as follows:-

| | |
|---|---|
| Non-Verbal Test | Fairly Good |
| Arithmetic | Fairly Good |
| English | Fairly Good |
| Intelligence | Fair |

I have arranged with the Headmaster of Christ Church Secondary Modern School, Southport for an application form for admission to the Supplementary Examination to be held on the 28th March to be sent to him. The form will be signed by Mr. Thompson and handed to your son. Please return the form duly completed, as soon as possible.

Yours faithfully, etc."

By this time I was settled at Christ Church, and I never re-sat the 11-plus examination.

It's strange how trivial events can influence a person's life in a big way. One afternoon, shortly after the 11-plus results became known to us, I was walking home along Hesketh Lane when, as I passed Tarleton fire station and the clinic, I noticed a pocket diary lying in water in the gutter. Out of curiosity I picked it up and looked to see if the owner's name was inside it. I discovered that it belonged to one of my friends, Alan Parkinson. Whilst flicking through the pages, my attention was caught by the contents of one page in particular.

Alan had written some highly derogatory remarks about my failure of the 11-plus examination, and he compared my future with his own at Hutton Grammar School. Those remarks hurt me badly and made me feel very inadequate, but they gave me a determination to prove myself as good as he might ever be in life.

From that day on I wore a huge chip on my shoulder. Even though it has shrunk quite a bit now, the chip is still there, and I have always campaigned against unfair selection in education and for all children to be given equal opportunities, with encouragement for them to develop their own individual talents. Many young people from my generation were equally damaged by this selection process, and they are still being damaged today by Local Education Authorities in places such as Trafford in Greater Manchester, where 11-plus selection is still used. I was very disappointed that the 1997-2010 Labour Government didn't abolish the 11-plus examination system.

Please don't get me wrong. I am not against measuring children's abilities, but the results should always be used in a positive way. As a result of the 11-plus selection process, I was denied many opportunities in my early education. At secondary school I wasn't able to become a competent speaker of a foreign language, which had consequences for me later. I was never given an opportunity to play a musical instrument, and I wasn't able to study any of the sciences as a single subject, which also had consequences for me later.

NOTES

1. Lily May Iddon was born at 3.55 am on Sunday 29 December 2013.

2. A good description of the area as it was in my early years can be found in the book *Lancashire Plain and Seaboard*, Herbert C. Collins, J. M. Dent and Sons Ltd., London, 1953.

3. Frank Hornby was born in Liverpool on 15 May 1863 and lived most of his life in Maghull; he died on 21 September 1936. He invented Meccano construction sets in 1902 (although the trade name was registered later, in

1907), Dinky Toys in 1934 and Hornby Dublo model railway sets, which were marketed after his death in 1938. He was the Conservative MP for Everton from 1931 to 1935.

## CHAPTER TWO

# TEENAGE YEARS - A WAKE-UP CALL

~

From the age of 11 onwards my life began to change significantly. My two closest friends, Stephen Melling and Martin Ashcroft, went off to other schools, along with Alan Parkinson and David Barron. My mother had won me a place at Christ Church Boys' Secondary Modern School in Southport, and I was required to travel the ten miles there every school day on the 8.05 am Preston to Southport double-decker Ribble bus and the ten miles back on the 4.35 pm, journeys I would make for the next seven years. These buses ran hourly.

The morning bus travelled slowly through Tarleton, then across the Southport New Road into the village of Mere Brow, back onto the Southport New Road before taking another detour and journeying through the village of Banks. It proceeded into Southport along Southport New Road and Cambridge Road, round Hesketh Park and along Southport Promenade before dropping me off at the Claremont Hotel (today Byng House, a convalescent home and a listed building), between Neville Street and Scarisbrick Avenue. Christ Church is on Lord Street; the school building is at the back of the church. Although the building is still there today, it closed as a school in 1974. It is accessed from Lord Street or Chapel Street down Corporation Street at the side of Southport Town Hall.

Lord Street is below the level of The Promenade at Southport and, just once when I got off the bus on The Promenade, I found the sea flowing down Neville Street and flooding Lord Street. On that morning we had to take our shoes and socks off, roll up our trousers and wade across Lord Street to get to school. Fortunately, the sea had not invaded our classrooms.

The three-storey building, the third school to have occupied this site, was Victorian, and the Headmaster's study and a second playground that was used by the older children were at roof level. The main playground and the outside toilet block were between the east end of the church and the school. Fewer than 500 boys attended the school until they reached the age of 16.

The access to the three floors of the school from Corporation Street was open to the elements, and it could be quite cold in winter when the wind was blowing through the school. We reached the classrooms on the upper floors by climbing up Victorian wrought iron staircases. On the ground floor was a hall which was equipped as a gymnasium and surrounded by a changing room and three or four classrooms.

Christ Church Boys' Secondary Modern School in Southport as it is today.

Details of the stone archway shown in the top picture (this entrance wasn't used when I was at the school): the plaque informs us that "Christ Church Higher Grade School was erected in 1898 when Reverend J. H. Honeyburne was the Vicar".

Mr R. H. Hill, who taught me geography.

Joan and Wilf Taylor.

 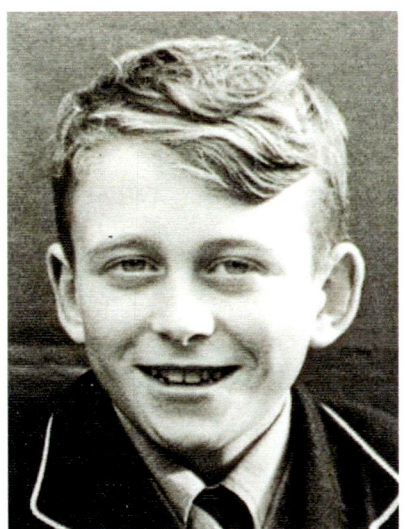

As a pupil at Christ Church Boys' School.

The main hall of the school, which was equipped with a stage for the daily assemblies, was on the first floor. Sliding partitions divided it from the four classrooms, two on each side of the hall. On the next floor up was the science laboratory, which had a high vaulted ceiling. Another short wrought iron staircase enabled access from there to the roof playground and the Headmaster's study.

When I was at Christ Church the Headmaster was Mr William Charles Thompson. Like all his staff, he was keen on maintaining strict discipline in the school. Teachers used a ruler, a cane or the slipper to hand down punishments to unruly pupils. I got the slipper once, from an eccentric teacher called Mr Snell, although I can't remember what for, and I got caned once by Mr Hill for misspelling 'woollen'. I didn't misspell it again.

## SCIENCE AND POLITICS: AN UNLIKELY MIXTURE

A six foot three inches tall 'gentle giant' called Wilfred Taylor boarded our bus at Mere Brow, and he became my closest friend during my secondary school days. Wilf's father was a lay preacher on the local Methodist circuit. Like my father, he was in the market gardening business and they were strong Methodists. The Taylor family went to the small Mere Brow chapel twice on Sundays. I was a regular visitor in their household on Sundays and regularly accompanied Mr and Mrs Taylor, Wilf and Wilf's sister Joan to the evening services.

When I arrived at Christ Church I realised within days how I had neglected my earlier education. But I wasn't alone. We 37 Form 1A boys sat for days and weeks at the beginning of our secondary education learning our multiplication tables by rote. I became numerate for the first time. In the Christmas examinations I was placed second in the form and remained in the top three of my class throughout my career at Christ Church, often being the top boy. In my first year the geography teacher, Mr R. H. Hill (we called him 'Pinhead'), was my form teacher. He had served in the navy and often smelled of alcohol in the afternoons, when he leaned over us to see what our exercise books contained.

During my secondary school days we had the feeling that the dark cloud that had hung over Britain during the years of the war and those immediately after was finally being lifted. The Coronation of Queen Elizabeth II on 2 June 1953 was a joyous occasion for the people of the United Kingdom. I remember watching the event on a black-and-white television set somewhere and receiving a Coronation mug, which I haven't kept, and I felt after that event that there was a new mood about in my country, one of hope rather than despair. The Festival of Britain, which was held in London in 1951, also helped to lift the mood of the British people at that time. Rowland Emett created the Far Tottering and Oyster Creek Railway in Battersea Park for the Festival, and I have been an admirer of his kinetic sculptures and those of others ever since.

'Once every Preston Guild' is an expression used in Lancashire to refer to a rare event. Preston Guilds come round once every 20 years and one had had to be cancelled during the war years. At the age of 12 my dad and mum took me to the Royal Preston Guild of 1952 to see at least two of the daily parades. It was celebrated in style as the new mood of hope developed after the war years. It is an occasion when every aspect of civic and industrial life is celebrated. The churches marched with their banners and brass bands, Proud Preston's industries displayed their wares and the military marched too.

Probably the second most influential person in my life, after my mum, was the general science teacher at Christ Church School, Mr R. E. Jones, although the English teacher there, Mr W. P. Pearson, who became my Form Teacher when I reached the age of 13 and remained so until I left the school at the age of 16, was also a great influence.

I have never liked gymnasiums or outdoor sports in winter, and my physical training marks always reflected this dislike of exercise. I tell my friends that people die trying to keep fit and that if I feel like taking exercise, I go to bed until the feeling wears off. Obesity was never a problem in my youth. I can't judge whether it was a lack of food or too much activity, as distinct from planned exercise, or both, that kept me thin. My greatest embarrassment was being sent by the school nurse to classes to correct my posture – flat feet and rounded shoulders.

The school's playing field was a bus journey away. The footballs in those days were made of a thick leather case that contained an internal rubber ball (my father used to keep pig's bladders for this purpose) that was inflated through a valve. The inner inflated ball was laced inside the outer leather ball. When these balls got wet they became heavier than usual, and kicking them was like kicking a brick. Occasionally I was expected to head one of these balls, which nearly laid me out on the ground and left my head spinning for several minutes. I had nothing but respect for the Tom Finneys, Stanley Mathews, Nat Lofthouses and Tommy Lawtons of that time. I hated playing football, especially on wet, cold winter days. I much preferred cricket in the summer.

Having got that off my chest I have to admit that, although it was exercise, I was extremely grateful that Mr R. H. Hill regularly took us to the Victoria Baths at the top of Neville Street on Southport Promenade, where I learned to swim, after a fashion. I have in my possession a 'Proficiency Swimming Certificate', awarded to me in 1953 by the Southport Education Committee. I enjoyed playing in and on water and had nearly drowned in my dad's 'pit' in my early years, but I have never been a strong swimmer.

I became extremely passionate about cricket in my youth. My friend Derrick Pickervance's home was opposite the cricket field on Carr Lane, Tarleton. Whenever I could find time in the summer months, I was there hammering balls all over the field, with my friends in pursuit. I was never any good at cricket, either as a bowler or as a batsman, but boy did I enjoy trying. The problem was that I never received any formal tuition in cricket and I could not keep my eye on the ball when I had a bat or ball in my hand. As in later life, my eyes gave me trouble as a young boy. I squinted badly. However, an eye specialist in Liverpool pronounced that I would grow out of the problem.

I had a most unusual bowling style, which my friends found very amusing. The ball seemed to appear from round the back of my neck. My main ability was as a wicket keeper. In my teenage years I graduated to be Tarleton second eleven's wicket keeper, although I had to serve as a scorer for many years leading up to that graduation. I must confess that my father was one of the selectors!

Victoria Swimming Baths on The Promenade at Southport.

'The Wine Cellar', Municipal Gardens, Southport, formerly an underground gentlemen's toilet.

My friend Martin Ashcroft played in the same team and, as a slow spin bowler, he was almost unplayable on a good day. I could stand on top of the wicket when he was bowling and God help any batsman who went down the wicket to play a ball and missed. On one occasion, Martin bowled and I ran out, stumped or caught ten of the visiting team players in one innings. Tarleton was in the Southport and District Cricket League, and we played on Southport cricket grounds, as well as on those in the villages of Bretherton, Croston, Mawdesley (which had a gently sloping outfield – good for high scores), Rufford and Hesketh Bank.

I could run, having picked up this skill escaping from a charging bull on more than one occasion. I hold sports day certificates from Christ Church School for coming second place in the senior 440 yard races in 1955 and 1956, and one too for the senior 880 yard race in 1956. But, neither I nor 37 other boys in my class could ever run like Mick Wyman. He could run like the wind, and he was one of the best young amateur football players I have ever known. I have often wondered what he did with his talent.

At school I enjoyed the art and craft lessons, where I picked up the skill of bookbinding. I bought copies of the National Geographic Magazine, bound several copies together in a leather binding and learned how to use gold leaf to apply the title on the leather front cover. At the age of 13 I was introduced to technical drawing by Mr Snell. I enjoyed drawing the plans and elevations of machines and buildings. I became fascinated by algebra and geometry and we were taught the skills of bookkeeping too, presumably because some of us were expected to run small businesses, like the market garden that my father ran.

The toilets at Christ Church School were outside in the school yard and quite disgusting. They were smelly, and freezing in winter. There were no seats on the toilet pans, the cubicle doors wouldn't lock, and there was no toilet paper, unless you brought your own from home. In 1969, when I presented the prizes at Christ Church School as one of their most successful pupils, I told the story of putting my hand up in a class, receiving permission to go to the toilet, then running like mad down Corporation Street, across the front of the Town Hall and Art Gallery and diving down the steps into the municipal toilets (now a wine cellar!) After the return journey, I was pretty exhausted, but I don't believe any of the teachers ever realised what I had been doing for those five years. That was exercise enough for me during my days at Christ Church School.

My reports are full of glowing praise from all the teachers, with the exception of the physical education teachers. One of them was involved with the *Eagle* comic, which introduced boys to characters such as Dan Dare, Pilot of the Future. It was produced initially in Churchtown, Southport. The first issue arrived on news stands on 14 April 1951.

Eventually, I became a prefect as a senior boy, and Wilf Taylor (also a prefect) and I became the official recorders of the Southport weather. On the roof of the school there was a small weather station, where we recorded the wind speeds, took the temperature and measured the volume of any precipitation there had been in the last 24 hours.

It was the general science lessons that interested me most at school. At the age of 11, my mother told me about a boy in Sutton Avenue, Tarleton who had a chemistry set for sale. It was one he had put together himself and not one of the boxed sets that were common at that time. It contained a good supply of glassware and chemicals and a small Victorian book of experiments (which I wish I had kept). The set cost me 14s and 6d (72.5p). The book, published in 1907, was written by Professor Roscoe, Emeritus Professor at the Victoria University of Manchester who, as well as being a chemist, became a Liberal Member of Parliament. He and I are the only two chemists to date who have published peer-reviewed papers in the journals of learned societies while serving as Members of Parliament.

Mr Jones advised me that Cave's the Chemist in Neville Street, Southport, conveniently situated on my route to the home bus stop at the Floral Hall on The Promenade, was a good place to supplement my set with more glassware and chemicals. I bought thistle funnels and beehive shelves, round- and flat-bottomed flasks, conical flasks of all sizes and all the chemicals that I needed from Cave's. It was a proper chemist's shop the like of which I never saw again, and it has long since disappeared.

At my home there was a porch with a solid floor behind the front door, which was separated from the hall by a partition. Apart from picking up the mail and the *Lancashire Evening Post* or the *Southport Visiter* which dropped through the letter box, my parents rarely used this small space. The electricity meter was also in a cupboard in there, and the top of the cupboard made a good laboratory bench. That became my laboratory, where I conducted all the experiments described in the book that I had acquired and many more besides.

Cave's the chemist's shop was in this parade of shops on Neville Street, Southport, adjacent to the Victoria Swimming Baths.

The Mecca Bingo Hall, Lord Street, Southport, formerly the Garrick Theatre. The entrance to Southport Bus Station was under the clock tower on the left of the picture.

I made and collected all the common gases, hydrogen, oxygen and chlorine, and tested their properties. I changed one chemical into another and distilled all manner of liquids in my 'retort'. The colour changes that occur as chemicals are mixed and react together fascinated me. I learned how to differentiate chemicals by their unforgettable smells. There was no fume cupboard, of course, but I propped open the large letterbox flap when the fumes became too much for me. At the age of 11, I decided that I was going to be a chemist.

I wanted to know how our bodies work too. So, I decided to buy *Teach Yourself Physiology*. The Teach Yourself series of books, published by the English Universities Press, provided an excellent source of knowledge and I bought quite a few of them as aids to my education.

Sadly, Mr Jones had met an untimely death by the time I returned to Christ Church in 1969 to present the school prizes.

It became clear to my teachers at Christ Church School that I shouldn't give up my education at the age of 16, and they persuaded my mum and dad to let the school enter me for several GCE examinations and consider enrolling me at Southport Technical College. In 1956, I achieved passes in the Joint Matriculation Board GCE Ordinary Level examinations in English Language, History, Geography, Mathematics Syllabus I, General Science I, Elementary Physiology and Geometrical and Engineering Drawing. For good measure, I also sat and passed the English, Arithmetic and General Knowledge Entrance Examinations of the Local Government Examinations Board which would have provided me with a local government career.

At home, I studied in the small bedroom above the stairs – the 'box' room – with the help of a single-bar electric fire to keep me warm in winter. I listened to a small radio and played 78 rpm vinyl records on an electrically-driven record player. The first vinyl record I ever bought was *The Dam Busters' March*. Every time I hear it played today, as it often is at Remembrance Day parades, it reminds me of my teenage years.

My obvious academic successes at Christ Church School, which were recognised several times at school prize-giving events, made me a sitting target for the school bullies, and there were plenty of those. Fights in the school playground occurred on what seemed to me a daily basis. I was often taunted and even hit in order to get me into a fight with other boys, usually bigger in every way than I was at that age. It was, of course, frightening. However, I had my very own bodyguard in my best friend, Wilf Taylor. He had a very mild temper and I never saw him hit anybody, but to have Wilf by my side was enough. Other boys were frightened by his presence. I owed him a lot. Wilf and I had the disadvantage too that we lived outside Southport.

Mr Thompson joined the school in 1920 and retired, with 40 years of service (25 of those as Headmaster), in 1960. He died suddenly in 1965. He was followed by Mr A. C. W. McIntyre, who served as Headmaster for the next 12 years. The Closing Service for Christ Church Boys' Church of England Secondary Modern School, which was opened in 1823, was held on 12 July 1974 in Christ Church. The Headmaster at that time was Mr D. Roy Strickland and his Deputy was Mr W. P. Pearson, who taught at the school for 25 years.

The children who remained at Christ Church School in its year of closure were transferred to Ainsdale County Secondary

School. Christ Church School was the last of the town centre schools in Southport.

In our teenage years Wilf and I often returned to Southport at the weekends and in the school holidays to go to one of the several cinemas on Lord Street but, most of all, we enjoyed watching the antics of Brian Rix in the so-called Whitehall Farces that visited the Garrick Theatre in Southport. The theatre was conveniently situated close to Southport's bus station at the Birkdale end of Lord Street, almost opposite the then very posh Prince of Wales Hotel. Much later, when I entered Parliament, I came to know Lord (Brian) Rix who, like me, was interested in helping children and adults with learning difficulties.

Wilf made his own puppets, and his skills as a puppeteer made him a popular attraction at many fetes and galas. I often accompanied him and I quite enjoyed his versions of Punch and Judy.

In my youth I saw all the Rodgers and Hammerstein films – *Oklahoma, Carousel, South Pacific, The King and I* and *The Sound of Music* – some of them several times. The 1961 film *West Side Story* (Robert Wise and Jerome Robbins) also had a big impact on me. I enjoy films – *Dr Zhivago, Gandhi* and *Lawrence of Arabia* are among my favourites. The 'Ealing comedies' (produced by the Boulting Brothers), the series of 'St Trinian's' films (starring Jimmy Wheeler, a pioneer of both radio and television, with his catch phrase: 'Aye, aye, that's your lot') and the classic 'Carry On' films, starring people like Barbara Windsor, Sid James, Hattie Jacques and Kenneth Williams, filled the cinemas in the 1950s and early 1960s. Any film starring Alec Guinness, Ian Carmichael, Terry Thomas or Leslie Philips was also popular.

Every school day my friend Wilf would go off at lunch time to a shop supplying herbs and herbal drinks, and he would drink one glass of sarsaparilla. Wilf discovered the Swan chip shop, one of the best I have ever known. My mum and dad enjoyed their fish and chip suppers there too. Its reputation is intact today.

At the age of 16, Wilf Taylor left school to join his father in his market gardening business. By this time his father was also acting as a produce merchant in the Mere Brow area, and Wilf followed in his father's footsteps. He also became a Methodist lay preacher on the local circuit.

Sadly, James Wilfred Taylor died from an aneurism on 21 April 2005 at the very early age of 64 (he was one day away from his 65th birthday). On the day of his funeral, 28 April, the small chapel at Mere Brow was packed, and Eileen (my second wife) and I listened to the service in the adjacent Sunday school. Wilf is buried in St Mary's Church graveyard at Tarleton. I visit his grave from time to time and try to keep in contact with his wife Mollie.

Entertainment in the 1940s and 1950s was dominated by the radio. We listened to programmes like *ITMA, Much Binding in the Marsh, Round the Horn, Music While You Work, Have a Go*, with Wilfred Pickles and his wife Mabel (which ran from 1946 to 1967 and generated a number of catch phrases, such as 'What's on the table Mabel' and 'Give him the money Barney'), and serialised drama programmes such as *The Thirty Nine Steps* and *Dick Barton, Special Agent*. Peter Sellers, Harry Secombe, Spike Milligan and Michael Bentine made *The Goon Show* famous. Most young people tuned in their radio sets to Radio Luxembourg until the pirate radio station Radio Caroline challenged orthodoxy.

Variety really was the spice of life in my youth. The list of comedians that entertained us is endless, with Arthur Askey ('Hello Playmates'), Norman Wisdom (who, later, I met briefly when he visited the Houses of Parliament), Tommy Trinder, Will Hay, Harry Worth, Charlie Drake, Peter Butterworth, Terry Thomas, Tommy Hanley, Hylda Baker (from Bolton), George Formby (from Wigan), Laurel and Hardy, Jimmy Jewel and Ben Warris, Abbot and Costello, Ted Ray, Charlie Chester, Michael Bentine and Frank Randle readily springing to mind.

The early television programmes were dominated by variety shows too, with *The Billy Cotton Band Show, Hancock's Half Hour, The Black and White Minstrel Show* (which wasn't 'politically correct' and fell out of favour), Max Bygraves, Morecambe and Wise (their first Christmas Show was broadcast in 1969; Eric Morecambe died in 1984), the *Val Doonican Show*, Des O'Connor, Mike and Bernie Winters and Benny Hill easily coming to mind. Everyone watched *Dixon of Dock Green, What's My Line*, with its chairman Gilbert Harding, and *Sunday Night at the London Palladium* (its first compere was Bruce Forsyth).

Later we were introduced to the 'Two Ronnies' (Ronnie Barker was one of my favourite comedians, especially in the classic *Open All Hours*), Michael Parkinson, *Monty Python, Dad's Army, Fawlty Towers, Top of the Pops*, with Pan's People and, later, Legs and Co (its first presenter was the now-disgraced Jimmy Savile) and Terry Wogan (*Blankety Blank* had a very long run). I was a big fan too of Les Dawson, Frankie Howerd (in *Up Pompeii*), Tommy Cooper, Rowan Atkinson (in *Blackadder* and as Mr Bean) and Roy Hudd and Emu (their appearance on *The Michael Parkinson Show* is a classic). But 'top of the pops' for me were Bill Owen in *Last of the Summer*

*Wine* and Richard Wilson in *One Foot in the Grave*. Variety had started to die a death in the 1950s when performers like Tommy Steele arrived on the scene.

My father decided to buy our first black-and-white television set in time to watch the last FA Cup Final that Preston North End FC featured in, which was played at Wembley on 2 May 1964, when they lost to West Ham FC (West Ham 3; Preston North End 2), but it was long after everyone else had acquired a set. The early television sets that I remember were manufactured by Bush. I watched television at 72 Hesketh Lane (where Stephen Melling lived) or at various other households, for example the home of Harold Aspey in Sutton Avenue.

My father enjoyed watching sport on television the most, especially cricket, which I often watched with him. He could never get his head round the phrase 'Dubbin Mixer' in the credits at the end of programmes. "What do they need a dubbin mixer for?" he often asked me. The only dubbin my father knew was the waxy substance that was applied to leather football boots to soften and waterproof them.

My parents were keen to see that I was not seduced by the demon drink, and I wasn't, until the age of 19. They signed me up in 1952 at Tarleton Methodist Chapel as member number 597 in the Star of Hope Tent (no. 55) of Southport Juvenile District No. 15 of the Independent Order of Rechabites. It cost them 1d (240d = £1) per week for me to belong and to receive their lessons. These must have had some impact because, in 1953, I was awarded a First Class pass in their Temperance Knowledge Examination.

From the age of 11 scouting became an important part of

my leisure activities. Along with my Tarleton friends Stephen Melling, Martin Ashcroft and Kenneth Klee, I joined the Rufford Scout Troup in the Owls Patrol, seven of us altogether. We cycled the five miles to the Rufford scout hut in Flash Lane and back. Joe Martland, a farmer from Burscough, was our scout leader. His half-cousin, Alan Martland (see later), was our patrol leader. When I left the scouts I had an armful of badges. We tied knots, we learned how to light fires without matches, we cooked food on camp fires and we sang all the camp fire songs that scouts sing. I always earned quite a bit of money on 'Bob-a-Job' days.

We also went on some interesting summer camps, to places like Wray Castle in the Lake District and to Llansannan in North Wales, which gave me experiences of life outside my

The Owl Patrol (left to right): Alan Martland (patrol leader), me, Martin Ashcroft, Stephen Melling, Kenneth Klee, Clark Chadwick and another boy.

immediate environment. Scouting became a passion, at least until I was parted from it by entry later into university. My visits to North Wales in my scouting days attracted me back later to visit its castles, such as those at Caernarvon and

Rufford Scout Group: Joe Martland (leader) is seated in the middle; I am sitting on the extreme left of the middle row.

Rufford Scout Group: I am sitting fourth left on the front row.

Conway, its seaside resorts, and inland places such as the Swallow Falls at Bettws-y-coed, the Denbigh Moors and the Llanberis Pass. Llandudno is one of my favourite seaside resorts. My mum and dad liked Llandudno too, and I often

Brother Graham and Muriel Pickervance visit our summer camp at Wray Castle.

Llansannan village.

Mum at Lytham.

returned to its shingle beach to admire the views of the Little Orme and Great Orme.

During my secondary school years I became involved a lot in market gardening and in helping my mother to run her 'club'. Mum supplemented our income by circulating the catalogues of Great Universal Stores. Because there were few shops in our village at that time, and because people didn't have the money to buy some of their goods outright, they joined my mother's 'club', which meant that they could have the goods up front and pay for them in 20 or more instalments. Usually on Friday nights, she cycled around the village to collect money from one 'round' of her customers, while the other 'round' was my responsibility. In this way I made many friends in our village.

Bill Pickervance (second left) with my mum (extreme right).

## SCIENCE AND POLITICS: AN UNLIKELY MIXTURE

One of the disadvantages of working on a small farm or market garden is that it is almost impossible to take a holiday. We 'day tripped' in our car to the Fylde coast and Morecambe Bay - Blackpool, Lytham, St Annes, Morecambe, Fleetwood, Sunderland Point, Glasson Dock and Grange-over-Sands were all 'ports of call'; to the Lake District – Kendal, Coniston and Windermere; to North Wales – Snowdonia, Llandudno, Rhyl, Prestatyn and Conway; and to Belle Vue, the 'Tivoli Gardens of Manchester'. I used to enjoy going through the Mersey tunnel to New Brighton, which was a lively holiday resort in my youth. My parents enjoyed taking me to Chester and Chester Zoo as well. Occasionally we went farther afield, to places like York.

As a result of living near the sea, and especially as a result of exploring the dangers of the Ribble marshes at Hesketh Bank as a young boy, I have always been interested in the sea and those who gain a living from it. I read about famous rescues and heard about wildfowlers being drowned on or rescued from the Ribble marshes. In 1954 and 1955, I received Certificates of Merit from the Royal National Life-Boat Institution for essays that I submitted to them about fictional rescues at sea.

Solitude for me as a boy was sitting on top of the bank at Slinger's farm watching the tide come down the River Ribble to flood the marshes until the water reached my feet, with the sound of the wind bringing the cries of wild geese to me and the sound of the curlews feeding on the arable land behind me. I have sat there too with my friends watching the test pilots across the river at Warton take off in the latest aircraft and land them safely again.

We learned how to walk safely on the marshes. When the cows that grazed on them from Slinger's farm turned for home, we knew that the tide had turned and was filling the deep gullies of the marsh. At that stage we had to get off quickly, otherwise we would be trapped by the gullies ahead of us filling up with seawater. It was a dangerous place to be at the best of times. A little-known delicacy that we collected on the Ribble salt marshes is the soft green plant sampi (usually called samphire), which needs to be pickled in vinegar to bring out its taste. My Uncle Dick thrived on it.

Almost on an annual basis my dad would drive us through Blackpool in the autumn to see the illuminations which, for young children, were just fascinating. We always looked forward to the fish and chip supper on the way home, with dandelion and burdock pop. There was no motorway then and we took the 'old road', though Penwortham and Preston to Lytham and St Annes. It was fascinating for me to get glimpses of men assembling the aircraft in 'Dick Kerr's works', the very aeroplanes that would be tested at Warton, which we also passed in Preston on our way to Blackpool. As we approached the coast there might be a prize for the first one who could spot Blackpool Tower.

My father enjoyed telling stories about coach trips to the illuminations. Those from the Liverpool direction used to stop en route at the public houses along the A59, at the Rams Head, an old coaching inn in Tarleton, or at the pubs further down the A59 road in Hoole and Much Hoole. The Rose and Crown and the Black Horse in Much Hoole were popular with the 'trippers'. After a lengthy stay in one of these places, the coach driver was able to drive his 'trippers' up and down

Fishergate and Friargate in Preston, which had become brightly lit by the new neon lights, and the 'trippers' thought they had been through the Blackpool illuminations.

My father often recalled the day he met the famous hangman Albert Pierrepoint on a train returning from one of his 435 public hangings. A hangman was allowed to keep the deceased person's last belongings, according to my father. It was Pierrepoint who hanged Timothy John Evans on 9 March 1950 (Evans received a posthumous pardon in 1966), and Derek Bentley on 28 January 1953 (he received a posthumous pardon in 1998). Later in his life Pierrepoint became an opponent of capital punishment.

When he retired, Albert Pierrepoint made a living by managing public houses. He was the landlord at the Rose and Crown in Much Hoole, near Tarleton, which later became an Indian restaurant. The place was smashed up one evening when a coach party from Liverpool called in on their way to Blackpool illuminations. On board was the brother of a man who Pierrepoint had hanged. After that incident it wasn't long before Pierrepoint retired completely to the outskirts of Southport, where he spent his last days living in a bungalow on Southport New Road (the A585).

Many people from the large cities were evacuated to the villages during the war years and stayed with people like my dad and mum, who had spare bedroom accommodation. Ron and Jen Jones stayed with us and we became great friends. It was like having an extended family. Ron was in the army and his unit of the Royal Engineers was stationed at Bank Hall, which was used as a control centre and military hospital during World War II. Ron Jones was a big man and an amateur boxer. The shapes of his nose and ears gave the game away.

Ron and Jen were very good to me; they had no children of their own and treated me as their own son. I remember a day when I was seven or less when they persuaded my dad and mum to let them take me on the big dipper at Southport's fairground. My parents were not keen on the idea; they felt it would terrify me. They were extremely surprised when I came off the ride laughing rather than crying and requesting another ride.

Bank Hall, a Jacobean mansion dating back to 1608, is on the opposite bank of the River Douglas from the village of Tarleton, at Bank Bridge, where many people have come to grief in road traffic accidents. The A59 goes over the canal and river and round a dangerous bend at this point. I always considered Bank Hall to be part of Tarleton but it is actually in Bretherton, which is part of the Chorley District of Lancashire. In the 1940s and 1950s it was a grand old building but became derelict in the last few decades. It featured in the 8 August 2003 BBC *Restoration* programme, which prompted serious attempts to save the building, and I understand that Urban Splash hope to convert it into apartments for sale.

I remember Ron and Jen Jones inviting me to some very enjoyable garden parties and fairs on the expansive lawns of the Hall. Before the war it was one of the homes of the local landowners, the Lilford family. From the hall towards Croston runs Carriage Drive, which we used as a shortcut to Croston on our bicycles.

When the war was over and Ron Jones was discharged from the army, Ron and Jen moved to live near Stanmore in Middlesex; fortunately for me their home was close to Queensbury Station, then on the Bakerloo Line but now part of the Jubilee Line of the London tube system. Ron got a job as a security guard in a huge factory at Wembley, where they made greaseproof wrappings for all manner of foodstuffs, Wrigleys chewing gum included. He showed me round the factory on one of my visits to stay with them during my school holidays. Later he became the doorman at the Westbury Hotel. Ron and Jen Jones introduced me to London.

My first trip to London was on a steam train with my dad to see a schoolboy cup final at Wembley Stadium. I was well impressed. I can't remember my mum ever visiting London and my brother Graham has been there only twice – in November/December 1999 and June 2003 - when he and Pam visited Eileen and me when I was a Member of Parliament. My mum and dad never travelled abroad.

Later, Ron and Jen took me to Wembley Stadium several times to watch the speedway and stockcar racing. I remember one very special outing that they took me on – to an airport, where I enjoyed my very first 'joy ride' in a De Havilland Rapide aeroplane, owned by Island Air Services (I have the tickets and photographs to prove that I made this journey). That airport is now known as Heathrow. I also went up with them in another four-seater aeroplane that used to take off on the expansive sands of Southport beach.

In 1955 I spent several weeks staying with the Jones family in Stanmore. I went all over London on that occasion. My photograph album of the time reminds me that I visited Hamley's Toy Store in Regent Street, Windsor Castle, Old Scotland Yard (where later I worked), Buckingham Palace, Piccadilly, when the traffic actually went round the statue of Eros, Parliament Square, the British Museum, the Science Museum and the Victoria and Albert Museum in Kensington, Westminster Abbey, St Paul's Cathedral, Battersea Park and its funfair, London Zoo, and the Monument.

# SCIENCE AND POLITICS: AN UNLIKELY MIXTURE

Ron and Jen Jones with Jen's mother.     David Barron at Laxey in the Isle of Man.

In 1956 I revisited London. Ron and Jen Jones took me to see Esther Williams in an 'Aqua-Spectacular' at the Empire Pool and Sports Arena at Wembley, and I visited the Tower of London and Hampton Court (by river), as well as returning to London Airport, which had officially opened as a major airport (Heathrow) in 1956. It was on Tower Hill that I first heard the Methodist preacher Donald Soper preaching socialism.

I remember too that I visited Greenwich by boat from Westminster pier. I also visited the BBC to see a radio show recorded, but I can't remember what it was at this distance in time. After the age of 16 I didn't visit London except for the occasional interview and business trip until I became a Member of Parliament in 1997. I had come to the conclusion that it was a far too busy place for me to consider visiting often.

When Ron Jones retired, Ron and Jen decided that they too

had had enough of the hustle and bustle of London life and they retired to Catterick, to be closer to Jen's family. It was a convenient place to stop off whenever I was travelling up and down the A1, and I visited them from time to time until they passed away, especially when I lived in Durham.

My first 'unsupervised' holiday was taken in Douglas on the Isle of Man with my friend David Barron. I think I was 16 years old at the time and I felt very grown up staying in a hotel. I didn't return to the Isle of Man again until September 2011. In subsequent years David and I went further afield, to Scarborough, which I became very fond of.

It was through knowing David that I learned about the hate there was at that time in Liverpool and the Lancashire villages towards Roman Catholics. David fell for a girl, but his father Bert discovered she was a Roman Catholic and stopped him from associating with her. I discovered later that Bert Barron, who was also a market gardener, was a member of a local Freemasons Lodge.

There was no Roman Catholic Church in Tarleton when I was born, but a priest arrived (probably in the 1950s) and bought a large house on Hesketh Lane, where the few Roman Catholics who lived in Tarleton at that time could go to worship. Eventually, enough money was raised to build a church on Hesketh Lane. There was considerable resentment towards this group of people at that time, which I could never understand. That this feeling of resentment towards Catholics in Lancashire extended beyond my village was demonstrated vividly one day in my youth when the Roman Catholic Archbishop was stoned in the streets of Liverpool, which the comedians have called over the years 'the capital city of Ireland'.

My Aunt Maggie loved music (she was brought up with an HMV gramophone constantly playing some kind of music) and she liked to believe that I had a musical talent. I was certainly interested in all forms of music, with the possible exception of opera. Consequently, she tried first to get me interested in playing the mouth organ, which she could play herself. Larry Adler was entertaining us all at the time. Next, she bought me a beautiful accordion, but it was extremely heavy to hold whilst trying both to control the bellows and press the right keys. I gave up. Later in life I regretted not taking more seriously the encouragement provided for me by Aunt Maggie to learn to play a musical instrument.

An enormous second-hand pianola arrived as a present from Aunt Maggie for Graham to encourage him to learn to play the piano, and the 'dresser' in the front room was displaced by it. Eventually, the pianola found a home in the community centre for older people in the centre of the village of Tarleton.

In the 'growing business', there are busy times and slack times. My father often helped the local farmers with their harvests. When the hay was ready or the corn was ripe it had to be gathered in quickly, especially if the sun was shining. I learned to drive tractors on the farms before I learned to drive a car. For several years after my birth the wheat and barley were cut by scythe and stacked down the field in sheaves tied up with binding string. Later, primitive cutting machines carried on the front of tractors did the job. Then, the really magnificent combine harvesters were introduced, which made the job much easier, although farmers had to pay contractors to do the harvesting for them.

The sheaves were collected by horse and cart, which took the loads to the farmyards, where mechanical threshing machines separated the wheat from the chaff. These machines also had to be contracted in by the farmer. The combine harvesters have the advantage that they not only gather the corn but thresh it as well.

My father was friendly with the Lowe family, who had an arable farm on the A59 at Lathom, near Burscough. As well as helping them with their harvests, we bought our Lancashire heeler dogs from them. My father liked these dogs because they had short legs and could go under his hen cabins to clear out rats' nests. One in particular, Sooty, which Dad gave to my brother Graham as a birthday present, lived to a ripe old age.

The famous entertainer George Formby also kept these dogs as pets and bought them from the Lowe farm, where I first met him. On one visit to the farm my father discovered that George had a car for sale, and I remember waiting with my father behind the Garrick Theatre in Southport for George to come out of the theatre during the interval to sell his car to my dad. He came and sat in the car with us, still wearing his stage make-up. I remember very little about him except that he was a very pleasant man.

I worked a lot for my father from a very early age, but I preferred to work for the other local market gardeners and farmers, who paid me by the hour for my labours. I always looked forward to the autumn, when the farmers took on extra labour to pick potatoes. Although this was back-breaking work, it paid well. Howard's farm employed me, to deliver their milk and to clean out their shippons (cow sheds) and provide fresh straw for their cows. Their milk was bottled fresh on the farm and I helped them too in the farm's small dairy.

With my father I learned how to grow tomatoes from seeds and prick out the plants into individual plant pots. When the plants were of a suitable height, we knocked them out of their pots and planted them with a trowel about two feet apart down rows in our greenhouses. They were tied to bamboo canes initially, then trained to grow up string tied to overhead wires running down the greenhouses. Before the introduction of trickle irrigation systems I would spend hours watering tomato plants, side-shooting them and even pollinating them.

Before the plants were planted the soil had to be sterile. A few times my father lost whole crops of tomatoes as a result of the plants becoming diseased from the soil. There were no fungicides to spray onto the plants to prevent fungal diseases destroying them, and the plant breeders had not bred disease-resistant varieties of tomato plants either. To lose a whole crop was a severe blow for any grower. It often meant borrowing money from the bank.

I enjoyed the week or two when the contractor visited our market garden and steam-sterilised all the soil in our greenhouses. Preferably, this was done on an annual basis, although sometimes we missed a year because of the cost or, alternatively, we sterilised the soil with a gas gun (firing methyl bromide into the soil) or by applying a strong solution of formaldehyde onto the soil with a watering can.

My father grew lettuces in his greenhouses too. Tomatoes and lettuce were the main money earners for us. Lettuces too had to be sown from seed, pricked out into boxes and the plants planted out in the greenhouses. Finally, they were cut when ready, packed loose in wooden boxes, watered to keep them fresh and sent off to market with the produce merchant, usually with Peter Guy. Later, they were packed individually in polythene bags and packed in dozens in disposable cardboard boxes.

Greenflies were the main enemies of lettuce. Lettuces full of greenfly had to be dug under, which meant total loss of the crop. In the late 1940s and early 1950s we placed piles of tobacco down the paths between the lettuce plants and set fire to them. The nicotine aerosols that were produced as a result killed some of the greenfly. Later, pesticides could be sprayed onto the lettuce plants whilst they were growing, which eradicated these pests altogether. We sprayed the lettuce plants heavily with water a few days before they were cut in order to remove the last traces of these chemicals.

Although my father used artificial fertilizers on his soil, he had to check the pH levels of the soils and apply lime from time to time if the soils became too acidic. I spent many weeks preparing the greenhouses with my father, double-digging manure from the local farms into the soil. I was pleased when he bought a mechanical 'rotatiller'.

Dad also liked to grow chrysanthemums and other flowers, particularly tulips and daffodils, which he imported as bulbs from Holland. These came in large wooden crates. We planted out the bulbs before the winter and buried them outside under layers of peat and soil on a bed of cinders. The boxes were brought into the greenhouses in the spring and the heat forced them to flower, hopefully just in time for marketing on Mother's Day. The daffodil bulbs were not reused but planted out in our garden instead or given away.

My father also produced mushrooms in one of his large sheds for a few years. I always enjoyed picking mushrooms, especially since they were grown on benches at hip height or higher, which meant less bending down than in the greenhouses.

The two main blocks of our greenhouses were heated by two coke-fired boilers that had to be looked after. They had to be 'clinkered' twice a day, once in the evening and again the following morning, before being filled up by shovelling coke into them. In the mornings the vents along the length of each greenhouse had to be opened, in the early days individually, then later using a lever that opened the vents all the way down one side of a greenhouse at the same time. They all had to be closed again in the evening.

On many occasions I was tasked with closing the vents at night and stoking up the two boilers. From our house I had to walk through my Uncle Dick's market garden to get to ours, and there were no lights along the paths apart from that provided by a torch that I carried. I found these journeys and the work that I had to carry out frightening in the dark of the winter months, although I never experienced any trouble from anyone.

Market gardening was hard labour, and in those days it tied you to the business night and day. In his younger days my father owned the land originally purchased when he set up his business and built his home on Hesketh Lane, but he rented quite a bit more land from Lord Lilford. The Lord Lilford, who my father had known all his life and who operated a system of fair rents, eventually died without a successor living in Britain to follow him. A relative came back to Britain from South Africa to inherit the estate and appointed Mr Bracewell as his agent. An instruction had obviously gone out to maximise income from the Lilford estates, which resulted in a significant hike (up to 200%) in the rent of his tenants. As a result, my father was forced to buy another plot of land and give up working the rest, which is now part of an adjacent school playing field.

This affair prompted me to write a critical letter to the *Lancashire Evening Post*, which was published. Shortly after his arrival in the area, this newly-arrived member of the Lilford family was seen at a local hunt meeting on a hunting pink-coloured tractor rather than on a horse, which caused great mirth amongst our villagers.

We had grown many outdoor crops – strawberries, potatoes, cabbages, carrots, cauliflowers and kidney beans, mainly – but we stopped growing these crops when we lost the rented land. I remember as a young boy watching my father plough his outdoor land with a horse-drawn plough but later, he would bring in a local farmer with a tractor and plough, or turn over the soil with the 'rotatiller' I previously mentioned.

There was an awful lot of weeding to be done, of course, both inside and out. The greenhouses had to be constantly maintained. From time to time we cleaned all the glass, the wooden gutters between each pair of greenhouses were tarred, as well as the various sheds, and the wooden spars were painted with white lead paint, both inside and outside the greenhouses. Occasionally, and more than occasionally if there had just been a storm, broken panes of glass were replaced. In the autumn we cleaned out ditches and cut the hedges.

All this hard labour meant that my father needed more help than ever I could give him. My mother always helped him when she was not doing her housework, and Dad hired labour in. Harold Aspey worked for Dad on a part-time basis for many years, and relatives and friends would come and give a hand when he was sick or really busy.

My parents allocated me other chores to carry out. Whenever I could, I mowed the back and front lawns at our home and dug the flower beds that surrounded them once or twice a year, and it became my job to paint the outside of the house. My mum and dad were keen on its two-tone cream and green effect, which made this job far more complicated than it need have been. I was fearless on the extendable wooden ladders, even after I fell off them one day onto the concrete below whilst painting the bathroom window above the back door.

On 3 September 1956, I enrolled at Southport Technical College (as Southport College, it has today expanded its footprint considerably). The next two years were the most important in my life so far, and I worked night and day to pull myself up by the bootstraps after finding out at Christ Church School that I had the ability to realise my dream, to become a chemist.

Mr Roberts taught me Advanced Level GCE pure and applied mathematics in the daytime, Mr Crossley taught me chemistry and Mr Morrell taught me physics. But, on three

Southport Technical College, now Southport College - August 2011; the main entrance was under the clock tower.

evenings a week in 1956-1957, I also attended night classes to study GCE Ordinary Alternative Level mathematics, chemistry and physics, which I passed in June 1957. I had the same three teachers in the evenings that I had in the daytime.

Without these three men I could not have achieved my dream. Mr Duncan Crossley had the greatest influence on me: he was a superb teacher of chemistry and the third most influential person in my life. Not only were his explanations of chemical phenomenon clear, but he used chemicals and glassware on his demonstration bench to demonstrate everything that he was talking about. Of course, we had laboratory classes as well in which we carried out our own experiments. Mr Crossley retired in 1971 after 50 years as a teacher, 26 of them at Southport Technical College.

Mr Roberts also became very interested in me because I showed a great interest in what he was trying to teach me. I caught him several times on a soap box on Southport Promenade preaching socialism to the small crowds that surrounded him.

Gwilym Edffrwd Roberts, born in 1928, contested the Ormskirk Parliamentary Constituency for the Labour Party in 1959 and Conway in 1964, before becoming the Member of Parliament for South Bedfordshire from 1966 to 1970, and for Cannock and Burtonwood from 1974 to 1983. He lost that seat in a Conservative landslide General Election to Conservative Gerald Howarth. After Westminster, he served as Leader of Cannock Chase District Council and, when I last made inquiries, was serving on Staffordshire County Council.[1] Neither Gwilym Roberts nor I knew at the time he was teaching me that both of us would eventually become Members of Parliament.

Despite my general science background, I was able to achieve marks of 78%, 71%, 60% and 65% in chemistry, physics, pure mathematics and applied mathematics, respectively, in the 1956 Christmas examinations on the A-Level courses at Southport Technical College. My marks got better as I absorbed more knowledge and one year later, they were 87%, 88%, 67% and 83%, respectively. "He has the makings of a Scholarship Candidate" Gwilym Roberts wrote at the bottom of my report at the end of 1957.

Whilst I was at Southport Technical College my friends decided that I should have a girlfriend. I had shown no interest in dating girls up to this point in my life. I was introduced to Jean Howard, who lived in Marshside, Southport, and we went out together for a few months, usually to the cinemas in Southport on a Saturday night, but we were not well-matched by our friends and the relationship ended after a few months. In any case I had my hands full with my studies and it was a risky business catching the last bus home to Tarleton after escorting Jean home.

At about the same time I decided that I wanted to learn ballroom dancing. The only dancing classes on offer were in the evenings at a primary school on Shore Road, Hesketh Bank, so I decided to enrol along with my Tarleton mates. This didn't go down well with the Hesketh Bank lads. They were not too keen on us dancing with the Hesketh Bank girls who they fancied. It was even worse when I fell for one of the local girls and started dating her. Irene and I started to go out together on a regular basis, catching the 'passion wagon' from Hesketh Bank station on a Saturday night and making sure that we caught the last train home from Southport. The carriages at that time had individual compartments, and the trick was to hang out of the window of the 'slam-shut door' on the platform side of the train to deter other passengers from climbing into the same compartment. The song *The Blackpool Belle*, written by Bolton singer and songwriter Howard Broadbent, always comes to mind when I think back to those days.

On one occasion we were met off the train at Hesketh Bank station by a gang of the Hesketh Bank lads, who followed us as I escorted Irene home. They were trying to provoke a fight all the way, and eventually took my bicycle off me and threw it over a fence. I was encircled by them and took quite a beating. It was frightening.

It didn't stop me seeing Irene and we started to visit the Floral Hall in Southport, where they had a regular Saturday night dance, and ballroom dancing became one of my passions. Irene was my first love, but I felt that our relationship had to end when I later enrolled at the University of Hull.

In my youth there was little salacious material for young men to drool over, no page 3 topless girls, merely pin-ups of famous film stars in one-piece bathing suits in the newspapers. The nearest we got to titillation in the media was in the publications *Tit-Bits* and *Reveille*.

At the age of 17, I decided to learn to drive my father's car and get my driving test out of the way. Cousin Harry agreed to sit in the passenger seat and give me instructions. He took me onto the roads of Tarleton Moss, which have deep drainage ditches on either side of them. I certainly kept on the road! I had learned to drive tractors on the farms, so using a clutch, a brake and a steering wheel was not too difficult for me. It was quite easy to find quiet roads on which to learn to drive in the 1950s, not so today. The expansive sands of Southport beach also provided plenty of space to learn how to handle a car. I took my driving test in Southport and passed first time.

Then along came the first really big setback in my life. I had been feeling ill for some months, but as I got out of bed one morning in the early part of January 1958, I collapsed and the doctor was sent for. I was very ill for the next six months, several of those weeks confined to my bed. My problem was eventually diagnosed as glandular fever, a disease from which young people, who it mainly strikes down, can recover slowly.

Fortunately, I had made several good friends on my travels by Ribble bus to Southport and back to attend school. One of them was Ethel Embley, who attended St Wyburn's private school for girls in Southport. Her father was also a market gardener, with a business at Much Hoole on the A59 Preston to Liverpool road, very close to the attractive Carr House, where the Reverend Jeremiah Horrocks, who ministered to the people of Much Hoole from 1639 to 1640, predicted and observed the transit of the planet Venus on 24 November 1639.

Ethel caught the same Ribble bus that I travelled on, and for several years we exchanged ideas about our school work. She helped me to understand academic concepts and I helped her in turn. We enrolled together and studied the same courses at Southport Technical College between the years 1956 and 1958, then went our separate ways. She very kindly lent me her well-kept notebooks and forwarded homework on to me using other pupils who travelled on the same bus and lived near me in Tarleton. I duly returned her notes and my completed homework using the same route.

I caught up with Ethel again many years later when I was elected to Parliament. She wrote to me as Ethel von Fritschen and we met again at her sister's house and at the Houses of Parliament before she returned to her life in Germany.

Around Easter, I can't remember exactly when at this distance in time, I was able to return to my studies at Southport Technical College, although I was by no means as well as I had been before glandular fever struck me down. I was determined however to succeed and, in June 1958, I passed the Mathematics Alternative A (Pure and Applied Mathematics), Physics Syllabus I and, more importantly for me, the Chemistry Advanced JMB GCE A-Level examinations. I also gained a pass in Scholarship Level Chemistry. I was ecstatic when I received the news, and so was my mum. For my dad it signalled that I was probably not going to follow in his footsteps, and I could feel his disappointment. Neither he nor I was to know at that stage of the tragedies that were to befall my family in the future.

In the summer term of 1958 I had been looking at the possibility of taking my career to the next level at a university. I sent for several application forms and syllabi and studied them. To my bitter disappointment I realised that most of the 23 universities in existence at that time including the many external colleges of London University, required a foreign language to satisfy their matriculation (entry) requirements, Greek, Latin or French in most cases. However, it seemed that one or two of the London Colleges and Hull University might interview me, so I applied to three of them.

I didn't get a response from University College, London. My visit to King's College, London was a disaster. Along with two other applicants I was sat down in a room and a woman with purple hair (I had never seen such a spectacle before) proceeded to put psychological aptitude test papers in front of us. I wasn't aware that they existed either. I was expecting to be interviewed about my scientific ability, not to be screened for entry by a psychologist. I never heard from King's College again. I didn't even see the Chemistry Department at King's College on that day.

At about the same time, I received a letter inviting me for an interview in the Department of Chemistry at the fledgling University of Hull (Hull had a long history as an External College of London University and was granted its own charter in 1957). At least I was probably going to be interviewed by a chemist. And I was, surprisingly by the Head of Department, Professor Norman Bellamy Chapman, for whom I came to have a great respect in my later years. I explained carefully to him about my long illness, and he was sympathetic. Nevertheless, he started to probe my understanding of chemistry. Fortunately, my lack of knowledge was outshone by my strong desire and my immense enthusiasm for the subject. He was extremely impressed by my non-traditional educational background too.

NBC, as I came to know him, admitted that Hull University also had a foreign language matriculation requirement but I could see that he wished it hadn't. He struck a deal with me – if I passed 'Ancillary German for Chemists' at the end of my first year in Hull, he would persuade the University's Registrar that that pass would constitute my foreign language requirement for matriculation there. Of course, I had to do well in my forthcoming A-Level examinations, and I did. I passed 'Ancillary German for Chemists' at the end of my first year in Hull. I felt extremely grateful to be given this chance, and I committed myself not to let NBC down. NBC was the fourth most influential person in my life.

NOTES

1. Gwilym Edffrwd Roberts also retired from politics in 2010 and lives with his wife in Rugeley.

# CHAPTER THREE

# HULL UNIVERSITY

∼

My dream was beginning to come true. I packed a large travelling trunk containing most of my belongings and dispatched it on the train at Hesketh Bank Station, addressed to Camp Hall, Harland Way, Cottingham, near Hull, where I had been told that a room would be provided for me. I was extremely pleased not to have to look for a place to live in Hull; the university was not well endowed with accommodation in the autumn of 1958. They had, however, made an effort to house most of the 'fresher students'. I followed my trunk a few days later, accompanied by my bicycle, on the train to Paragon Station Hull.

My first year at university was a very difficult time for me for several reasons. I arrived at university as a boy of 18 and ended my first year as a young man.

Camp Hall was just that. Most students lived in an ex-army camp on a large site that accommodated a lot more Hull students in the next few years. The building of Ferens Hall was almost completed and I was one of the first inhabitants of one of its four wings, built round a small, green quadrangle. Jim

Treherne was its first Warden. Freshers started on the ground floor of each block and worked their way up to the third floor in their final year.

Most of my colleagues on the BSc Special Honours Chemistry Degree course lived in the Nissen huts of the old army camp or in Needler Hall in Cottingham village. Women were housed in Cleminson Hall or Thwaite Hall, also in Cottingham village. From Ferens Hall to the Chemistry Department was a cycle journey of about five miles.

It's a different picture today in Cottingham. All the halls of residence are mixed and, where Camp Hall stood, there are several halls of residence, with a central service area containing a bar, meeting rooms and a refectory. It's a sizeable student village. In 1958, Hull University's main campus on Cottingham Road consisted of two blocks dating from University College days, a new Chemistry Department building in the middle of the campus, a student union building beyond that and, across a cricket field, a sports pavilion on Inglemire Lane with more sports fields across Inglemire Lane. Next door to the university was an independent teacher's training college, today part of the university.

Conscription into the armed forces ended gradually from 1957. Camp Hall was well named, because it was full of ex-servicemen when I arrived. Chas Gosling, who had a handlebar moustache, was President of Ferens Hall, which included all the Nissen huts in the surrounding camp. He regularly had us marching up and down Harland Way outside the campus and round the roads of the old camp. I felt as if I had joined the armed forces after all. The ex-servicemen wanted to make sure that those of us who had missed conscription were going to experience it anyway. They treated us like fags in a public school.

This was a very macho environment to live in and one that I had not been used to before. It was intimidating. Fresher students were made by these older men to run round the quadrangle of Ferens Hall, sometimes naked, whilst the contents of dustbins were thrown at them. Fortunately, I wasn't one of those chosen to be humiliated in that way.

We were told to get ready to put on a 'show' for the second and third year students in the refectory hall, which was covered for the purpose with large tarpaulins, on the walls as well as the floor. If the audience didn't like the act, the slop from the evenings meal came our way; in fact they threw it anyway, whether the act was good or not. The bar was, of course, open

The University of Hull (circa. 1957).

Feren's Hall, University of Hull, in 1958

before the show. These were the fresher's initiation rites which were prevalent at most of the universities in those days. I hope these traditional introductions to life at university have long since been abandoned.

There was great rivalry too between the Ferens Hall men and the Needler Hall men. Each Hall had a mascot, and these were regularly stolen from the Junior Common Rooms, where they were kept, then recovered in another raid.

I soon discovered why fresher students were given the ground floor rooms. Officially we were 'gated' after 11 pm, but those who were late coming back home knocked on the windows of the ground floor rooms to gain entry to the Hall. This was especially troublesome at the weekends. This was also a route to 'smuggle' women into the rooms.

Although I went to the fresher's fair I only joined one club or society, the Student Chemical Society. I also attended the Fresher's Ball that was held in the hall in the student union building. In those days we had dance bands playing ballroom music and a quartet played during the intervals.

In my three undergraduate years I worked hard, night and day, throughout Wednesday afternoons, reserved for sport, and over the weekends too. A small number of us formed a discussion group, which I found most helpful. Anyone who had had difficulty following a lecture or understanding the concepts that were being introduced to us could raise the matter with the others who might have understood. Being lectured at by lecturers in a university, as all students know, is quite different from being taught by teachers at school.

Food was a problem initially for me, because Ferens Hall and the university refectory did not cater for people who didn't eat meat. Vegetarians were rare individuals in the 1950s. At Ferens Hall there were formal dinners at 6.30 every evening and we served the food from the end of the table. The sight of jugged hare was not very appealing to me. In the end I caved in and started to eat small portions of meat, though never pork or liver, which made me feel sick.

Undergraduate students had heated discussions at these formal dinners. It was at this time that I realised that my political views were different from those of most of the students around me at dinner. All my close family (cousins included), with the only exception of my brother Graham, have been lifelong supporters of the Labour Party in what was mainly a Conservative village. My father once stood as a Labour candidate in an election for the Parish Council, and I 'campaigned' for him on my bicycle. Despite the fact that my family were well-known and respected in Tarleton, he got thrashed, which was expected. I stoutly defended my left-wing principles against the ideas propagated by those students who I considered to be on the right of the political spectrum.

1958 was the year in which the Campaign for Nuclear

Disarmament's (CND) first Aldermaston March was led by Canon Collins and Michael Foot MP. I was never persuaded to join CND; I have always believed in multilateral disarmament.

Hull University broadened my interests in other ways too. I had never met a black or Asian person before living there. At that time Hull was attracting a large number of foreign students. Although there were few in the Department of Chemistry, other departments had considerable numbers of students from across the world. The Law Department attracted Nigerian students, and I became very friendly with Ben (Benedict) Ekigwe Okafor, who lived in my block at Ferens Hall – six students in each block, or house, with a communal bathroom on each floor and a communal kitchen for each block.

Vijayanathan Venkatasamy, who was studying for a Joint Degree in Physics and Chemistry, also lived in my block; he was from the island of Mauritius. To my surprise, when I was elected to Parliament in 1997, another student who I had known in Hull, also from the island of Mauritius, Professor A. S. Kasenally, wrote to congratulate me. Geoff Holt, another student in my block, was remarkably keen on astronomy. His hero was Professor Sir Fred Hoyle, the physicist. I learned a lot about the world and other disciplines by getting to know these students.

The first thing I noticed about Hull when I arrived was the swarms of bicycles on the city's streets. The landscape was so flat that it was difficult for those learning to drive to find an incline on which to demonstrate a handbrake start. Hull was unique in that all the telephone boxes were painted cream and green, unlike the red boxes throughout the rest of the country.

The city owned its own telephone system, which made calls out cheaper than elsewhere.

I enjoyed rag days when I was an undergraduate. This was a chance to let off steam. Ferens Hall always built an elaborate float. I remember one year when we built a Mississippi showboat, complete with paddles on its sides which were turned by hand from the inside, and an elaborate chimney. I was persuaded, as the only chemist involved in its construction, to devise a system for producing smoke. I used a complicated system for generating smoke from a Winchester full of concentrated hydrochloric acid and another Winchester full of 880 ammonia solution.

Ben Ekigwe Okafor with a Nigerian friend.

All went well for most of the journey. Of course, I was very careful to keep others riding on the float away from these potentially dangerous chemicals. The problem was that the driver kept coming to a halt rather abruptly. In Newlands Avenue he halted more abruptly than I expected, and the residual acid and ammonia solution mixed together all at once. The whole float was covered in what looked like, to an observer, real smoke. We were on fire, and it wasn't long before a fire engine

# SCIENCE AND POLITICS: AN UNLIKELY MIXTURE

Visit of the Queen Mother to the University of Hull on 20 June 1960 to open the University Library.

Selling 'rag mags' on the corner of Jameson Street and Paragon Square, Hull in 1959.

arrived. My face was the colour of beetroot, and I had to apologise profusely to the firemen. They were quite amused by it all and pleased that nobody had been hurt. That might not be the situation in the 21st Century.

After the Fresher's Ball I regularly attended the union dances on Saturday nights along with some new friends. My closest friends on the chemistry course were Bill (actually Derek McHardy) Brewis, who was older than the rest of us and from Scarborough, and Michael Graham Rodgers, always called Mike, whose family lived in Halifax. I was friendly too with another older student, Alan Buckley, and with Dave Jackson. There were only three women students in this male-dominated group of first-year chemists.

The union dances attracted women from outside the university, local trainee nurses, women from the teacher training college and women from all walks of life in the city of Hull. The Saturday night dances were lively affairs and it wasn't long before I attracted girlfriends. The first inconveniently lived on the opposite side of the city to where I lived in Cottingham, actually in the then thriving fishing community of east Hull, and it was too much hassle to escort her home and travel back to my halls of residence late at night. For a while I dated a trainee nurse from Ireland but she was deeply religious and too strait-laced for me.

On the occasions that I visited my parents I escaped on Saturday nights to Southport Floral Hall, which I had frequented a lot before going up to university, but I was now able to drive there and back rather than catch a bus or a train. One Saturday night I foolishly agreed to call off on the way home with some friends at the Riverside nightclub on Southport New Road at Banks. Today this is a popular caravan site.

With Gillian Wales and John Payne (they later married), dressed up for rag day.

Joyce Ayres aged 16, in 1958.

The club was raided by the local police, who arrested everyone with an alcoholic drink in front of them, several of my friends included. Fortunately, I was in the toilet at the time and my thin body allowed me to escape through a small window, just before the local constabulary realised that this was an escape route from the club. I didn't drink a lot of alcohol in those days, so it would have been difficult for the local police to charge me.

Later, again at a student union Saturday night dance, I met an attractive young girl (she was almost 16 when I met her, although she looked older) called Joyce Ayres, who conveniently lived on Harland Rise right next to Camp Hall. Joyce went to the secondary school opposite her own home. That was the beginning of a long relationship which lasted into my postgraduate years in Hull. She was born into a Roman Catholic family, which was a disadvantage for us at that time because we both knew that marriage was out of the question unless I converted my religion.

Just before Christmas in my first term at university, I received a telephone call from home to say that my father had collapsed with a coronary heart attack and was in the Promenade Hospital at Southport. He had smoked most of his life and had eaten a lot of fatty foods (he was a pig butcher). But, as I discovered later, heart disease was common on the male side of my family.

My mother never learned to drive and she travelled to see him on a Ribble bus ten miles there and ten miles back most days. Friends and relatives were kind and took her as much as they could in their cars. This was a time when my mum was under considerable stress. Dad was in hospital in Southport for about six weeks altogether in the early months of 1959 and, after that, in a convalescent home near Hesketh Park.

Mum also had the market gardening business to look after. My brother Graham was just 11 and had started attending Christ Church Boys' Secondary Modern School that term. I had serious thoughts about packing in my studies at Hull University and coming home to run my father's business. My mind was in turmoil. Should I take a year off? I came home for the Christmas vacation and visited my dad with my mum as often as I was able. Frankly, I never expected him to recover; he was really quite ill.

My relatives, and especially my mum, were keen for me to continue my university studies; Mum above all people knew how hard I had worked to get there in the first place. With a strong feeling of guilt, which is within me to this day, I returned to Hull after Christmas and continued my studies. But there was worse to come. For several years Mum had been suffering from colitis. She managed, with the help of friends and relatives, to bring in the Dutch bulbs, which we sold every year as Mother's Day approached, and the tomato and lettuce plants got planted with outside help. My father was able to come home after spending several weeks in the convalescent home in Southport to recuperate, but he was unable to labour as he had always done before his illness. He packed up smoking altogether after his heart attack.

At the beginning of the summer it became obvious to all who knew my mother that she was ill herself, probably as a result of all the strain that she must have suffered whilst running the business and visiting my dad in Southport.

She became quite sick and was diagnosed with ulcerated colitis and admitted to Southport Infirmary as the summer vacation of 1959 approached. I was able to come home from Hull and visit her in hospital almost daily, because I had essentially completed my first year at university. I remember that she was in great pain and I became quite desperate because the doctors didn't seem to be treating her. Her stomach filled with gas and became an enormous size. She died on 22 July 1959, having contracted septicaemia. She was only 53, and it broke my heart.

For years afterwards I painfully wondered whether there was anything I could have done to save her. Should I have been harder on the doctors? Should I have demanded an inquiry as to what had really caused her death? She was gone, and there was nothing any of us could do about that. One of life's cruel blows had struck us.

After Mum's funeral – I remember that it was a very hot July day – I attended the funerals of my aunts and uncles, and even those of some older cousins, on quite a regular basis. All five Iddon brothers and many of my cousins too were struck down by heart diseases.

At the time of my mother's death my Uncle Dick and Aunt Ada were living in a bungalow they had built next door to 76 Hesketh Lane. Their son Frank and his wife Bessie and two adopted children, June and Michael, lived at number 76. When Mum died Uncle Dick and Aunt Ada invited my father and my brother Graham to their home for Sunday lunch most Sundays, and I joined them when I was home from university. She continued to entertain my family on Sundays long after my Uncle Dick died.

My Uncle Dick was quite a character. I have mentioned before his achievements as a footballer. Without his drive, Tarleton would not have the pavilion, actually a community centre, that it has today at the bowling club. Along with his friends, Uncle Dick spent years fund-raising to replace the old wooden bowling green pavilion with a brick-built structure. Aunt Ada was still attending the Saturday night dances there in her 80s. Uncle Dick raised turkeys for slaughter at Christmas and he also raised pheasants for the Lilford estate, which had annual shoots on their land surrounding Bank Hall.

I was even more determined to succeed in Hull because I knew that that was what Mum had wanted from me. My father soldiered on and brought up my brother on his own. I can only imagine what impact losing his mum had on my brother, at the age of 11. Slowly time healed some of my emotional pain, although it has never disappeared completely.

Brother Graham didn't only follow in my footsteps at Christ Church School; he followed me into the market gardening business as well. Now he was my father's main source of help as he grew up, and he left school at the age of

15 to help Dad run his business. Life at Christ Church School wasn't easy for him either, because the teachers regularly compared his ability with mine, which was extremely unfair on him. I have often wondered whether the events of 1958/1959 stopped him from pursuing another career pathway that he might have yearned for.

After earning some money by working on farms or market gardens during the summer vacation, I returned to Hull University, in October 1959, with a heavy heart, to begin my second-year studies. At least I had managed to pass my three ancillary subject examinations in German for scientists, physics and mathematics, which allowed me to concentrate on and enjoy studying chemistry.

By this time I had become involved in events that the Student Chemical Society organised. A brewery trip was the

Tarleton bowling club – Aunt Ellen Johnson, Grandma Iddon, Uncle Dick and Aunt Ada are sitting in the middle row starting third from the left; my father is sitting second left on the front row.

# SCIENCE AND POLITICS: AN UNLIKELY MIXTURE

Tarleton Bowling Club – my father is seated in the middle of the front row with my Uncle Dick sitting on his left shoulder (the Reverend L. N. Forse is sitting on the extreme right of the front row).

Undergraduates at Hull University: Professor N. B. Chapman is sitting in the middle of the front row (sixth from the left); Dr Ken Clarke is third from the right on the front row; Professor Roy Baldwin is seated immediately to the left of NBC and I am standing in the third row immediately above NBC.

event of the year, although we held dances and other social functions. Outside lecturers were invited to speak during the year, and we organised annual dinners outside the university at places such as the Beverley Arms in the small town of Beverley, where there is a wonderful minster, not to mention a racecourse. We also visited the chemical industry, who entertained us like royalty after we had received their presentations and toured the plant or laboratories.

I was full of energy in the late 1950s and early 1960s. The Mersey Sound was emerging and the Beatles began to hit the headlines. Elvis Presley turned out one hit after another. The Twist became a favourite dance and I became quite adept at twisting. An essential part of returning from our Student Chemical Society outings was to call at a public house, where I would be invited by my student colleagues to demonstrate the twist. It didn't stop at that; I was able, with a bit of help, to stand on my head whilst drinking a pint of beer. I could never down a yard of ale though. I worked hard and I played hard in those student days. Bill Brewis and Mike Rodgers told me that I should pay attention to what happened to people who 'burned the candle at both ends'.

Bill persuaded me to join him on an evening out at a nightclub in the New York Hotel, close to Paragon Square, on Anlaby Road. It is now derelict and boarded up. There were six chemists, Alan Vickery, Dave Jackson, Harry Diamond, Bill, Dave Viney, and me in the party altogether plus one of Bill's close friends, Lance Naylor, who was studying economics.

Lance had seen the cabaret on a previous visit to the club and told us all about it before the acts came on stage. We were out for a laugh, and the lads persuaded me to volunteer to help the conjuror. I was more than a bit inebriated (two pints of beer was enough) by this time of the evening, and the conjuror wasn't too pleased when I spoiled some of his tricks. Well, I could see exactly what he was up to from where he placed me on the stage. But there was worse to come. A comedian followed the conjuror and, as he approached his punch lines, one of us (not me; I had done enough damage) would shout it out before he could get it out. The audience loved it; I am sure that they thought all this was part of the act. That was the end of the evening. We were ejected from this high-class nightclub.

In the early 1960s David Barron introduced me to the clubs he was visiting in Liverpool. We especially liked the new Cavern Club. It was a dump which defied all later health and safety laws. There was one way into this old former fruit cellar, down a narrow flight of stone steps, and only the same way out. The toilets were a disgrace. But it was magic. It got so full and sweaty that condensation on the vaulted ceilings dripped back down on us. There was something about the buzz down there that I have never felt anywhere else. I suppose we were out to enjoy ourselves, which helped to make a good atmosphere, and enjoy ourselves we did.

Later, in the student union at the University of Hull, I heard the Spinners, the Liverpool folk group, sing their folksongs and sea shanties, and I got to know them since they were from my part of the world. I discovered that they had formed as a skiffle group at the height of Lonnie Donegan's career. In looking for somewhere to play, they had cleaned out an old fruit cellar in Mathew Street, which became a rock venue when skiffle died out (it didn't last more than a few years). That became the Cavern Club. It was demolished in 1973, then reconstructed and reopened in 1984, so the present Cavern Club is not authentic. Several times I visited Gregson's Well public house in Liverpool, where the Spinners established a regular audience for several years. It's now derelict.

At the University of Hull I remember attending a demonstration lecture called 'Explosives' which greatly impressed me. It was given by Lt. Colonel B. D. Shaw of Nottingham University who, I learned later, had won several shooting trophies at Bisley. He brought part of the physics lecture theatre ceiling down on that occasion. His most impressive demonstration was when he took an old rifle (he collected antique guns), loaded it with gunpowder, then stuffed a candle down the barrel and fired the candle through a 'barn door', actually a sheet of five-ply plywood. Altogether, I saw this famous lecture 13 times. 'BD' was still presenting it long after his retirement at Nottingham, indeed into his 90s, often with the help of his colleague Dr Frank Palmer. His TV appearance was a classic performance. I hope that a recording of it has been kept in the BBC archives.

Professor N. B. Chapman (NBC) was very keen to recruit young undergraduate chemists to become student members

Cabaret at the New York Hotel Hull (left to right): Lance Naylor, Alan Vickery, Dave Jackson, Harry Diamond, Bill Brewis, Dave Viney and me.

Thornwick Bay, Flamborough Head.

of the Chemical Society, whose headquarters are in Burlington House (next to the Royal Academy of Arts), Piccadilly, London, and I signed up in my first year at Hull. Thus began a long relationship with this organisation which later morphed into the Royal Society of Chemistry (RSC).

NBC introduced us to the new theories that had been proposed by Ingold and Hughes at University College in London to explain why organic chemicals undergo reactions – mechanistic organic chemistry was catching on with undergraduate students. On 12 February 1959, at a lecture given in the Department of Chemistry at Hull by the revered Professor Ingold, I signed the Chemical Society's membership book.

I achieved high marks in my chemistry examinations throughout my undergraduate days in Hull. On 15 December 1958, which was the day of a 'pea soup' fog in Cottingham and also the day of an examination in organic chemistry, the shuttle bus for the university failed to turn up. We dashed back to collect our bicycles and arrived at the examination hall some

20-25 minutes late. I still achieved a score of 75% in that examination.

My third year in Hull was as successful as the other two had been. I was told that I was expected to graduate with a First Class Degree, but it wasn't to be. The numbers in our Special Honours group had diminished somewhat by this stage. Students who failed examinations on these Special Honours courses were demoted to attend other degree courses instead – an Ordinary Degree course usually – or they were asked to leave the university. Students who didn't do well in the final year were given a Pass Degree.

Throughout my Hull undergraduate years I was allocated Professor Roy Baldwin, a physical chemist, as a mentor. He was there as my pastoral mentor should I have any problems that I needed to talk over with someone. As the final examination approached, I got myself into quite a state and felt that I needed to talk to him, so I plucked up the courage to go and see him. He gave me an excellent piece of advice. "Take a day off and go to Flamborough Head", he said. I did, and returned many times after that.

About 50 students started our course in 1958. In the summer of 1961, two students gained a First Class Special Honours Degree in Chemistry, and they deserved that recognition. Six of us gained a Class II (Division I) Degree, 11 gained a Class II (Division II) Degree, seven gained a Class III Degree and eight were awarded a Pass Degree. Only 26 students finished the course with a Special Honours Chemistry Degree, about half the number who had started in 1958.

In the year I sat for my finals examinations the staff of the Chemistry Department decided to introduce a 'problem solving paper' in addition to examinations in the three main branches of the subject, organic, inorganic and physical chemistry. On the day I faced the extra paper, my brain would not communicate with the rest of my body. In any case, I was not familiar with the style of these questions, and the problems were set in areas of chemistry which I wasn't too familiar with either, such as nuclear chemistry. Most of my student colleagues were similarly tripped up by this paper. My poor performance probably cost me the loss of a First Class Degree but, nevertheless, I was extremely happy to be awarded a good Class II (Division I) Degree in Special Honours Chemistry.

On 1 July 1961, four days before my 21st birthday, I received my degree at a congregation held in the magnificent City Hall of Kingston-upon-Hull. In the audience sat my father and brother and Joyce Ayres, then my fiancée.

Now I was a qualified chemist, but what next? I wanted to join a research group; organic chemistry was my greatest interest of the three main branches of chemistry, so I filled in an application form. Success depended upon how many research scholarships the university was awarded that summer by the Science Research Council (SRC). The university allocated its scholarships on the basis of how well each applicant had done in their degree examinations.

My relationship with Joyce Ayres was now very close; we were engaged. During my three undergraduate years I came to know Joyce's family remarkably well and was a regular visitor at their home. My father and my brother Graham stayed with the Ayres family in Cottingham at the time of my graduation, and Joyce travelled over to Tarleton to meet my friends and wider family. I was convinced that I had found a partner for life. That wasn't to be either.

Joyce joined the Transport Police and, during the first year of my postgraduate studies in Hull, our relationship began to

My Convocation at Hull City Hall.

Dave Jackson and Bill Brewis on the lawn in front of Feren's Hall, Cottingham.

Granted a Special Honours BSc Degree in Chemistry at last.

develop tensions. She met a Transport Policeman with whom she established a relationship, and my first long-term relationship was over.

Professor Chapman used to say that "there are more kicks than ha'pence in this world", which I took to mean more downs than ups in life.[1] How right he was.

During the summer of 1961 I worked for six weeks at ICI Dyestuffs Division at Blackley in north Manchester, where I was given a research project on rubber additives. I had applied for jobs in the chemical industry just in case I wasn't accepted to undertake research for a Doctor of Philosophy (PhD) Degree in Hull, and this was one of the places where I had applied to work. It was a very large research and development department with a world-class reputation. Whilst it was officially within ICI's Dyestuff Division, the laboratory carried out a wide cross-section of research and development work.

ICI had two major sites in the north of England for the production of dyestuffs at that time, Blackley and Huddersfield. I was also interviewed in Huddersfield with a view to working there for ICI. The Blackley plant was adjacent to the research and development laboratories, Hexagon House, the Headquarters of the Division and also adjacent to the operating theatres at Crumpsall Hospital. The hospital's air intake system dragged in particles of a pigment called Monastral Blue when it was being manufactured, with inevitable results. This pigment is used as a vascular label in medicine so, presumably, is not toxic in small amounts. Dyestuff production at Blackley was transferred a few years later to the Huddersfield site.

I had an interesting interview after my graduation in 1961 with the Calico Printer's Association (CPA), who had a laboratory on the top of a building in Oxford Street, Manchester, where they developed Terylene. Ironically, because they were involved in what was then still a profitable cotton textile trade, they sold their patent to ICI. CPA transported me to one of their mills south of Manchester to show me their manufacturing processes. At the time of my visit they were printing patterned curtaining material on both sides at the same time. They seemed quite proud of the process and the machines they were using, and I assumed they were recently acquired. But this was 1961, and the date stamped on the machine was at least a decade before that. The Lancashire cotton industry made its mistakes and went into sharp decline in the following years. CPA must have regretted parting with their patent on the discovery of Terylene.

I felt a great sense of relief when Hull awarded me one of their SRC Research Studentships, and I was assigned Dr Ken Clarke as my immediate supervisor to work in Professor Chapman's (NBC) medicinal chemistry group. My friends Bill Brewis, Mike Rodgers and Alan Buckley joined NBC's reaction kinetics group. In our first year we all worked in one large laboratory at the top of the Department of Chemistry, where we had studied as undergraduates. The new research wing was being built next door and we were looking forward to moving into our new laboratories. After he left Hull University Alan Buckley undertook postdoctoral research in Canada, then he returned to Britain to work for ICI before leaving to work in the USA, where he became Research Director for Celanese in New Jersey. Sadly, he died at the early age of 53. Whenever I saw him he always seemed to have a cigarette in his mouth.

An older PhD student, Keith Bowden, was completing his studies with Dr John Shorter in this laboratory when I was allocated a place in it. He was a mischievous kind of guy who enjoyed sending undergraduate students to the stores for daft things such as a mercury hammer (mercury is a liquid at ambient temperature) or a bottle of benzene rings (the molecular formulae of benzene is $C_6H_6$, six carbon atoms joined together in a hexagonal ring, each attached to a hydrogen atom). When those students arrived at the Chemistry

Department's stores the store keepers merely laughed and told the students that they had been had.

Keith wired balloons onto taps and, just as students were about to turn the taps on, he diverted their attention, with the result that the balloons rapidly filled with water and burst. He also filled balloons with Cardice (solid carbon dioxide), put them in a drawer and waited for the startled reactions of people close by as the explosion of the pressurised balloon occurred. Dr Keith Bowden taught chemistry most of his life at the University of Essex in Colchester.

At the height of anxiety over the possibility of a nuclear war, I received a letter headed 'Civil Defence Programme 1962: Yorkshire C.C. Civil Defence Committee (NE Division)', allegedly signed by the Chairman of the Civil Defence Sub-Committee [Area 4(a) – 22: Section 576], which read:

"Under the direction of the Civil Defence Programme, we are entering into extensive training to organise both civilian and industrial corps., for the purpose of fire fighting in the event of the danger of atomic raids becoming imminent.

As a citizen whose loyalty to the Government is unquestioned we believe that we may count on you, as a patriot, for full co-operation. We have therefore taken the liberty of appointing you atomic warden for:

District: University

Training will be confined to one night per week for the next six months.

Thanking you for your kind co-operation in this matter. Please accept the thanks of our committee for your part in the enterprise which we feel is vital to the best interests of us all. Enclosed is a list of the equipment necessary for each warden."

The 'List of Equipment for Atomic Wardens' for the 'Yorkshire NE Division' consisted of 16 items, starting with reasonable items such as a respirator, an axe and a stirrup pump and proceeded through other reasonable items, but the last item was 'a broom to be inserted in the only available place, so that Warden may sweep floors as he progresses'.

Several years later, when I was at the University of Salford, I received an almost identical letter, probably from the same joker.

Unknown to me, in the autumn of 1963, Michael Rodgers *et al* wrote to the then 'agony aunt' Evelyn Home at *Woman* magazine on behalf of my fictitious wife expressing concern over the fact that the compounds I was preparing during my PhD studies were being tested on animals as potential new drugs. I received a very nice letter from Evelyn Home, addressed to Mrs B. Iddon at 102 Cottingham Road and dated 24 September 1963, which explained why I shouldn't be as concerned by my husband's work as I appeared to be. Such was the humour of my postgraduate colleagues!

Early in my postgraduate career I was introduced to the dangers of perchlorates when Alan Underhill, a postgraduate student who was working for Dr Brian Hathaway, an inorganic chemist, lost a finger in an explosion whilst handling one. Brian Hathaway was more 'matey' with the students than most of our staff members; he flirted with Maureen, one of our laboratory technicians and in summer, they disappeared to the roof sunbathing. At one of our Student Chemical Society functions, Brian Hathaway's racy open-topped sports car was carried over some concrete bollards and parked inside the physics block quadrangle.

Bill Brewis was one of the few students who could afford to run a car in those days and he often went home to Scarborough at the weekends. His late father had been a distinguished doctor there, and the family was brought up in a very large house at 55 Esplanade Road, near to the South Cliff in Scarborough. Bill's father was one of the first doctors to X-ray his patients and his original X-ray machine was still in the house when I stayed there with Bill.

I had already visited Scarborough on holiday with David Barron, but staying with Bill enhanced my fondness of this Yorkshire resort. We journeyed out to Primrose Valley and to the North Yorkshire Moors, as well as to other places, and we regularly attended dances at the Spa Ballroom on the South Cliff. Bill knew a couple of local girls, who we dated, and I tried to take off on water skis, not very successfully, in the harbour at Scarborough.

The hormone serotonin was discovered by two independent groups a few years before I began my research, one in Italy and the other in the USA, in some cells in the gastrointestinal tract as well as others in the brain, where it plays an important role in determining whether a person tends to be highly excitable or, at the opposite end of the mental health spectrum, extremely depressive. By developing synthetic compounds (called antagonists) that counteract the actions of serotonin in people whose brains contain too much of it or by developing synthetic compounds (called agonists) whose actions are similar to those of serotonin, the theory was that we could normalise mentally ill people.

Serotonin is part of the indole group of heterocyclic organic compounds (compounds containing more than carbon atoms

With Bill Brewis and Mike Rodgers at Southport.

On the North Yorkshire Moors, 1962, with Penny and Wendy Bamford (Bill Brewis was the photographer).

in rings; sulfur or nitrogen atoms, for example), so NBC set me the task of synthesising specific indole compounds. I struggled for a year to make them and gave up. The problem was that the final stage in the synthetic pathway involved the use of a strong acid, and indoles are notoriously susceptible to destruction by strong acids.

I was 'mentored' by Bert Hughes, one of NBC's third-year PhD students, who was willing to try any chemical reaction under the sun. Bert's laboratory was in the basement of the Chemistry Department. One day he came to see me in our laboratory and a phone call came through from the Chemistry Department's stores, also in the basement, to say that there had been one almighty bang in his laboratory next door to them. He had been trying a literature recipe to obtain some of the nitroindoles I required as my starting materials, as they were not available commercially. Any organic chemicals with nitro-groups in them are potentially explosive compounds (TNT or 2,4,6-trinitrotoluene, for example). I tried an alternative route to the same compounds, and we had another explosion in our laboratory. This was another reason for abandoning the indole line of research.

These early experiences of indole chemistry led Mike Rodgers to give me the nickname 'Emil', after the German chemist Emil Fischer who carried out the early research on indoles.

I persuaded NBC and Ken Clarke to let me work instead on a series of compounds, called benzo[b]thiophenes, in which the nitrogen atom present in indoles is exchanged for a sulfur atom. This allowed me to synthesise analogues of the original target compounds, which were sent off to the company with whom we were collaborating at that time – Australian-based

Aspro-Nicholas - for screening for biological activity. The Nicholas Research Institute was in Slough, where our contacts were Dr John James and Dr Bob Parfitt.

To our surprise, one compound, codenamed AGN 1414, displayed significant anti-tumour activity. The Nicholas Research Institute entered it into chemical trials on terminally ill patients in a hospital in Glasgow, and it was shown to significantly reduce the size of certain tumours. However, the compound proved to be too toxic for safe application and therefore was not considered marketable. Nevertheless the anti-tumour activity of these compounds was patented, and that discovery resulted in quite an effort at the University of Hull to find similar but safer compounds. None were found to be better than AGN 1414. At that time about one in every 15,000 compounds that were screened for potential biological activity reached the market as a useful drug, so we were not too dismayed by this outcome.

I decided to purchase a portable typewriter and in the summer of 1964, I began to type up my PhD thesis, which consisted of a review on serotonin and the role it plays in our bodies and a description of the chemistry that I had been involved in, along with the screening results provided by the Nicholas Research Institute and the experimental procedures that I had completed, all accompanied by the relevant literature references.

Professor Mike Martin-Smith of the University of Strathclyde examined my thesis and conducted an oral examination. He was impressed enough to recommend that the University of Hull award me the Degree of Doctor of Philosophy (PhD), which they did on Friday 2 July 1965. 14 postgraduate students received their PhD Degrees at that congregation, again held in Kingston-upon-Hull City Hall. My father attended to see his eldest son gain a second degree. Later Mike Martin-Smith offered me a postdoctoral position to work in his laboratories, but I went to the University of Durham instead.

Whilst I had to work hard during my three postgraduate years, there was less pressure than there had been when I was an undergraduate student. I decided that I had no wish to continue living in a hall of residence and, along with Mike Rodgers sought private accommodation as close as possible to the university.

Almost opposite the university there is a crescent-shaped road called Newland Park, and Bill Ross, the manager of Bladons, a large department store in Hull, was advertising a large room at a reasonable rent, so we decided to live there for a while until we could find a place of our own. Altogether, three Hull students shared one enormous room in a very large Victorian mansion which was divided up into flats. Mike and I shared the room with Noel Parker-Ashley for a few months, then with Graham Hemming, a psychiatry student. This address was very convenient for Mike because his girlfriend, later his wife Shirley, lived just round the corner with her parents.

It proved to be an interesting year. Bill Ross, the store manager and owner of the flat, was openly gay and we met a number of his gay friends during the year. One of his visitors was from the Royal Ballet Company, and I was invited to watch him dance Pineapple Poll at the New Theatre in Hull. Bill and his friends escaped to York most weekends, where a considerable number of gay people met in the Kings Arms pub, near York Minster. Bill and his friends could see that the three of us were straight and we all became good friends. In fact, I visited Strathclyde with Bill and met his parents. Towards the end of our stay in Newland Park Joe Quinn, who was a friend of Bill Ross, managed the flat.

It was during this first year as a postgraduate student that my relationship with Joyce broke down. After that I had several girlfriends, but I was cautious of becoming too involved with any of them.

Eventually we moved out of Newland Park to an upstairs flat almost next to the university campus, at 102 Cottingham Road. I shared this furnished flat with Mike Rodgers and a young MSc student, who was also studying with Ken Clarke, called Dave Harvey. He was the son of the Vicar of Looe in Cornwall. In the downstairs flat resided two other chemists, Roger Pinder and John Payne. We all became great friends.

This was a happy time. We held regular parties at 102 Cottingham Road on Saturday evenings, which were attended by a wide cross-section of people, almost exclusively students. Our neighbours were very tolerant people.

Mike Rodgers, Bill Brewis and Alan Buckley worked on the same floor – the third floor - as I did in the new research laboratories, and I often visited them. We worked a lot in the evenings. The nature of their work required them to visit the laboratories at unusual hours to take readings as their chemical reactions occurred. The three of them acquired a lot of general knowledge because they were always quizzing one another, a sort of perpetual pub quiz. "I say Emil, here's your starter for five", Mike would say as I walked into their laboratory.

Mike Rodgers edited the three editions of volume 6 of Gooch, *Journal of the Hull University Student Chemical Society*, which paved the way for his lifelong career in publishing.

In August and early September 1963, Bill Brewis, Mike Rodgers, me and Dermot (one of Bill's friends) set out on a three-week camping holiday across the continent in Bill's car. I had never been abroad before. The weather was atrocious and we were forced to stay in a lot of cheap guest houses and hotels. I wasn't too impressed by the French which, together with my other experiences of France in later years, discouraged me from regularly visiting that country, but we enjoyed driving down the Rhine Valley and through Bavaria. We visited Munich, with its beer cellars, including the Hofbrauhaus, and listened to the 'umpa' bands. We visited Berchtesgaden and the site of the Berghof, Hitler's mountain residence in Obersalzberg, which was destroyed at the end of World War II, and Oberammergau, the village where the Passion Plays are produced.

After Germany we invaded Austria, visited Salzburg, and drove down the Inn Valley to Innsbruck. It was in the Inn Valley that we stayed on a camp site at Solbad Hall next to an Olympic-style swimming pool complete with a diving board. I was game for anything in those days, and my mates knew it, so they told me they would give me ten shillings (10s or 50p in today's money) if I dared to jump off the diving board into the pool. When I got to the top of the steps and onto the platform of the board and looked down at the water, it seemed half a mile away. I jumped and, as I hit the water, my arms were almost torn out of their sockets. It felt like hitting concrete. My back was damaged for the rest of the holiday and for weeks after that. I had learned my lesson. They paid up, but it wasn't much consolation for the pain I suffered.

On our return journey we enjoyed a day out on the River Mosel. The boat stopped at several villages on the banks of the river, where we sampled the local wines.

Working long hours in the laboratories brought our activities to the attention of the local police. We all received a letter from the university authorities to ask whether we worked outside normal hours and, of course, we admitted that we did. A policeman called round at our Newland Avenue flat and insisted on searching our wardrobes, which caused us great concern. As he left, he told us that a girl had been raped on the Inglemire Lane playing fields during the previous weekend. Obviously, she had been able to tell the police what clothes her attacker was wearing. Fortunately, the police didn't call again.

In between the two NBC laboratories Dr George Gray, another Hull Lecturer in Organic Chemistry, had a laboratory.

Clockwise: Munich City Hall, Salzburg, Baden Baden and the diving board at Solbad Hall.

His research group worked on a series of compounds called biphenyls, mainly recording their spectra and other physical properties after their synthesis. At that time this work didn't seem very interesting to me.

George mixed well with postgraduate students, and we were regular visitors at the Haworth Arms at the junction of Cottingham Road and Beverley Road. I never in a month of Sundays thought this laboratory would become as famous as it did a few years later. I don't think George Gray knew the significance of his work at that time either. George and his students were carrying out pioneering work that led to the use of liquid crystals in electronic (LCD) displays that are very familiar to us today – in televisions, mobile phones, etc, etc. He wrote a seminal book on the synthesis and properties of biphenyl compounds which attracted the attention of Japanese scientists who were developing LCD displays.

The Hull compounds were patented, and the development work was done at the University of Hull, at the Royal Signals Establishment and at Poole in Dorset in the development laboratories of British Drug Houses (BDH; later Merck bought this plant). That work helped to put the Chemistry Department in Hull on the international map and George proceeded to win several international prizes for his work.[2]

We were allowed to become 'postgraduate student demonstrators' in the undergraduate laboratories, which provided us with a small amount of money to top up our SRC grants. This involved a three-hour stint each week during each of the three undergraduate terms. We allocated the experiments, marked the books and demonstrated laboratory techniques to the students.

Once, we were convinced that one of our students was fiddling his experimental results. Students in the organic chemistry teaching laboratories were expected to reach conclusions about the identity of so-called 'unknown compounds' that we gave them in numbered containers. Those who wanted to fiddle persuaded a second or third-year student to hand down their laboratory record book to them and merely copied the results from the older students into their own notebooks. Of course, these students learned nothing.

We decided to catch our 'fiddler' out by giving him a crushed Polo Mint to analyse in a numbered glass ampoule. He came back with an almost perfect analysis for the numbered compound. That student did not survive on the Special Honours Chemistry Degree course; he was hopeless all round.

A practical experiment was allocated to first-year students that really tested their ability to handle chemicals carefully. The

The postgraduate school at Hull University: Professor N. B. Chapman is sitting in the middle of the front row, Keith Bowden is on his left (in the picture) and I am sitting on his left. Dr Mike Scrowston is standing between Keith and me on the second row and Dr Ken Clarke is on his right (in the picture).

Joyce and me at Hull University's Summer Ball with friends.

synthesis of *para*-nitroso-*NN*-dimethylaniline is straightforward enough; the problem was that the product is a bright green dye. The majority of students dyed either themselves or their notebooks. I remember receiving a letter from a student's landlady complaining that he had arrived home with green hair and that he had turned his pillow and bedclothes bright green as well. She washed them and all her washing turned green too.

NBC was keen to see his postgraduates attend the welcome meetings for chemistry fresher students, which were held in the library of the department. On one occasion he asked a fresher where he came from, to which the student responded that he didn't think Professor Chapman would know the town he came from. "Where's that, laddie?" asked NBC. "It's Barnsley" replied the fresher. The look on NBCs face said it all! He spluttered out a list of famous people who had been born in Barnsley, but he didn't mention that he too hailed from that town.

I had not felt 100% fit since my bout of glandular fever in my Southport Technical College days and I was advised to have my tonsils removed. So, in the summer of 1962, I had my first-ever operation at Hull Royal Infirmary. Although the operation went well, I wasn't pleased at being expected to eat hard foods, including toast, almost immediately after. The university had just opened a new medical centre on the opposite side of Cottingham Road to the main campus and back-to-back to where we lived in Newland Park, so I persuaded my friends to get me transferred there to recuperate. I think I was one of their first ever in-house patients. The sister was wonderful and plied me with jelly and cream, rice pudding and other soft foods until my throat recovered. Since that date I have hardly had a day off work.

About half way through my postgraduate studies a young lecturer was appointed to teach organic chemistry in Hull and he was given a place to establish a research group in our laboratory. Dr Michael (we called him Mike) Scrowston gained a PhD Degree at the University of Leeds under the supervision of Professor Lythgoe. His favourite story about Lythgoe was when he overheard his research students talking about Marilyn Monroe. "Who's she?" he asked. "Has she published?" He thought they were talking about another scientist, which demonstrated how insular some academics could be at that time.

For a while Mike carried out the same research in Hull. His branch of 'natural product chemistry' required him to visit a lot of churchyards to collect several sacks filled with yew tree leaves, from which he extracted the chemicals in huge stills with organic solvents. Many of our best medicines have been discovered in nature in this way. The Leeds group carried out the pioneering work on the taxane group of compounds, which has provided us with some anticancer drugs that are used in the treatment of breast cancer.

However, after my discovery of the anti-cancer compound AGN 1414, Mike's research interests were diverted into heterocyclic sulfur chemistry. During the short time we worked in the same laboratory he introduced us to the idea of 'lab trips', which involved taking a day off now and then to escape to the seaside on a glorious summer day. We visited many places on the east coast, from the River Humber to Bridlington and Flamborough Head, and I was introduced to places such as Hornsea and Withernsea on this rapidly-eroding coastline.

Mike came from Walkington, a small village at the foot of the Yorkshire Wolds on the Hull side of this lovely and largely unknown countryside. He was full of tales about life in this small village and he seemed to know all its inhabitants by strange nicknames. 'Crummy Oliver' was one of them. Life in Walkington revolved around the local pubs (I visited the Ferguson Fawsitt Arms several times), the church and the duck pond. On one occasion Mike persuaded a group of us from the postgraduate school in Hull ('egg heads', as the villagers might have called us) to challenge Walkington's best brains to a general knowledge contest. I was useless at remembering unnecessary knowledge in those days, so I just cheered on our team from the sidelines. With people like the knowledgeable Mike Rodgers in our team of six, we thought we would walk it. But quizmaster Mike Scrowston had some tricks up his sleeve. We had several rounds of 'identify this object', and he had trawled the village for some very odd objects that none of us had ever seen before. "What is the meaning of the following saying?" quizmaster Mike would ask, with a mischievous smile developing on his face. We hadn't a clue; most of the sayings were known only to country folk. It was great fun, but we lost, albeit marginally (if the score can be relied upon, it was Walkington 83 to Hull University 82).

I was most impressed with Mike when, for their summer fete one year, he persuaded Pat Phoenix (Elsie Tanner in Coronation Street) to open it.

When I left Hull I stayed in close contact with Mike and Shirley Scrowston. I invited Mike to examine my PhD research students and he invited me to examine his. On more than one occasion I performed my demonstration lecture The Magic of Chemistry (see Chapter 8) in Hull and we kept each other informed about our research activities. We researched and published two 'reviews' together.

Mike presented an interesting public lecture on his interests in natural product chemistry entitled 'Myth and Magic to Modern Medicine'. He explained how medicines had been discovered in a variety of plants; colchicine in the flowers of the Autumn Crocus, salicylic acid (sodium salicylate is aspirin) in the bark of willow trees and atropine in deadly nightshade or belladonna, for example. He demonstrated how effective a blowpipe, which he obtained from the Amazon Basin, could be in injecting poisons into an unwanted visitor by firing the arrow at a balloon.

Before Mike began his popular lecture he displayed a row of the plants that he talked about along the front of the demonstration bench or table provided by the organisers. On one occasion after he had spoken to a Women's Institute branch, all the plants disappeared. His attention had been diverted by a conversation he had with some of those who attended his lecture. Before Mike left for home, the chairwoman of the branch thanked Mike profusely for allowing their members to raffle the plants that he had brought along with him! There had been a complete misunderstanding. Little did she realise that it had taken Mike years to put his collection of plants together; some of his collection were quite rare plants.

Sadly, Mike contracted pancreatic cancer and died at a very early age. I am still in contact with his widow Shirley, who lives in Walkington.

I came to love the countryside around Hull. One of my girlfriends in my Hull days had a van, and Jean and I enjoyed visiting all places to the north and west of Hull. We drove the full length of Spurn Point, explored the Yorkshire Wolds and tripped off to the seaside places too. I came to know a lot of the public houses in the area. After completing my studies in Hull I revisited the city a lot for different reasons, and I always tried to take an indirect route from the M62 motorway through all the villages that I had come to know so well.

During most of my time in Hull, however, the M62 did not exist, and the journey by road across Lancashire and Yorkshire through Rochdale, Halifax, Pontefract, Castleford, Goole and Hessle was long and tedious. I remembered later in my research career a smell rather like new-mown hay that I picked up every time I passed the Yorkshire Tar Distiller's chemical plant in Pontefract.

Hull docks were very busy when I was a student there, but business had started to decline. There were docks even in the city centre, but the one closest to the City Hall (Queens Dock) was filled in during my stay in Hull and converted into Queens Gardens, with the College of Further Education at its east end and the headquarters of Hull police on its north side.

## SCIENCE AND POLITICS: AN UNLIKELY MIXTURE

The old city of Hull had a charm of its own, with some good jazz and folk evenings in pubs such as the Ye Old Blue Bell in Market Place. I bought one of Cliff Richard's first records, which is still in my possession, in a small shopping arcade in that area and I bought Joyce's engagement ring in that arcade too. William Willberforce's house, now a museum, is in the same area and well worth a visit. A famous pub, Ye Olde White Harte in Silver Street, only admitted men until Hull University's female students laid siege to the place.

The river front in the city was an interesting place to take a walk. The ferries began their journeys there to take people across the River Humber to New Holland in Lincolnshire. They were paddle steamers. The ferries were very busy until Transport Secretary Barbara Castle decided during the Hull North Parliamentary by-election campaign in 1966, which was won by Labour candidate Kevin McNamara, to build the magnificent Humber Bridge, considered an expensive white elephant at the time.

At weekends student groups hired a ferryboat to paddle up river to Goole and back, with a jazz band on board and, of course, a bar. I enjoyed several evenings on these boats myself. When I was elected to Parliament I was invited to a function on a boat that is permanently anchored on the River Thames close to Embankment underground station. To my surprise, I found the Tattershall Castle to be one of the ferry boats from the Hull-New Holland crossing, now a restaurant and bar.

After my relationship with Joyce ended, I was introduced, I think by my Tarleton friend David Barron on one of my trips home, to Marjory Ball, who lived in Chorley. She attended Young Conservative socials, and I believe that I met her at one of those in the Royal Oak Hotel in Chorley. We struck up a serious relationship which lasted through part of my second and through my third year postgraduate days in Hull. She became my second fiancée.

NOTES

1. Strictly speaking this expression, according to *Brewer's Dictionary of Phrase & Fable* (18th Edition), means scant gratitude for one's efforts (and therefore not worth the trouble).

2. Professor George Gray died on 12 May 2013.

SCIENCE AND POLITICS:
AN UNLIKELY MIXTURE

# PART 2

~

# A CAREER IN CHEMISTRY

CHAPTER FOUR

# STARTING MY CAREER AS A CHEMIST

~

During my last postgraduate year in Hull, I considered my next move. I had an open invitation to return to the research and development laboratories of ICI at Blackley, but my research work in Hull was tempting me towards a career in the pharmaceutical industry. It wasn't too difficult for a chemist with a good degree to get a job in the 1960s.

Then I came across an advertisement in a chemistry journal for an appointment as a Senior Demonstrator in Organic Chemistry at the University of Durham. I applied for that position, as well as for a postdoctoral position to work with Professor Ron Haszeldine at the University of Manchester Institute of Science and Technology (UMIST), which would have taken me closer to Tarleton. Haszeldine had a formidable international reputation as a chemist. His very large research group was prolific in its rate of publication of papers in the chemistry journals, mainly, although not entirely, in the developing field of organofluorine chemistry.

Unusually, my first interview was in the evening in

Manchester. I arrived at the allotted hour and was asked to wait on a chair outside Haszeldine's office. People were going in and out of his office at regular intervals. Something like an hour later, it could have been up to two hours, I was ushered in to meet the great man. He made it quite clear that if I joined his group, I would be working night and day in the laboratory, and that I wouldn't get much time off. Who could argue with that? I knew that association with his group would stand me in good stead later for getting a job in the chemical industry, and he had excellent connections with a lot of industrial companies. I was offered a place in his research group.

Next I travelled by train from Hull to Durham. I had a dreadful vision of Durham in my mind as I undertook that journey, of coal mines and slag heaps and a despoiled industrial landscape. Nothing could have been further from the truth. As the train pulled into Durham station on the elevated east coast main line, I saw this beautiful vision of Durham Cathedral and the castle standing prominently across the River Weir on Palace Green. Durham must be one of the most beautiful places in England, and it was a joy to live and work there.

Employment in Durham is dominated by three institutions, the university, the cathedral and the high-security prison, an unusual mixture for such a small city.

On the morning of my Durham interview I heard from a BBC news bulletin on my radio that there had been a big explosion in the Department of Chemistry at the University of Durham the evening before and that there was a 'missing person'. I was curious to know what had caused it.

On the day of my interview I was joined by Dr Jim Feast, who was being interviewed for a permanent appointment as a

Lecturer in Organic Chemistry. Our paths crossed again after I left Durham, when Jim became President of the Royal Society of Chemistry (2006-2008) and I was elected to Parliament.

My interview with Professor Ken Musgrave and Dr Richard D. Chambers went well, and I was offered a job as the first-ever Senior Demonstrator in Organic Chemistry in the new science laboratories. My job was to organise and supervise laboratory classes for the third-year undergraduates and to join the organofluorine chemistry research group. I also prepared interesting demonstrations for visiting schoolchildren to see on the open days that the department organised.

I was over the moon when they offered me a job, and I accepted it on the spot. It was a fixed three-year contract. I realised how fortunate I had been, and I have always been extremely grateful to Ken Musgrave for giving me an early start in my academic career, and in such a prestigious chemistry department at the age of only 24. Professor William Kenneth Rogerson Musgrave died at the age of 92, in December 2010.

During my first year in Durham Dr Dave Clark, a newly-appointed lecturer, decided to take a one-year sabbatical with Professor J. D. Roberts in the USA to learn more about the rapidly-developing method for determining the structures of organic compounds – NMR or Nuclear Magnetic Resonance spectroscopy - which also led to the discovery of Magnetic Resonance Imaging (MRI) scanners later (they left the 'Nuclear' out because of fears that it might put patients off subjecting themselves for examination in these scanners). I was asked to undertake Dr Clark's lecture load whilst he was away, which provided me with further academic experience when I was appointed as a Temporary Lecturer for one year in addition to my other duties.

The offer of a job at Durham meant that I had to turn down Professor Haszeldine's offer. Little did I know then that Ken Musgrave and he had shared a laboratory together in Professor Tatlow's pioneering organofluorine research group at the University of Birmingham, during which time they had not been very friendly with each other.

After the interview I was shown round the impressive facilities I would be using. A combined research laboratory and office was reserved for me at the end of the third-year teaching laboratory in a recently-built extension to the department. Whilst walking down a corridor in the older wing of the department I caught a glimpse of a laboratory that had been completely destroyed by the previous evening's explosion. My curiosity overcame me, but Dick Chambers was completely open about what had happened.

The chemist involved had been carrying out a reaction between pyridine and phosphorus pentachloride in a 'bomb' (an autoclave) at high pressure and at a temperature of over 200°C to prepare pentachloropyridine, the starting material from which pentafluoropyridine was prepared. The 'bomb' was a thick, cylindrical stainless steel container into which the chemicals were placed before a top carrying a safety valve was bolted on. Huge amounts of hydrogen chloride gas are produced during this reaction and pressure builds up inside the reaction vessel. Ordinarily the pressure could be released by venting off the gas in a fume cupboard, but we discovered that the phosphorus pentachloride sublimed and blocked the safety valve. I was shown the remains of the 'bomb' or reactor which had exploded; it was nothing more than a flattened piece of thick stainless steel.

Fred Drakesmith, the research worker who had been reported missing in the BBC bulletin, was eventually found to have been in a local hostelry. The UMIST group, which I later discovered were in competition with the Durham group in exploring the chemistry of the new and interesting chemical pentafluoropyridine, also had explosions in making pentachloropyridine. The rivalry between the Durham and UMIST groups was so intense that it spilled over into footnotes at the bottom of the research papers that the rival groups published in the *Proceedings* and *Journal of the Chemical Society*, until the Editor refused to publish any more of these rather bitter exchanges.

Before I left Durham to travel back to Hull I was keen to know in which area of chemistry they would prefer me to carry out my research whilst in Durham. To my initial shock Dick calmly announced that he and Ken Musgrave would like me to work on the chemistry of pentafluoropyridine and similar compounds, and I did so.

Durham University has a collegiate system, although the teaching is carried out in departments and not in the colleges, at least for science subjects. When I first arrived in Durham I lived as a don in Grey College, which is on a hill overlooking the science laboratories and the city. I had a suite of two student rooms interconnected by a door, which was adequate. I only had to roll down the hill to get to work. Students, as in Hull, were 'gated' at night. If we caught an undergraduate climbing through a ground-floor window after hours, walking on the lawns or committing other misdemeanours, we could issue a fine. These were used to buy books for the college library.

Grey College had a Junior Common Room (JCR) and a Senior Common Room (SCR) where dons could book in for lunch. Grey was quite a popular college with railway buffs because, from the SCR, they could see trains coming and going into Durham Station, across Palace Green. Its Master in 1964 was a mathematician – Sid Holgate, if my memory serves me correctly.

Dinners in the evening were formal gown-wearing affairs and I had to buy a gown before I could sit on the top table with the Master and the resident and visiting dons. We paraded in with the students standing and grace was presented in Latin. Successive generations of dons in the Durham colleges had laid down plentiful supplies of good wines in their cellars, and these could be purchased at dinner with a charge added to our monthly account. The colleges charged the original cost of the wine with a small additional charge, so these wines were ridiculously cheap. Most resident dons, with the exception of our Master, who had a family house on site, were single men. As at Hull, the colleges were single-sex colleges when I started to work at Durham. The college across South Way, St Mary's College, was for women only.

I met some characters during my stay in Durham. One of the Grey dons, a geographer, was a specialist in continental drift and the shift of tectonic plates. Another, Ogilvy Angus Milne Buchan, son of an Aberdeen doctor, was a philosopher. Og was a stocky man who always seemed to be pushing his glasses up from the end of his nose. He was very funny and I took an instant liking to him; we became great friends. He had a cat called Chatty Samuel Smith.

Before arriving in Durham Og had been in Jamaica at the University of the West Indies, which I visited later in life. Once, when I visited his flat, the door was open and he called me in. He was marching up and down naked in the bath, stamping on a mixture of his dirty clothes and soap powder. It was wash day. Eccentric he definitely was.

Shortly after the 'moors murders' trial of Myra Hindley and Ian Brady was over, Brady arrived at Durham gaol and decided to take an interest in philosophy. Og was a Lecturer in Philosophy in the Department of Extramural Studies at Durham. He was dispatched to any college or organisation that showed an interest in philosophy. Consequently, Og was invited to meet Brady with a view to Brady gaining a degree in the subject. I discussed Og's interview with Brady with him when he returned from the gaol. Og turned down the request from the gaol to be Brady's tutor because he would not have been allowed to bring any of Brady's work out of the high-security gaol to mark, which seemed entirely reasonable to me in view of the media's intense interest in Brady.

Punting on the River Weir was one of the joys of being in Durham, and Og enjoyed punting, especially if another person was using the pole. I hadn't realised that punting in Oxford was so different to punting in Cambridge until I met Og. The person with the pole can either stand on the stern platform of the punt or, and this is safer, stand in the well. We always punted from the stern platform. It was great fun; we never fell into the river. Of course, bottles of wine to drink and a picnic were a must on these sunny days out on the river.

When I had moved out of Grey College, Og arrived at our house one evening to dine with us in quite an agitated state. He had set out from Grey College in his van quite inebriated and struck a stationary vehicle as he passed it. What should he do? On another occasion, equally agitated, he told me that the Grey College cleaners were talking about the number of whisky bottles they were finding in the waste bin in his flat, so he had begun to go up to a lay-by on the A1 and unload them there. Life was not dull with this man around.

One day, he announced to me that he was getting married; I was surprised, if not a little anxious. I hadn't met the woman involved at that stage. I was invited to 'stand in' at his wedding in the Durham City Register Office, and gladly attended. I thought this would see a change in his behaviour. No such thing. The next news that we received was that he had died, after only a few years of married life.

Durham was full of interesting characters in those days, none more so than the Professor of Music. The Music Department was up on Palace Green, very close to the magnificent Norman cathedral and castle. Professor Hutchinson didn't believe in music examinations; people were either born musicians or not. Rumour had it that he posted up the written examination papers in his department for all to see because he didn't believe in examining his students in that way. He had a dislike too for some musical instruments. When the Department of Music was endowed with a Welsh Harp, he left the crate in which it had arrived standing unopened in the foyer of the department.

Professor Hutchinson lived on Quarryheads Lane, near St Mary's College and close to the New Inn at the junction of South Road and Stockton Road, a pub very popular with those of us who worked on the science site, also at this junction. Professor Hutchinson was a regular at the New Inn and was a well-known character in that neighbourhood. He wore a 'Wee Willy Winky' outfit as his bedclothes – striped, with a pointed hat carrying a bobble – and was caught before bedtime, wearing his bedclothes, on more than one occasion climbing over his neighbour's fences to pick their flowers. Imagine the sight!

One night he was walking the short distance home on Quarryheads Lane from the New Inn when the Dame (appointed from the Ministry of Agriculture) in charge of St Mary's College was walking her dog in the opposite direction and called across to him, "Drunk again Professor Hutchinson?", and he called back "So am I, Mary (not her real name), so am I".

David Bellamy, who became a famous television presenter and later a leading campaigner on environmental issues, was a member of the Department of Biology when I arrived in Durham, but hardly anyone saw him in the department. I have never understood why he campaigns against the generation of electricity from windmills.

The Professor of Inorganic Chemistry, Professor Geoffrey Coates, was quite a character himself. He was Head of the Department of Chemistry when I arrived in Durham. At student socials they sang the words of a TV cider commercial, "Coates comes up from Somerset where the cider apples grow", and he did. When he was lecturing to students, he couldn't keep still and played with the long wooden tapered pointer that was provided in every lecture theatre in those days, and pretended to swing on the handles of the blackboards when he was pulling one down. He attempted to climb the pointer as he spoke. He also fiddled with the taps on the demonstration bench and had this remarkable habit of sticking his head in the sink. This behaviour earned him the nickname of 'the Ostrich' from the undergraduate students.

Professor Coates and his research group worked on selenium compounds, and he is the only person I have ever heard of who had a paper refused for publication by the Chemical Society (which became the Royal Society of

Chemistry) because it stank. After I left Durham he departed in 1968 for the University of Wyoming in the USA.[1]

The Chemistry Department at Durham was a good place to work. The laboratories were well equipped and my colleagues were very friendly. I was allocated a research student, Tony Story, who I supervised for Professor Musgrave. By an analogous route to the one that we used to synthesise pentafluoropyridine, Tony synthesised heptafluoroquinoline and heptafluoroisoquinoline and carried out some reactions with them. We protected our work on these innovative systems by taking out patents.

Also working in our laboratory in the fluorine group was a young PhD student called Jack Cunningham, who I met up with again in the House of Commons when he was the Member of Parliament for Copeland (1983-2005). He became Baron Cunningham of Felling, a Labour Peer in the House of Lords.

I began to prepare some pentachloropyridine for my own work. The university's insurance company no longer allowed us to do this work inside the Department of Chemistry. Instead, we were allocated a laboratory in some old huts at the back of the main building, where Professor Paneth had, in earlier years, established for the first time the existence of some highly reactive species in chemistry called free radicals (nothing to do with politics!)

I went down to the laboratory one Saturday night to switch off one of these reactions, with the intention of 'working it up' on the following Monday morning, only to find that another catastrophe had occurred. The room was covered – the benches, the fume-cupboard in which the 'bomb' was sat, the ceiling and all the walls – in pentachloropyridine, and there was a gap between the top of the 'bomb' and the top, which had been securely bolted on. At this time we were taking the precaution to line the inside of these 'bombs' with nickel to prevent pitting of the stainless steel that had been occurring previously, in the belief that this was weakening the strength of the 'bombs' or reactors.

Clearly, we could no longer use that room, so my next reaction was attempted in an old concrete-built chamber up in the woods behind the science laboratories, which had been used in earlier years for the pioneering radiation chemistry that was carried out at Durham. At my first attempt in this new environment the reaction vessel remained intact, but getting its top off was a hazardous business. Our engineers had built a metal cradle with long handles attached, which enabled us to capture the 'bomb' and carry it into the open air, where we carefully loosened the bolts until the pressure began to escape from inside. I was able to take the contents to my own laboratory and pour them onto ice in a 5-litre glass beaker in a fume-cupboard. 'Smoke rings' of phosphine gas could be seen coming off which spontaneously burst into flame in the air above the beaker. This was exciting chemistry but a little more exciting than I had anticipated. I had enough pentachloropyridine at last to prepare my basic starting material from it – pentafluoropyridine.

But the excitement did not stop there. My next embarrassment was to cause an evacuation of the whole Department of Chemistry. I converted pentafluoropyridine into 4-methyltetrafluoropyridine, then into 4-bromomethyltetrafluoropyridine. All these reactions were carried out in a well-ventilated fume-cupboard. When I worked up my reaction, extracted the product with ether and tried to remove the ether on a rotary evaporator, there was nothing left in the Buchi flask. Where had my product gone? It had gone through the fume-cupboard exhaust system into the air outside, where a fraction of it was taken in by the air intake system for the entire department's ventilation system, situated some yards away. That caused evacuation of the entire Department of Chemistry.

This compound proved to be so volatile that it was almost impossible to keep it, even at room temperature, in the liquid state. Even worse, it was the most lachrymatory chemical that I ever handled, so much so that we informed Porton Down that it might be a useful riot control agent.

Whilst Dave Clark was in the USA I was given the responsibility of organising the colloquia for postgraduate students and staff members of the Organic Section of the department. I became aware that Professor Ron Haszeldine had never given a talk on his research work at the University of Durham, so I suggested to Dick Chambers that he should. I was aware by this time, of course, that there were tensions between Musgrave and Haszeldine, but I hadn't realised how bad they were until that moment.

Nevertheless, mainly because I thought it would heal old wounds but also because I thought that the postgraduate students should be given the chance to come face-to-face with one of the most prominent chemists working in their field, I persevered with this idea. Eventually, agreement was reached for Haszeldine to visit Durham. I had to ask all the postgraduates to turn round all the bottles on their shelves containing the novel organofluorine chemicals that they were working on so that as we showed Haszeldine round (which was usual when visitors came to the department), he couldn't get any indication as to the type of research activity that was being carried out in any of our laboratories.

At the age of 24 the transition from a postgraduate student to a don felt strange. I felt more like a student than a don when I began my academic career, which gave me the advantage that I could talk to and understand the concerns of the undergraduates whom I was now teaching more than could some of my older colleagues. But I knew that I couldn't get too close to them. In my first year, my third-year group of undergraduates tried very hard to get me to date one of the women in their group. She used to wear strong Blue Grass perfume whenever she came close to me, and there was a buzz in the lecture room when I walked in and she was there. One day, an apple appeared on the demonstration bench. I ate the apple but resisted the other temptation. In any case, I was engaged.

When I started to present lectures to undergraduate students, I remembered how bad some of those who lectured to me had been at putting their subject matter across in a manner that could be understood by their student audience, so I made a special effort to present my subject in the clearest manner I could in all the years I was an academic. The first time a lecture is presented is not usually the best. The lecture improves as it is presented a second time, then, at the third attempt, it will be as right as it will ever be. My two-plus years in Durham provided me with a good start for my later career in Salford.

In 1966, my first publication – on the work carried out in Hull – appeared in the *Journal of the Chemical Society*.

All my staff colleagues seemed to be in keep-fit mode in Durham and they made a couch potato like me feel very guilty. So, when an Inorganic Lecturer, Dr Mel Kilner, invited me to be his regular squash partner, I agreed to give it a go, even though I had never played the game before. I kitted myself out and, much against my inner instincts, found that I quite enjoyed chasing a small ball round a smallish room.

I should have listened to those instincts. I twisted one of my ankles so badly that I ended up in the A&E Department of Dryburn Hospital, where they fitted me with a 'pot' and gave me an arm crutch, which enabled me to walk for the several weeks I wore it. When the new plaster dried out I spent hours with a long knitting needle trying to free the hairs that were trapped in the plaster.

Durham was a special place for me in more ways than one. I met Merrilyn Muncaster at a dance in the old student union building, which was demolished later to build the new bridge across the River Weir in Durham. Merrilyn was training to be a teacher at that time at a teacher training college in Darlington, which is ten miles to the south of Durham. The women from the college came to the Saturday night dances at the student union in Durham. As our relationship became very close she decided not to proceed with her course.

Merrilyn and I were married at Headingly Methodist Church in Leeds (Dr Roger Pinder was my best man). Following our reception, which was held in the back garden of the Muncaster's home, we leapt into a hired car and headed north to drive as far as we could that day. I was exhausted by the time we reached Berwick-upon-Tweed, where we stayed the night at the Kings Arms Hotel. Our honeymoon was spent in a static caravan in a field on a farm near to Inverewe Gardens in Wester Ross, Scotland.

In Durham we rented a furnished former miner's terraced house on Nevilles Cross Bank, close to the A1 (now the A167 Newcastle to Darlington Road). I could walk from there to the science laboratories.

# SCIENCE AND POLITICS: AN UNLIKELY MIXTURE

My marriage to Merrilyn Muncaster. Left to right: my father, best man Dr Roger Pinder, Elizabeth Waterhouse, me and Merrilyn, chief bridesmaid Jennifer Walker, Annabelle Foxcroft and Evelyn and Cyril Muncaster.

I remember well the time that Merrilyn was 'carrying' our eldest daughter Sally and the days leading up to her birth. There came a point when I shopped, using lists provided by Merrilyn. One day, she provided me with a very long list and wrote a 1, 2 or 3 opposite each item. Although she had explained what these numbers meant, I merely gave the list to the shopkeeper, who proceeded to put all the shopping into boxes. I was surprised to see the amount of shopping I was expected to carry home but the shopkeeper very kindly offered to deliver the boxes.

When they arrived and Merrilyn started to unpack the boxes she was surprised to see three packets of items such as lentils on the kitchen table. We were eating lentil soup for months after that. Of course, the number 3 meant that the item was of the lowest priority and not that we needed three packets, jars or tins of those items.

On the days leading up to the birth of Sally the roads became impassable with heavy snowdrifts. The snow ploughs managed to keep the main roads clear, but we lived on a bank. It remained impassable, as did the road (now the A690) that crossed the A1 and led to Dryburn Hospital. When the time came for Merrilyn to go to hospital, I was amazed when the ambulance managed to reach our home.

It wasn't common in 1965 for husbands to be present at a birth, but I was keen to be there, and Merrilyn wanted me to be with her. Husbands were seen by the midwives as a bit of a nuisance. Nevertheless, Dryburn Hospital agreed to telephone me at work. However they never did, and I have always regretted not seeing Sally Jane born or being there in the final stages of labour to comfort Merrilyn.

Sally was born on 30 November 1965. It was a difficult birth, as I discovered later, because the umbilical cord had wrapped itself round Sally's neck in Merrilyn's womb. Sally's early days were spent in a Moses basket, which we kept for the birth of our second daughter Sheena three years later.

Our Neville's Cross home was freezing cold that winter, and the snow remained on the ground for many days. We also had trouble with the hot water boiler, which put carbon monoxide into the kitchen. Nevertheless, we managed to cope, penniless though we were.

In 1964, I joined the Durham Student Labour Club in unseating the cigar-smoking Tory Member of Parliament for Darlington, Anthony Bourne-Arton, who was replaced by the Labour candidate Edward Fletcher in the General Election of that year.

## SCIENCE AND POLITICS: AN UNLIKELY MIXTURE

When I lived in Durham most of the pits were working and the big occasion of the year was the Durham Miners' Gala, which was held on the second Saturday of July. Miners assembled with their elaborate banners and individual colliery brass bands at various meeting points around the city and proceeded to march into the city centre, where they combined into a single parade. They marched past the County Hotel, where the miners' leaders and official guests gathered on the front balcony to salute them and their families, and proceeded to march onto the huge cricket field on the banks of the River Weir.

I enjoyed listening to the platform speakers at the end of the march. MPs Dennis Skinner, Michael Foot and Tony Benn were regulars at the Durham Miners' Gala when I lived in Durham. After the speeches, those attending enjoyed the amusements provided on the cricket field or toured the numerous stalls put up by people from all around the country.

Margaret Thatcher came to power in 1979. The Durham pits began to close and there was a period when it was considered that the Durham Miners' Gala might come to an end. Ironically, Margaret Thatcher convinced everybody concerned that it should be kept alive, and it became a reminder to the people of Britain of the damage she and her Government had caused to the mining industry in Britain. Today it is as big an event as ever and puts a lot of money into the Durham businesses. I have been back to the Gala a number of times since leaving Durham.

In 1965, the whole of the organofluorine group was invited by Ken Musgrave and Dick Chambers to accompany them to Munich, where several papers were presented by the group at an International Conference on Fluorine Chemistry. This was the first conference that I attended outside the UK. By this stage the work that I carried out in Hull was being published in journals of international standing, and several patents had my name on them.

Professor Hans Suschitzky.

Eileen and me on the River Weir in Durham.

Attending the Durham Miners' Gala; Tony Benn MP is on the balcony of the County Hotel.

I had followed the work of Professor Hans Suschitzky at the Salford Royal College of Advanced Technology (there were ten CATs, essentially polytechnics, at that time); he had prepared fluoroquinolines and fluoroisoquinolines, and I was eager to meet him. I discovered that he too was at the Munich conference and I introduced myself to him. He learned that I was in the organofluorine group led by Ken Musgrave and Dick Chambers in Durham, and I discovered that Salford's Department of Chemistry and Applied Chemistry was about to appoint seven lecturers, three in organic chemistry. Hans suggested that I apply for one of these posts, and I did. Hans Suschitzky had not met Ken Musgrave and Dick Chambers before. That visit to Munich secured my immediate future.

This was the post-Robins era, which gave way to a rapid expansion of the university system; not only were existing universities expanding but new universities, like Lancaster and Keele, were emerging on green field sites, and all the ex-CATS became universities too. We began to use terms such as 'redbrick universities' and 'the new universities' more and more to differentiate the different ages of creation of the universities. Slowly, a pecking order of academic achievement started to emerge, and in more recent times the elite Russell Group of universities was formed.

NOTES

1. Professor Geoffrey Edward Coates died on 10 January 2013.

**CHAPTER FIVE**

# CONTINUING MY CAREER IN SALFORD

~

I began working in Salford in the autumn of 1966. It was a place I had been through, mainly en route to Manchester on the A6, several times before in my life. Each time I passed 'Hanky Park' (Walter Greenwood based his play *Love on the Dole* on this area of extreme poverty) I thought places like Salford were places where I would never work.

Shortly after I arrived in Salford 'Hanky Park' was demolished (there were a lot of rats around during the demolition period), to be replaced by a mixed public sector housing development, which stands there today. The tower blocks, one named Walter Greenwood House, eventually became unpopular with the local people and several of them became managed accommodation for university students.

Clifford Whitworth steered the former Royal College of Advanced Technology at Salford into university status in 1967 and served as the first Vice-Chancellor of the new university until 1974. He was followed by John Horlock (1974-1981), John Ashworth (1981-1990), Tom Husband (1990-1997) and

Michael Harloe (1997-2009). The present Vice-Chancellor is Martin Hall.

HRH Prince Philip, Duke of Edinburgh, served as the University of Salford's first Chancellor (1967-1990). He was followed by Sarah, Duchess of York (1991-1995), who had a rather turbulent social life shortly after her appointment, Sir Walter Bodmer (1995-2005), Martin Harris (2005-2009) and Irene Zubaida Khan, the present Chancellor.[1]

I spent the next 31 years teaching chemistry at Salford in what became the largest Department of Chemistry (and Applied Chemistry) in the UK at its peak, with over 70 academic staff plus support staff. In those days the department housed biochemists, a rapidly developing subject area, polymer chemists, dyestuff chemists and nuclear chemists. The research carried out was mainly of an applied nature. Many lecturers were not involved in research or scholarship; in the vacations they just disappeared. However, over the following years a significant change was to occur in the new university.

When I arrived in Salford the university was centred on science, technology, engineering and mathematics (the STEM subjects). There were very large Departments of Civil, Electrical and Mechanical Engineering. Most of the electrical engineers who maintained the National Grid at that time were trained at Salford.

Sadly, after Salford became a university in 1967, and especially after the cuts in finance that were applied to the university by the Conservative Government in 1981 (Salford's budget was cut by a massive 44%), the more expensive courses that required laboratories and engineering workshops for their teaching declined, and the university filled its places by developing courses that were cheaper to run. To be fair, by then students were faced with a plethora of choices and chose to enrol on courses which appeared to lead more easily to the prospect of a degree, and hopefully employment.

I have always believed that we should have kept the polytechnics and CATS and allowed them to develop their status as higher education institutions which specialised in providing the scientific and engineering talent this country has always needed, as well as carrying out the applied research which is valued by industry, rather than encourage them to become like all other universities.

John Ashworth, who bore the brunt of the cuts made in 1981, was a strong supporter of the SDP. After he left Salford he became Director of the London School of Economics and after that, was appointed as chairman of the British Library Board. Before John Ashworth took up his appointment, the university was managed by one of the engineering Professors, Tom Constantine. Tragically, he died not long after the 44% cut in the university's finances was announced, and many academics believed that the pressure he was under at that time contributed to his untimely death.

Prime Minister Margaret Thatcher had the cheek to visit the University of Salford on 15 January 1982, when she opened a building on the campus for Salford University Industrial Centre Ltd. There were no cheers for her on that day; students and staff stood in a dignified silence as she stepped out of her car. She was 'frozen out' by a small band of demonstrators who turned their backs on her as she appeared from the car.

An early observation I made was that the library was better for chemists at that time in Salford than the library at the University of Durham. In Salford there were long runs of journals and many excellent books that research chemists needed to access. Some members of staff had made a reputation by writing books. Rudi Diamant, a physical chemist, for example, was a prolific writer of textbooks.

Rudi became engaged in litigation with publisher Robert Maxwell when Maxwell heard that Rudi had accused him of not paying up all the royalties that were owed. At that time I shared an office in the Tower Building (see later) at Salford with Dr Basil J. Wakefield and Dr Douglas Maass. As I picked up the shared phone one day, I recognised the unmistakable voice of Maxwell on the other end of the line. He wanted to speak to Basil, who had become embroiled too in Rudi's accusation. Rudi Diamant was able to settle his dispute with Maxwell out of court to his satisfaction. Amazingly, he conducted his own case.

Rudi was quite a character. He spent some time with a scientific expedition to study whales. When one of the whales was landed on board the ship and found to be pregnant, Rudi decided to preserve the baby whale in formalin in a tin trunk and bring it back for a museum in the UK. On arrival at customs a customs officer spotted the trunk and demanded to know what was in it. When Rudi responded "a whale", the customs officer found it hard to believe. Nevertheless, Rudi managed to talk his way out of the situation and the whale was admitted to Britain.

My career at Salford began in the Maxwell Building of the Royal College of Advanced Technology. There were 13 of us in the office where I had a desk, and it was almost impossible to do any serious work in there. The Head of Department when I arrived was a likeable older man called Professor George Ramage, who had carried out some distinguished research in organic chemistry on terpenes in his lifetime. I believe that he was engaged during the war years on developing the industrial production of penicillin.

George Ramage is remembered for the ankle-length laced-up boots he wore. He travelled to Salford every day from Kirkburton, near Huddersfield, and back by bus and train. He was a true Yorkshire man. Instead of getting off the bus from Victoria railway station on the Crescent at the university, he got off at the stop before, which was a fare stage, all to save a halfpenny on each journey.

George Ramage was a strong supporter of the Royal Institute of Chemistry (RIC) and often travelled to their meetings in London and back in the day. To save the RIC money, he never stayed in a hotel overnight; he arrived back in Huddersfield early in the morning on what we called the 'milk train' (actually the mail train). George Ramage had interviewed me for the job I was seeking at Salford and I was grateful to him for appointing me.

In the 1960s we taught many part-time students at Salford, mainly mature men and women, in the evenings and even on Saturday mornings. The university was heaving with students and there wasn't enough accommodation on the campus to teach all who had to be taught. We used old chapels, old workshops and school halls, and had to walk considerable distances to reach our students. I took great exception though when the university allocated me classes in the Masonic Hall across the road from the university.

Our department was the only one in the UK at that time where students could study full-time for the Part II examination of the Graduateship of the Royal Institute of Chemistry (GRIC). There was more chance of passing this examination at Salford than studying it part-time elsewhere. It was a tough examination to take and the students who passed it were highly valued throughout the chemical industry. Consequently, we had over 100 students on this course alone.

As well as some very hard theory papers, the students endured three days of practical examinations. At the end of the last day George Ramage brought ice creams into the large teaching laboratories and handed them out personally to each student as a reward for their efforts. We also taught part-time Part I GRIC students. Sadly, after the expansion of the university system, this route to a qualification in chemistry ended.

The four-year Applied Chemistry Degree course, which provided students who were 'job-ready', was also popular with students at Salford. This included a year out, spent working on paid employment in the chemical industry or a related one. As the years went by it became more and more difficult to place our students in industry, and these courses were dropped.

Salford University's buildings are built on either side of the River Irwell, where it forms a crescent and surrounds Peel Park, the subject of some of L. S. Lowry's paintings. The two parts of the campus today are linked by a footbridge over the river. Shortly after my arrival in Salford the Department of Chemistry and Applied Chemistry moved into a new building which was constructed between the first of the buildings built on the site in Victorian times, the Peel Building and the then Salford Art Gallery and Museum. It was called simply the Tower Building. Although our department was by far the largest housed in this building, there were other departments in the building too. Chemistry was first taught at Salford, in the Victorian era, on the top floor of the Peel Building in a laboratory with a very lofty roof.

The Tower Building gained a reputation as one of the few buildings in Britain which had paternoster lifts installed in it – two banks of linked continuously moving open-access cabins, which gave rapid access to the upper floors. Stepping into them could be quite daunting for those who had never used these lifts before. I remember the occasion when Prince Philip was shown round the Tower Building. Towards the top floor of the building he stood gazing with amazement at these continuously moving lifts. A student acknowledged him on his upward journey and came down within a short time standing on his head!

I have already referred to the hard-working Professor Ron Haszeldine at UMIST; it was rumoured that he never slept. However, when my colleague Dr Feodore Scheinmann attended a conference, he caught Haszeldine asleep in the daytime lying on a lawn behind a hedge, and snapped a photograph.

When Feo was responsible for organising the Organic Section's colloquia at Salford, he invited Haszeldine to speak and during the traditional introduction of the guest speaker, Feo showed a slide of a sleeping Ron Haszeldine. After the lecture, as they both stepped into the same paternoster lift cabin on the ground floor of the department, Feo dropped the slide and it disappeared into the underground cavern below the lifts, never to be recovered.

L. S. Lowry taught art in the Peel Building at Salford before his paintings became widely known. Some staff members in our

University of Salford (left to right): The Peel Building (behind trees), the Tower Building and Salford Art Gallery and Museum.

Our organic chemistry research laboratory in the Tower Building at the University of Salford.

department purchased his paintings before he retired; John Noble, for example, picked up a painting for about £100. Salford's collection of Lowry paintings were hung next door to the Tower Building in the Salford Art Gallery and Museum, which was a good place to show visitors. Salford City Council constructed an old street inside that building, Larkhill Place, which demonstrated the lives of rich and poor people in Victorian times. This building housed the first library in the country that loaned books to the general public without a charge being made. Lowry's paintings are housed today in the Lowry Centre at Salford Quays, formerly Manchester Docks (actually situated in Salford), where there is also a shopping mall.

The River Irwell, which flows through Salford and forms a boundary between the cities of Salford and Manchester, was diverted to form the main water flow for the Manchester Ship Canal when it was constructed in 1894. The Ship Canal joins the River Mersey close to Liverpool, 36 miles away from Manchester. This canal allowed large ships to reach Manchester, with cargoes of cotton coming in and all the products of the cities and towns of Lancashire being shipped out. The docks were still very active when I arrived in Salford in 1966, but they fell into decline and, today, have been the scene of a major regeneration project, the latest phase of which is Media City. Manchester United Football Ground, the largest in Britain with its 76,312 seats, and the War Museum of the North are across the Ship Canal from Salford Quays.

Across the A6 from the university is Joule House, in Acton Square, where James Prescott Joule lived for the seven brief years of his marriage. Using a beer barrel from his father's brewery, he constructed an experiment that allowed him to study the relationship between mechanical energy and heat energy, which led to the term 'Joule' being used as a unit of energy.

Trafford Park was the largest industrial park in Europe from the 1940s through the 1960s, but it also fell into decline. Tens of thousands of people worked in its factories and on its chemical plants. There were so many people working on Trafford Park at its peak that the companies agreed to work different shift patterns to avoid congestion on the roads when the shifts changed. Whilst there are factories, including chemical factories, there today they employ far fewer people. The Department of Chemistry and Applied Chemistry at Salford University always had close links with the chemists of Trafford Park, with firms like Ciba-Geigy and ICI, for example. The Trafford Centre, which attracts 32 million shoppers per annum, has been constructed at the western end of Trafford Park, adjacent to the M60 Manchester ring road.

The Salford Department of Chemistry and Applied Chemistry was one of only two chemistry departments in the UK housed in a high-rise building, the other being that at UMIST. I could never understand why those who designed the Tower Building decided to put a room for carrying out high pressure reactions, albeit strengthened by concrete and steel, on the fifth floor of a building clad with glass. The Chemistry Department's stores were in the basement of the building, as was a laboratory for carrying out special operations. The main lecture theatres were on the ground floor and the tutorial rooms were scattered throughout the building. We had an excellent mechanical engineering workshop, which was organised by a technician called Joe Delaney (brother of playwright Sheila Delaney), and an excellent glassblowing workshop, where Ken Bullock constructed glassware to order and repaired broken glassware, both housed in the Peel Building.

The University of Salford was provided in the 1960s with one of the best nuclear teaching and research facilities in Britain for handling low- and high-level radioactive materials. The Cockcroft Building, built adjacent to the Tower Building, was a multidisciplinary building used by the engineering departments as well as by scientists. It had a 'cold side', which housed teaching and research laboratories, and a 'hot side', which housed a cobalt-60 source (this retracted below ground when not in use) and special fume-cupboards in which highly radioactive materials were handled remotely. Our department trained most of the chemists for the nuclear power industry, and many of the students came to Salford from abroad, ironically a significant number from Iraq.

When Merrilyn, Sally and I arrived in the Manchester area in 1966 we lived for a short time in an upstairs unfurnished flat in Didsbury, close to Wilmslow Road. Apart from a bed, a table, a few chairs and a cot for Sally, we had very little furniture in those days. The woman who owned our flat lived downstairs with a large dog. One day she went out and left her washing on the line and put the dog out in the garden. When she came back there was no sign of the washing. Later, she discovered that the dog had buried every item of washing in the flower beds of her garden.

Travelling across the City of Manchester to the City of Salford by public transport was most inconvenient, so I decided to approach my father for a loan to help me to purchase my first car. John Morris, the son of Ronnie Morris - another market gardener in Tarleton - and my brother Graham's best friend, who lived very close to my Tarleton home, had a red Morris Mini for sale, and I purchased it, I think for £400. It made getting to work a lot easier, and we were able to see more of my family in Tarleton and Merrilyn's family in Leeds.

With the loan to repay to my father and an overdraft which I had accumulated at a branch of Barclays Bank on Cottingham Road, Hull, I was in debt, but not by as much as students are today when they leave university. I was angered when Barclays Bank started to charge me what I considered to be an unreasonable interest rate on my overdraft, so I marched into their headquarters in Manchester to complain. I was ushered in to see a senior manager and told him that if they didn't remove or significantly reduce this charge, I would transfer my account to another bank. He found that remark quite funny until I told him that the Co-operative Bank had agreed to accept my account without charging for the overdraft, if I agreed to pay it off at an agreed rate. That wiped the smile off his face and Barclays lost my custom.

In my first year at Salford, George Ramage was very generous to me and offered a SRC grant to recruit a research student. We had some excellent students graduating with the GRIC qualification in 1966, and I recruited Roger Dickinson, a mature student who had worked in the pharmaceutical industry at Benger's Laboratories, Holmes Chapel, before enrolling on the full-time GRIC Part II course at Salford. Roger was interested in a PhD in medicinal chemistry, so I explained the significance of my Hull research which, essentially, was the preparation of benzo[$b$]thiophene analogues of biologically active indole systems.

Roger was one of the best research students I ever had the joy to work with and produced an excellent PhD thesis. He went on to work with Pfizer at their research laboratories in Sandwich, Kent, and I received many complimentary comments from those who worked with him there. He retired many years before I did!

Roger was a stamp collector and he persuaded me to take up my childhood interest again; I had even kept my childhood collection. I started to collect First Day Covers carrying the stamps of Elizabeth II, and I have kept up this collection until the present day. I must be one of the few people with a complete collection of the *Philatelic Bulletin.*

In his attempts to prepare pure 3-substituted benzo[*b*]thiophenes, Roger Dickinson discovered an interesting ring-opening reaction. I pursued this intriguing discovery with other research students, work that involved me in a long-standing friendship with Professor Salo Gronowitz at the University of Lund in Sweden. This work required us to synthesise highly air-sensitive and water-sensitive compounds, such as n-butyl-lithium, that were not available commercially until a few years later. They caught fire in air or on contact with water and all reactions had to be conducted under a blanket of dry nitrogen gas.

The parent molecule benzo[*b*]thiophene was difficult to obtain commercially (it came from coal tar) and when it was available, it was costly to purchase. We spent many hours preparing it from other chemicals. To my joy, one of Dr Otto Meth-Cohn's Postdoctoral Fellows, Dr John Ashby, who worked in a laboratory that Otto and I shared for a few years when we moved into the Tower Building, came in and announced that he had found a prolific supply of benzo[*b*]thiophene 'rock' (it was a solid at room temperature), in Blackpool of all places. I roared with laughter when he gave it to me, sticks of Blackpool rock in which he had persuaded the manufacturer to replace the word 'Blackpool' with 'benzo[*b*]thiophene' throughout its length. I didn't eat it; I kept it until this day as a souvenir of those pioneering days.

Otto was working with the chemical thiophene at that time and it was also expensive to purchase. It had a smell like that of new-mown hay in my nostrils, and I remembered where I had come across that smell before – passing through Pontefract on the way to Hull. I gave that information to Otto, who acquired his thiophene thereafter in larger quantities from Yorkshire Tar Distillers Ltd. They were pleased to donate it to him. Later, I became involved in the chemistry of other condensed thiophene rings; we prepared the two isomeric thienothiophene ring systems, for example, and exploited their chemistry.

Hans Suschitzky seemed surprised that I had not asked Roger to work on a project related to his own interests, so I suggested that I prepare some pentachloropyridine and that we start to examine its chemistry and those of polychloroheterocyclic compounds in general. It wasn't clear how much work there was in the literature on this subject, so we set about reviewing the work already published. A book, *Polychloroaromatic Compounds*, edited by Hans Suschitzky, was subsequently published in 1974, and in 1981 we organised a conference on organic polyhalogen compounds. Altogether, Hans and I and Basil Wakefield published over 50 research papers in this area of chemistry.

Professor George Ramage was forced to retire in September 1972 when he developed a serious cancer, from which he died a month later. George was so ill before he retired that some of my colleagues had seen him lying on the floor in his office.

Professor Hans Suschitzky, who was Head of the Organic Section in our department, succeeded him as Acting Head of Department. He was succeeded by Professor Glyn Phillips, Professor Orville-Thomas, Professor George Gamlen, Professor Evan Wyn-Jones, Professor John Spencer and Dr Austin Barnes (who was Head of Department when it was forced to close).

Our work on organochlorine compounds at Salford mirrored the similar work on organofluorine compounds that the research groups in Durham, Manchester and elsewhere were engaged in, but there was one big difference – determining the structures of our reaction products was more difficult. However, we learned how to overcome this problem.

Large international companies, such as ICI Plant Protection at Jealott's Hill and Dow Chemicals in the USA, were exploiting this branch of chemistry too. Some of the products of our research did show interesting herbicidal activity and were protected by patents. However, polychloro-organic compounds fell out of favour as commercial products when the organochlorine pesticides, such as DDT and Dieldrin, were shown to cause problems in the environment.

Considering the difficulties I had experienced preparing pentachloropyridine in Durham, I was greatly relieved when I discovered that ICI had patented an industrial-scale process for preparing our starting material by passing pyridine in the vapour phase with chlorine over a catalyst. It became available to us from ICI at Runcorn in kilogramme quantities.

It seemed logical to follow up all the work I had done on polychloroheterocyclic and polyfluoroheterocyclic systems with similar work on polybromoheterocyclic systems. The first compound we prepared and worked on was tetrabromothiophene. This led us to discover an interesting double ring-opening reaction of dilithiated thienothiophenes, which provided a route to some very interesting enediynes. Unfortunately, I was unable to exploit this discovery to its full extent, because I was elected to Parliament in 1997.

We also prepared and exploited the chemistry of polybromo-imidazoles, -pyrazoles, -thiazoles and -1,2,3-triazoles.

Several compounds containing bromine atoms are used as flame retardants to prevent household and other materials, such as the plastics used in vehicle manufacture, from burning. We organised the first international conference on 'The Chemistry and Applications of Bromine Compounds' at Salford in the autumn of 1986 and published a book, *Bromine Compounds; Chemistry and Applications*, edited by me, Dr Dennis Price and Dr Basil J. Wakefield, in 1988.

Shortly after I arrived at the University of Salford and acquired a car, Merrilyn and I started to search for a house to buy so that we could settle down for a while. Eventually, we moved to 41 Stetchworth Drive in the small mining village of Boothstown. Our home was conveniently situated close to a junction on the East Lancashire Road (the A580), which led directly into Salford.

That junction, where Ellenbrook Road crosses the East Lancashire Road (the A580) and becomes Newearth Road was, I soon discovered, one of the most dangerous on the entire length of the A580 between Manchester and Liverpool, especially during foggy weather. It became so dangerous that the ambulance service kept first-aid equipment and a stretcher in the house on Ellenbrook Road closest to the junction for local residents to deploy when we heard the very loud bangs of colliding vehicles.

I helped to pull many people out of their vehicles at that junction and I looked after them until the blue light services arrived. One night we had to break the back window of a car to pull the driver out through it, because the front of his vehicle was on fire. We rescued a policewoman on one occasion whose foot was trapped under a foot pedal of her burning vehicle. Eventually, the Local Authority provided traffic lights at this junction, which reduced but did not entirely eliminate the number of collisions there.

Mosley Common colliery, one of the largest remaining coal mines in Lancashire in 1966-1967, was close to our house. The Red Lion pub, across the East Lancashire Road, remained open almost 24 hours a day to meet the demands of the coalminers working the different shifts at the pit. Mosley Common was closed before we left Boothstown for Bolton. The machinery was left down the pit, the debris from the demolished buildings and other machinery was tipped into the pit and the shaft was sealed with a plug of concrete. There is a housing estate on the site today.

On Ellenbrook Road, Boothstown was the Lancashire Mines Rescue Station and, in the village of Worsley, the entrance to one of the first coal mines can be seen at the Delph. The Bridgewater Canal was built from there to carry coal into Manchester to fuel the factories of the industrial revolution.

People who visit the village of Worsley are amazed to find that the water in the canal is orange. The colour is from the iron oxide which is washed out of the 47 miles of underground canals that transported the coal out of the underground coal seams to the Delph. This underground canal system extends to Farnworth, near Bolton, about seven miles from the Delph.

The father of my next-door neighbour (Alan Grundy) in Stetchworth Drive was responsible for continuously inspecting this underground canal system for roof collapses. If they become blocked, the water table rises considerably, with the likelihood of flooding occurring on land above the canals.

From 1966 onwards I realised that I was becoming increasingly deaf in my right ear. If I was lying on my good left ear when the alarm clock went off in the morning, I couldn't hear it. In a large lecture theatre I sometimes couldn't hear questions being asked by students on my right. Therefore, I decided to approach my general practitioner, who referred me to an ENT consultant at Hope Hospital, Salford in 1967. At the end of the consultation I decided not to proceed with an operation when he told me that the chance of success was only 50:50.

Several months later the Physics Department at Salford sent all staff members a letter announcing that they had built a new

41 Stetchworth Drive, Boothstown, Worsley.

# SCIENCE AND POLITICS: AN UNLIKELY MIXTURE

Sally and Sheena Iddon.

anechoic chamber and asking us if we would like to test our hearing in it. I readily volunteered. As I came out of the chamber I was met by Mr A. Tumarkin, Visiting Emeritus Professor from the School of Medicine in Liverpool, who told me what I already knew and asked me if I had done anything about my hearing fault. He recommended that I should go to see Mr H. Zalin at his rooms in Rodney Street, Liverpool (the Harley Street of Liverpool) and I did seek such a meeting. It turned out that our Visiting Professor had taught most of the ENT specialists then consulting in North West hospitals. He compared his former student at Hope Hospital with Mr Zalin by comparing a bricklayer with a clock maker, an expression which has stuck in my mind ever since.

A stapedectomy operation was performed on me in the summer of 1968 at Bootle Hospital, which was in the process of being closed. Mr Zalin had just come back from the USA, where he had learned how to undertake very delicate operations on the inner ear with very small instruments at high magnification. I was given only a local anaesthetic, because Mr Zalin required me to switch my position on the operating table several times as he operated.

Three bones in the inner ear, the anvil, the hammer and the stirrup, are responsible for conducting sound from the ear drum. Two of mine had become detached and Mr Zalin reunited them with the help of a Teflon peg, which is still in place all these years later. I gathered that this was a new kind of operation at that time. I was advised not to dive into water or take part in any contact sports that might dislodge the peg. The after-effects of the operation were very unpleasant. I couldn't stand up straight for weeks, and nausea was a problem too. However, with the help of anti-nausea drugs my balance slowly returned, as did my hearing. Mr Zalin invited me to return to see him at any time should I experience any difficulties. Fortunately, I have never needed to. Mr Zalin passed away a few years ago.

Our second daughter, Sheena Helen, was born in M3 Ward at Hope Hospital, Salford, and I was present when she was born at 10.17 pm on the evening of the 4 December 1968. Midwife Gloria Byron delivered a healthy baby weighing 6lb 13oz, with long black hair and very dark blue eyes.

When Sally reached the age of five we enrolled her at St Andrew's Church of England primary school in Boothstown village, but she received most of her education in Bolton.

I recall that life in Stetchworth Drive was a happy one. The children made lots of friends and it was safe for them to play out in the street; Stetchworth Drive is a cul-de-sac. As a family we often walked across the fields between our home and Worsley Old Hall and I often played with my rapidly growing children. They were particularly amused by my version of Jake the Peg, when I marched up and down the lounge, swinging a table leg between my two real legs and singing Rolf Harris's magnificent song. My puppet shows were enjoyed too by my children and their young friends. I constructed a puppet theatre using Merrilyn's ironing board and some curtains.

My guilt over my lack of exercise prompted me to join the badminton club at the University of Salford, and I played the sport for several years, then dropped out as I realised that I was no good at competitive sport.

I have always been attracted to the sea and one of my regrets in life is that I have never had the opportunity to take up sailing as a serious hobby. The student union at Salford hired boats occasionally. One summer the staff member who skippered them could not get enough students to crew a large catamaran he had hired in Brixton Harbour. When I was invited to join them, I jumped at the opportunity and those two weeks at sea proved to be two of the happiest weeks of my life.

On the day we planned to set sail out of the calmness of Brixton Harbour to our first port of call, Cherbourg, the wind was getting up. To make matters worse one of the two engines failed as we approached the open sea. Our skipper, who was an experienced sailor (he owned a boat which he anchored on the coast of North Wales), managed to get us back into the safety of the harbour, but it was quite frightening at the time. By the following morning, when repairs had been carried out to the engine, we set sail again on a calmer sea. Nevertheless, dodging all the shipping in the English Channel was a new experience for me.

We rested in Cherbourg and filled the ship up with wine and food. Our intention was to sail next to the island of Alderney in the Channel Islands. The experienced sailors in the yacht club in Cherbourg told us that with our catamaran, the Alderney Races would carry us straight past the island, and they did. We ended up anchoring in Dixcart Bay on the tiny island of Sark. When we mounted the steps leading from the bay onto the island, the profusion of wildlife - birds, insects and flowers - that we saw reminded me of my early years in Tarleton.

The highlight of our stay on Sark was attending the Saturday night dance. We took a short cut back to the boat across the meadows and I wasn't sure whether I was falling over sleeping cows or courting couples.

With our boat we were able to explore most of the Channel Islands, including the other small islands, such as Herm with its magnificent shell beach. It was glorious weather to sail in and out of these islands. On the way back across the Channel I was able to observe for the first time in my life bioluminescence as I lay on the net across the bows of the catamaran. As the bows stirred oxygen into the sea, algae glowed in the dark. Later, when I visited Africa and other tropical countries, I was able to observe the magic of fireflies dancing in the air at night (see also Chapter 8 - The Magic of Chemistry).

Now that I was back in Lancashire I saw a lot more of my family in Tarleton. On Sundays when there was a Sunday League cricket match at Old Trafford I picked my dad up in Tarleton and took him to watch Lancashire play. These were enjoyable outings. Not only did they reconnect me with the game I have loved most in my life but they gave me a chance to spend more time with my father in his old age.

At one match in the late 1960s he seemed to have something on his mind all day. Eventually, I discovered what was concerning him. I had established myself in a career and he was worried about the future of my brother Graham, who was running our father's market gardening business. "Would you be upset if I made a new will leaving the house and business to Graham?" he asked me. I had already taken it for granted that he had already done that, so I readily agreed to his proposal.

These were busy days, with a young family to bring up and a career to carve out. Some extra earnings were essential. Merrilyn worked on the bar at the Greyhound pub in Boothstown, which had a well-known wrestler as its landlord. Tommy Pye was one of a famous wrestling family. Later, she worked on the bar at the Excel bowling alley in Walkden and at the Bridgewater Hotel in Worsley village.

For a while I also worked at the bowling alley, but on different evenings to Merrilyn. I got the sack there for showing the manager how to change the carbon dioxide cylinders on the beer line safely. She had acquired the habit of letting the full pressure of the new cylinder into the cylinder head, whereas I insisted on turning off the needle valve of the cylinder head before I opened the new cylinder - then I adjusted the cylinder head to 15 psi of pressure.

I joined Worsley Branch of the Farnworth Constituency Labour Party when I lived in Boothstown and worked at the Emlyn Hall in Walkden when General Elections were called. I helped John Roper to become elected to Parliament as a Labour and Co-operative Party candidate in 1970, something I regretted later when he defected to the SDP, formed in 1981 by the 'gang of four': Roy Jenkins and MPs Shirley Williams, Dr David Owen and Bill Rodgers. At the General Election in 1983 he was replaced by Labour MP Terry Lewis and elevated to the House of Lords.

The road that runs between the villages of Boothstown and Worsley, Leigh Road, is known locally as 'millionaires' row'. The large houses that have been constructed along it on its north side are set on a hill looking south over open land, across the Bridgewater Canal towards Cheshire. They have long drives leading uphill to their front doors. My Labour Party colleagues thought I was mad when I told them I delivered our election leaflets to these houses and canvassed the people who lived in them, but I received a good reception at some of these homes.

Following my failed exploits in the bar trade, I decided to apply to abstract the chemical literature for Chemical Abstracts, published in Ohio, USA. This is one of the main sources of literature searches that a chemist must carry out when they are engaged in research. Today, several online search engines make this task a lot easier. For several years I abstracted patents. It was a tedious job but it brought in a small amount of extra income. I worked for a short period carrying out the same task for Derwent Patent Abstracts.

I was also an examiner for the Joint Matriculation Board's (JMB) GCE examination in Ordinary Level Chemistry for five years. In June, hundreds of papers arrived by registered post and I began the tedious task of marking them. After about a hundred had been marked I was required to attend a 'regulating meeting' at the JMBs headquarters, which was on the campus of the University of Manchester. The Chief Examiner went through the paper with us line by line, and mark by mark, in an attempt to ensure a consistency in the marking of the papers.

On one of these papers the question was asked, "What colour is sulphur?" That was how it was spelt then. The only acceptable answer was yellow. Flowers of sulfur, of course, are yellow. "But what if a student puts blue?" I asked the Chief Examiner, "Do they get a mark?" He looked at me as though I had gone mad, and asked me for an explanation. "Colloidal sulfur is blue", said I, "Just as colloidal gold is red. The question does not refer to flowers of sulfur". The following year I was no longer employed by the JMB.

When Doug Maass and I arrived in Salford, at about the same time in 1966, Dr Malcolm Spencer, a Lecturer in Inorganic Chemistry at Salford, who had a close association with the Royal Institute of Chemistry, persuaded Doug to put a new demonstration lecture together to present to schoolchildren and members of the general public the following Easter, and he persuaded me to put together another one to present as the Christmas Lecture at UMIST in 1968. That was the beginning of The Magic of Chemistry, which I discuss in Chapter 8.

Early in my career at Salford I was invited by the Chemical Society (which was amalgamated with the Royal Institute of Chemistry, the Faraday Society and the Society of Analytical Chemists in 1980 to become the Royal Society of Chemistry [RSC]), to peer review (referee) papers for publication in their journals. This is an unpaid activity that most professional scientists undertake. It ensures that only papers of the highest quality are accepted for publication by the learned societies. The more prestigious journals reject the largest number of submitted papers. Those who submit papers for publication do not usually become aware of the identity of the two peer reviewers.

I made a mistake with the first paper that arrived; it was from my former colleagues at Hull University. When my comments, all made in good faith and none of them derogatory, were returned to the authors for their consideration, they could tell from the tone of my comments that I had been the referee of their paper, which I had accepted while suggesting a few modifications. After that experience, I refused to peer review any further papers that were sent to me from research groups with whom I had an active collaboration. During my career I was a peer reviewer for hundreds of papers sent to me from a large number of journals.

At the beginning of my career, scientists' papers appeared mainly in the journals of the various learned societies. It wasn't long before the commercial publishing houses realised that there was money to be made from this form of publishing.

Their journals cost significantly more than those published by the learned societies and inflated the costs of running libraries considerably. The Dutch company Elsevier moved into the market and Robert Maxwell launched Pergamon Press at Oxford. Of course, the attraction for academics to support the commercial journals was the pay received by their editors, usually academics. It was seen also to be a prestigious appointment to accept editorial control of a commercially-produced journal.

It seemed at one stage as though there might be a journal for every element in the periodic classification of the elements. A *Journal of Fluorine Chemistry* arrived on the scene, as did an *International Journal of Sulfur Chemistry*, to name two of many. Few of these new journals failed and scientists were expected to read more and more of them, if they were to keep abreast of their subject's development. Eventually, a pecking order of journals developed, and scientists who want to be noticed today try to get their papers published in what are perceived to be the highest quality journals, those with the highest citation ratings.

My interest in medicinal chemistry continued at Salford. I developed an interest in the idea of separating the addictive properties of the opiate alkaloids, such as morphine and heroin, from their pain-killing properties. As far as I know, this ambition has never been achieved. Nevertheless, with the help of some able research students, I set about preparing some new compounds related to the opiate alkaloids which might possess similar pain-killing properties without the accompanying problems of addiction. Reckitt and Colman's research laboratories in Hull had a strong interest in this research area at the time.

Our work on polybromoimidazoles provided a good route to polysubstituted-imidazoles through a sequence of bromine-lithium exchange reactions. Imidazole chemistry had become important at that time. Metronidazole, for example, is an important antibiotic, active against anaerobic bacteria, that is used to protect patients undergoing operations from becoming infected internally.

The first antiulcer drug cimetidine (trade name Tagamet), which was approved for use in 1976, was discovered in the laboratories of SmithKline & French at Welwyn Garden City by James W. Black and William Duncan, two people who had been well versed in the skills of pharmacology previously in the laboratories of the ICI Pharmaceuticals Division at their Alderley Park laboratories in Cheshire, Mike Parsons, another pharmacologist, and by three chemists, Robin Ganellin, Graham J. Durant and John C. Emmett. I had the privilege of visiting the SKF laboratories on 9 June 1992 to make a presentation on our imidazole chemistry and to hear about their continuing work on imidazole chemistry. I kept in touch with Robin when he transferred to academia at University College, London, where he is now an Emeritus Professor.

Prior to the discovery of cimetidine, the only way to deal with serious ulceration was through surgery. Despite the high initial cost of cimetidine, it proved to be cost effective and kept most ulcer patients out of hospital. It has since been succeeded by other antiulcer drugs.

Cytokinins are plant growth hormones, which are produced at the time of the fruiting of a plant. Just before I left Salford for Westminster as a Member of Parliament we had successfully prepared some cytokinin analogues in which we inserted thiophene rings between the imidazole and pyrimidine rings of the purine ring system ('stretched purines') that is present in the naturally occurring cytokinins. Our aim was to prepare some synthetic analogues of the cytokinins that might improve crop yields, putting more peas in a pod or more tomatoes on a truss, for example. Again, we were not able to exploit this work further. My new career had begun.

My work on sulfur heterocyclic compounds continued. I continued also to collaborate with Dr Mike Scrowston at Hull University, and we published two 'reviews' together.

Professor Hans Suschitzky was working on some very reactive chemical intermediates, called carbenes and nitrenes, and I proposed a joint collaboration with him in this area whereby I would investigate the generation of nitrenes through the photolysis (reactions induced with light such as ultraviolet light) of compounds called azides. The first starting materials we prepared were various azide derivatives of my old 'friend' benzo[$b$]thiophene, a piece of work that led to some very interesting chemistry which we exploited extensively.

A number of my colleagues in the Organic Section of the Department of Chemistry and Applied Chemistry at Salford, Professor Suschitzky, Dr Otto Meth-Cohn, Dr Bob Smalley and Dr Alan Fitton, for example, were also exploring various aspects of heterocyclic nitrene chemistry, and the Salford group's work became recognised internationally. I collaborated with Professor Suschitzky in a number of other areas of research too.

Our department appointed two Welsh Professors; Professor W. J. Orville-Thomas, who joined us from the University of Aberystwyth, studied infrared spectroscopy, whilst Professor Glyn O. Phillips, who came to us from the University of Cardiff, was interested in the damage radiation can cause to sugars and other systems that are found in nature. Both men became Head of our Department of Chemistry and Applied Chemistry in succession. Jokingly we called this the era of the 'Welsh Taffia'.

I had a brief collaboration with Glyn Phillips which was an extension of my Hull studies on indoles. We irradiated various indoles and drugs containing the indole ring with gamma rays in order to see what the products were. If damage was non-existent, which I believed unlikely, drugs containing the indole ring could be submitted for radiation sterilisation before marketing them. Sterilisation is essential for aqueous eye drop preparations. As expected, irradiation of substances containing an indole ring in aqueous solution produced a plethora of products.

I think Hans Suschitzky felt at one time that the two Welsh professors were making a take-over bid for members of the Organic Section in our department. I did have one meeting with Professors Orville-Thomas and Glyn Phillips when they told me that, if I was going to work for them, it would have to be by "body and soul". I thought they were joking.

Glyn Phillips was one of the more colourful of the characters I knew in my days at the University of Salford. He was a good publicist, and enjoyed working with television companies. On one occasion he was called to a studio in Cardiff just before bonfire night to show children how to light fireworks safely before a live audience. A table had been prepared for him covered with heat-resistant sheeting. Glyn walked in wearing his cotton laboratory coat and safety glasses, carrying the fireworks in a biscuit tin. He proceeded to tell those watching that it was most important to put the lid back on the tin after removing a firework.

Glyn removed a rip rap and proceeded to light it. As he placed it down on the heat resistant mat it jumped, as rip raps do - straight back into the biscuit tin. Glyn had forgotten to put the lid on! The rip rap proceeded to light the other fireworks, which began to fly all over the studio and fill it with smoke. The cameramen ducked, the audience ducked and all hell was let loose. This happened in the days of black and white television.

That might have been the end of the matter. However, Cliff Michelmore was producing the *Tonight*, or perhaps it was the *24 Hours*, programme for the BBC at the time, and his researchers became aware of Glyn's misfortune in Cardiff. They decided to put out the coverage on national television, and Glyn tried to get an injunction in the courts to stop them. The output was seen by millions but I missed it.

The Student Chemical Society came to me when I was their staff contact and asked me if we could spice up their Christmas social. I related this episode in Glyn's life to them. Their intention was to borrow a clip of the broadcast from the BBC and show it at the social. It wasn't to be. After he heard about this proposal Glyn came to me and insisted that I stop them. In fact, he was extremely bad-tempered with me for even making the suggestion to the students in the first place.

On a Saturday evening many years later, when colour television had arrived, I was sitting in our lounge with my family watching *The Noel Edmonds Show* when I heard a familiar name, and there was Glyn Phillips on national television again.

Glyn invited various members of the Organic Section of our Chemistry Department, Dr Jim Clark, Dr Feodore Scheinmann and me, amongst others, to the dinners he organised for important visiting dignitaries. One of these was a chairman of the Science Research Council, who Glyn Phillips was very keen to impress. We met one evening at seven in the Maxwell Building private dining room and the staff served us drinks from a trolley, but there was no sign of Glyn or our distinguished guest. It wasn't until about 8 pm that Glyn arrived with our guest. We had quite a bit to drink during the dinner that followed. Then, just as everyone thought about departing, Glyn announced that he would take us all to the Brown Cow public house on Chapel Street to meet Manchester United stars George Best, Pat Crerand and several people from the Granada TV studios which were nearby. I don't think anybody believed him until we arrived in the pub and all the stars were there for everyone to see.

After eight years at Salford Glyn Phillips announced his retirement to the Departmental Board on 29 January 1975 and became Executive Principal at the newly created North East Wales Institute (NEWI) in Wrexham, now Glyndwr University.

In the December 2010 edition of *RSC News* I noticed that a 'Glyn O. Phillips Hydrocolloids Research Centre' had been opened the previous month at Hubai University in Wuhan, China, named after a centre by the same name at Glyndwr University. Clearly he was still active.

At Salford I supervised altogether three Postdoctoral Fellows, a Royal Society Visiting Fellow, a British Council Honorary Visiting Fellow from Czechoslovakia, two visiting scholars from Denmark (one continued his studies at Yale University), 25 PhD students, four MSc students (two continued to study for PhD degrees, one in the UK and one in Heidelberg) and numerous final year undergraduate research projects. A Royal Society Developing Country Fellow visited my group from Nigeria, and Professor Ross Grimmett - from the University of Dunedin in New Zealand - spent a sabbatical in Salford, which led to a fruitful collaboration in the area of imidazole chemistry.

One autumn I made a considerable effort to construct an MSc research project for a young student arriving from India. One of his relatives in Bolton had promised to pay his tuition fee. He arrived in the laboratory at the beginning of October and disappeared for good after a few days, much to my annoyance. Of course, I reported his 'disappearance' to the university authorities, but I am not sure what they did about this student's behaviour. Later, this became a common route of immigration into Britain, mostly for education at bogus colleges.

The work of my research group is covered by 152 publications in the chemical literature. When I was elected to Parliament I became one of only two chemists who published papers, three altogether in my case, during their career in Parliament. The other was the Liberal Member of Parliament for South Manchester, Sir Henry Enfield Roscoe. Before his career in Parliament began in 1885 he was Professor of Chemistry at Owens College, which became the Victoria University of Manchester, where there is a building named after him today.

Altogether, I organised or helped to organise five international conferences at Salford, in 1968, 1969, 1981, 1986 and 1987. When Emeritus Professor Hans Suschitzky turned 80 on 14 December 1995 I helped to organise a conference in Salford to celebrate this event, and arranged for

# SCIENCE AND POLITICS: AN UNLIKELY MIXTURE

Some of my research students: I am on the extreme left, Dr Basil Wakefield is third from the left, David Carr is third from the right, Peter Gallagher is on the extreme right and Nikki Colburn is seated at the front.

With Professor Hans and Judith Suschitzky at a Degree Congregation at the University of Salford.

# SCIENCE AND POLITICS: AN UNLIKELY MIXTURE

Professor Suschitzky in his office.

Professor Suschitzky's 80th birthday celebration. Left to right: Professor Gary Procter, Professor Stan Roberts, Dr Bob Smalley, HS, Roy Davies (one of my PhD students), and Dr Otto Meth-Cohn.

## SCIENCE AND POLITICS: AN UNLIKELY MIXTURE

Professor Suschitzky's 95th year - John and Wendy Suschitzky are standing, with me in between, and Hans and Judith Suschitzky.

a significant number of papers to be published in the journal *Tetrahedron* by those who had been associated with him. He continued to work as an Emeritus Professor well into his retirement, and I was invited to his 90th birthday party at his home in 2005 along with other former Salford colleagues. In the summer of 2010 Eileen and I, Hans and his wife Judith and their son John and his wife Wendy had lunch together at the Bridge Hotel in Prestbury village. Hans was 95 on 14 December 2010.[2]

Hans Suschitzky was born in Czechoslovakia, brought up by his grandparents, and studied medicine at the University of Vienna from 1934 to 1939. One of his lecturers was Sigmund Freud. His studies were interrupted when he escaped Austria in the late 1930s by swimming four kilometres in the River

Danube until he reached Czechoslovakia. There he acquired forged papers which enabled him to travel by train across Germany to Holland, from where he crossed the Channel to Britain. During the war years he worked on the estate of the Duke of Hamilton at Holsworthy in Devon, which provided him with fond memories, and was interned on the Isle of Man. Later he was shipped to Canada along with German prisoners of war.

In 1948, after returning to Britain, he was awarded an Honours Degree in Chemistry (First Class) from the University of London, which was followed by the award of a PhD degree in 1953 and a DSc degree in 1965. After a brief period in industry he lectured at West Ham College of Technology from 1949-1954, then joined the Royal College of Advanced Technology in Salford.

It was in London that Hans met Judith, whom he had known in Vienna. Judith, along with her older sister Ruth and their mother – the Maier family – fled Austria in 1938. Judith and her mother came to Britain, but Ruth went to Oslo to complete her education. There she was captured by the Nazis on 26 November 1942 and transported to Auschwitz. Judith learned of the fate of her older sister in 1947 when she was tracked down in London by Ruth's best friend Gunvor Hofmo. Later, in 1995 when Gunvor died, Ruth's diary was discovered amongst Gunvor's personal effects by her biographer Jan Erik Vold (Gunvor was a distinguished Norwegian poet) and was first published in Britain in 2009 by Harvill Secker. Ruth Maier is today regarded as the Anne Frank of Norway and there is a museum dedicated to her in Oslo.

Hans Suschitzky was a serious man with a 'specialist' sense of humour. Anybody who travelled in his car knew that he didn't take too kindly to people who slammed his car doors. On one occasion he invited me to lunch with one of his former PhD students; however, the 'he' I had known had been transformed into a 'she'.

I was very pleased when the University of Hull invited me to speak at a symposium in September 1982 to mark the retirement of Professor N. B. Chapman. Four of his former PhD students were invited to speak at that very special event.

I lectured on my research activities in Innsbruck, Linz, Graz and Vienna (Austria); Heidelberg, Kaiserslautern and Paderborn (Germany); Leipzig, Halle, Dresden and East Berlin (then in the DDR); Kosice (Slovakia); Paris (France); Lund and Stockholm (Sweden); Poona, Bombay, Hyderabad and Aurangabad (India); Bologna and Potenza (Italy); and Dar-es-Salaam (Tanzania) as well as at several venues across Britain (see later about attendance at international conferences).

I established active collaborations with Professor Fritz Sauter and his colleagues at the Technical University in Vienna, Dr Jan Becher at the University of Odense in Denmark, Professor Mikael Begtrup at the University of Copenhagen, Professors Paolo Zanirato and Pierro Spagnolo at the University of Bologna and Professor Richard Neidlein at the University of Heidelberg.

My relationships with Denmark resulted in me joining a four-person international panel, appointed by the Danish Minister for Education, to 'evaluate the international competitiveness of Danish chemical engineering education at university level'. In October 1989, the panel visited the Danish universities and talked to students, staff and the senior management of them in the daytime. We returned to our hotel in Copenhagen in the evening to a put a report together with administrative help provided by the Minister. It had a significant effect on improving the way in which the subject was taught in the Danish universities.

I was a Visiting Professor at the Universities of Bologna (1991) and Potenza (1993) in Italy and Liverpool (2002-2007), and a Visiting Associate Professor at the University of Dar-es-Salaam (1990 and 1992).

I examined a significant number of MSc and PhD theses from a cross-section of British universities, as well as from universities in New Zealand, India, Sweden, and Tanzania. In Sweden, a PhD student is expected to produce hundreds of printed copies of their thesis. Not only are fellow chemists invited to the oral examination, which is held in public, but friends and family are invited as well. Each person attending receives a copy of the student's thesis. It's all rather like attending a wedding.

The external examiner has to be very familiar with the PhD thesis, because they are expected to present its contents and convince the audience that public money has been well spent before cross-examining the student. The tradition is that the external examiner and the internal supervisor, along with senior members of the department, withdraw after the presentations to a separate room for their deliberations. These are deliberately drawn out as drinks are taken. Then the announcement is made.

In May 1985, I was privileged to be invited to the beautiful city of Stockholm by Professor Jan Bergman of the Royal Institute of Technology to conduct one of these examinations in the hall in the Swedish Royal Academy, where Nobel Laureates present their lectures (the awards are made in the City Hall). This experience was daunting enough for me, never mind the student, Borje Egestad. Fortunately both of us were able to put on competent performances. On this visit I was shown the room where Nobel Laureates are selected by the Academicians.

The family of the successful student invited me to a dinner that evening, which was conducted just like a wedding celebration, with speeches from me and the student on the top table. Nobody had told me before I left Britain that I would conduct a Swedish PhD examination in this way; fortunately I had brought with me a small gift for the student. It was the Student Chemical Society tie from Salford, which was designed by Dr Otto Meth-Cohn, a blue tie with thiophene rings emblazoned on it. The pentagonal rings were red with a yellow sulfur atom. This was very appropriate for the student since he had carried out research in this area of chemistry.

I was more prepared for the next Swedish PhD examination I conducted, in April 1989 at the University of Lund, near Malmo in the south of Sweden. The oldest building at the University of Lund is fronted by magnolia trees. When the first flower is seen to bloom on one of these trees, a celebration that spring has arrived is held across the university, an age-old tradition.

At a Degree Congregation held in July 1985, I presented the Salford East Member of Parliament, the Rt. Hon. Stanley Orme, with an Honorary Doctor of Science Degree at the University of Salford.

I decided to submit all my research contributions to Hull University in a bid to obtain the Degree of Doctor of Science (DSc), which required the work to be peer reviewed by fellow chemists of both national and international standing. I

## SCIENCE AND POLITICS: AN UNLIKELY MIXTURE

**PhD examination of Borje Egestad in Stockholm.**

Brian, Borje Egestad and Professor Jan Bergman.

Borge Egestad and his wife.

The dinner afterwards.

John Ashworth, Vice-Chancellor of the University of Salford, presents an Honorary Degree to Stan Orme MP.

considered at that time that acquiring this prestigious degree would help my promotion chances at Salford. It was a pleasant surprise when the peer reviewers that Hull University appointed recommended that I be awarded a DSc degree - for 'significant contributions to the study of heterocyclic compounds' - which I received on 11 December 1981.

I was promoted to a Senior Lectureship in Organic Chemistry at Salford in 1978, to a Readership in 1986 and received my Certificate of Long Service from the university in 1991 with an accompanying gift of £25, one pound for each year of service. The Vice-Chancellor at the lunch on 18 July was Tom Husband and his Registrar was Stuart Bosworth.

Professor Salo Gronowitz at the University of Lund in Sweden was appointed by the University of Salford as an examiner of my work when I applied for promotion to a Readership, as were Professors David Ollis of Sheffield University and Professor Charles Rees of Imperial College, London.

David Ollis was seen by his contemporaries to be a 'hard man', with very high standards. He was often highly critical of the work of other chemists when they presented their work at

## SCIENCE AND POLITICS: AN UNLIKELY MIXTURE

Dinner after the Convocation Lecture presented by Barbara Castle MP
(I am seated on the extreme right).

conferences. He had put me under pressure at a conference, but I was rescued by Professor Charles Rees, who everybody liked. Surprisingly, David Ollis copied to me his recommendation to the University of Salford that I be promoted to the grade of Reader. It was highly complimentary.

For a number of years in the 1970s, a Convocation Lecture was held in the large Chapman Lecture Theatre at the University of Salford. I remember presenting The Magic of Chemistry as one of these and attending other lectures by Barbara Castle, then Member of Parliament for Blackburn, the climber Chris Bonington, whose lecture on 6 December 1974 was entitled Changabang, and Professor Magnus Pyke, then a hugely popular television presenter of popular science programmes.

The theme of Magnus Pyke's lecture was sustainability in

agriculture. I particularly remember that he went on quite a bit about how meat production was bad for the human race, and I concluded that he must be a vegan. Since I was to join the dinner party after the lecture I didn't expect that steak would be on the menu, but it was, and Magnus seemed to enjoy his steak more than anyone else present.

In October 1980, I became a Chartered Chemist and was elevated to a Fellowship by the Royal Society of Chemistry (FRSC) when Professor Sir Ewart R. H. Jones was President of the RSC and Dr R. E. Parker was its Registrar and Secretary for Public Affairs.

I served for two terms on the Senate of the University of Salford (1984-1990) and served on the university's Academic Staffing Sub-committee (1990-1996). This committee was responsible for all promotions to the grades of Senior Lecturer and Reader across all university departments. Whilst its serving members, who came from a wide range of departments, debated each applicant's attributes extensively, in the end it wasn't that difficult to come to conclusions on the list of those who deserved promotion.

Throughout my academic career at Salford and my involvement in local politics I insisted that I should carry the same teaching load as the rest of my colleagues. However, I was grateful that those responsible for arranging my timetable arranged it in such a way that I could attend daytime council meetings.

My brother Graham was married in St Michael's and All Angel's Church, Croston on 12 June 1971 to Pamela Mary Lingard. They lived with my father at 74 Hesketh Lane where Graham was running my father's market gardening business. Pam's mother and father, Tom and Mary Lingard, managed the Lord Nelson public house in the heart of Croston.

Croston (the cross town), as the name implies, was where most people worshipped in earlier times, before churches were built in the surrounding villages. It was where people met, gossiped and exchanged goods with each other. I have always been amazed that such a small village could support 13 public houses, as it did in my youth. Croston was the spiritual heart of our part of West Lancashire then. I remember taking part in a huge pageant there when I was about seven years old, which we rehearsed for weeks on the rather grand rectory lawn.

Following his serious heart attack in the autumn of 1958, my father suffered a series of strokes. I was home on one of these occasions. I heard him collapse in his bedroom during the night and rushed to see what had happened to him. He had collapsed immediately behind the bedroom door and I couldn't gain access. I woke Graham up and together we were

My father with Aunt Maggie (Stazicker) at Brother Graham's wedding in Croston.

My nephew John Iddon.

able to push the door open and get him back into bed before we called for help. We never had a telephone installed at home, so neighbours had to be knocked up on these occasions.

As Sally and Sheena grew up we started to visit the town of Bolton on shopping expeditions. We were struck by the friendliness of its people and by the excellent service we received in the town's shops and on its excellent markets. When it became apparent that our house at 41 Stetchworth Drive was becoming too small for a growing family, we decided to look for a larger house in Bolton and sold it for £5,850 in March 1972. We didn't want to live on one of the new sprawling housing estates that were being built on the outskirts of Bolton and preferred instead to live on a smaller estate of new homes closer to the amenities of the town centre.

Quite by chance we discovered that the site of the former home of the Starkie family in Castle Hill, Tonge Moor, Bolton, had become a small enclosed housing development of four-bedroom and five-bedroom houses. One in particular attracted our attention, in Woburn Avenue. It was a four-bedroom house overlooking the attractive hamlet of Firwood Fold, where Samuel Crompton, inventor of the spinning mule, was born in 1753. The garden behind sloped down into the Fold and there were excellent views across the Jolley Brows, a large tract of open space, to Harwood and beyond. An added attraction was a horse riding stable in the Fold. It seemed like an excellent place to bring up our girls, so 19 Woburn Avenue, Bolton became our new home.

## NOTES

1. Irene Zubaida Khan retired from this position in 2014.

2. Hans Suschitzky died on Friday 23 March 2012, aged 96, just a few days before Judith Suschitzky's 90th birthday on 27 March 2012.

CHAPTER SIX

# EXPERIENCES AS A SAFETY OFFICER

For 13 years (1982-1995), I was Safety Officer in the Department of Chemistry and Applied Chemistry at Salford University. I collaborated closely with the University Safety Officer, Dr Alan Craig. An important part of my job was to give safety talks to the fresher chemistry students, including those embarking on Joint Degrees (chemistry combined with another subject), and I gave more advanced safety talks to the postgraduate students at the beginning of their first year of study. On one occasion I received a complaint from Dr Tony Sommerville, who was responsible for the Joint Degree courses, that a female student had requested a change of course immediately after attending my safety talk.

I tried to cover everything I thought the students needed to know to protect themselves and others from the risks involved in handling the more hazardous chemicals. My talks, especially those to postgraduate students, were illustrated by real-life examples. Most people, for example, are unaware of the hazards that the generation of clouds of dust can bring. Whilst the general public were probably aware in the early part of my career that coal dust could explode in coal mines, they were less aware that explosions are possible with dust clouds generated from metals, flour, wood, cotton, etc.

The *Billy Cotton Band Show* was a famous radio show which became a well-known television light entertainment show. A dramatic effect was planned whereby, as the pianist sat down to play his piano, it exploded as he touched the keys. It did, and the pianist died. The sides of the piano were unscrewed to allow them to blow off more easily and the explosion was generated by pouring flour into the inside of the piano. Tragically, too much flour was used.

During my term of office as Safety Officer I introduced the Control of Substances Hazardous to Health (COSHH) Regulations of 1988 into our department. This was no easy task. It required a carefully-monitored system whereby all students and members of staff conducted safety assessments on all experiments they were about to carry out, so that the experiments could be carried out as safely as possible without putting anybody at risk. Initially, staff and students alike resented the extra burden that this placed upon them.

I was also responsible for conducting regular safety checks throughout the department, including in staff offices, and an Annual Safety Inspection in collaboration with Dr Craig. We had the authority of the university to close laboratories down if we declared them unsafe or, at the very least, suspend an experiment or project until it had been made safe to our satisfaction. I was required to submit a report to each operator/laboratory, which detailed anything that we had found to be unsatisfactory, and I was responsible for ensuring that everything detailed was made safe. In a department housed in a tower block, and one which was the largest chemistry department in Britain at its peak, this was a very onerous responsibility for me and I did it to the best of my ability.

We held unannounced periodic evacuations of the Tower Building. I appointed floor wardens, whose job it was to ensure that everybody in our department obeyed the evacuation procedures. The problem was that we had great difficulty in persuading all who left the building to proceed to the safe place designated for them to gather – away from the building. They never seemed to realise the potential danger of falling glass from our glass-clad Tower Building in the event of a fire or explosion.

I was involved in investigating some quite serious incidents as Safety Officer. On one occasion I was called to one of the two paternoster lifts, which had come to a grinding halt. One of the university's maintenance team had tried to step into a paternoster cabin with a wooden ladder that was quite clearly not going to go into the cabin. Fortunately, he was unhurt and the cabin was only slightly damaged, but the ladder was in pieces.

I went to great lengths to teach students how to handle the various gas cylinders safely. Unused cylinders were kept in a compound in the basement of the Tower Building or, later, behind the Cockcroft Building. I explained why grease should never be used to lubricate the fitting of a cylinder head to an oxygen cylinder and showed photographs of the damage that could be caused if a gas cylinder fell over and became detached from the cylinder head as a result. Jet-propelled cylinders can penetrate brick walls and cause anyone in the way serious injury. Consequently, I was very keen that they were kept in the proper stands and chained to a bench or wall, as appropriate.

One day, when a large chlorine gas cylinder was being used in a ground floor laboratory in the Cockcroft Building, the postgraduate student found that he could not shut off the valve. It was frozen open. Huge amounts of chlorine poured into the laboratory as a result and an emergency was declared. The fire brigade arrived and a fireman went into the laboratory wearing a breathing set and threw the cylinder through a window onto the grass outside, which was bleached over a wide surface area as a result.

On another occasion a student placed a large unstoppered conical flask containing a large quantity of a volatile solvent into a refrigerator in his first floor laboratory in the Cockcroft Building. A few hours later there was a huge explosion, one of the biggest that we ever had in the department; all the windows were blown out onto the roadway outside. There was a scene of considerable devastation inside the laboratory, which I photographed from every angle, to use the resulting photographs in my safety talks. The people who occupied this laboratory purchased a domestic refrigerator without realising the dangers that an internal spark from the thermocouple mechanism could cause. Laboratory refrigerators and freezers are made in such a way that they do not generate sparks internally.

Even in teaching laboratories there are dangers, as I well knew from my Hull days. Pouring ether (or any other solvent that is not miscible with water) into sinks is a silly way of waste disposal. When undergraduates did that with ether, with other undergraduates using Bunsen burners elsewhere on the same island bench, inevitably there would be a flashback. Many are the fires I have put out in undergraduate laboratories.

One of the tricks that some students learned was to make a

mixture of iodine and ammonia and allow it to dry out slowly. When it was almost dry, the resulting wet paste of nitrogen tri-iodide was applied to toilet seats, to staircases, anywhere where it would cause a small explosion when it received a small shock.

On one occasion, when I was demonstrating to a student practical class in Salford, I came across an agitated group of students, with one student amongst them looking more worried than the rest. I readily ascertained that there was a large pile of wet nitrogen tri-iodide in his laboratory equipment drawer, drying out on a watch glass. Knowing of the potentially explosive nature of this highly shock sensitive substance, especially when it is prepared in such large quantities, I felt that I had to send for the 'Michelin man' suit that was kept in UMISTs Department of Chemistry, a bomb disposal outfit, complete with visor and thick handling gloves.

After evacuating the area, I cautiously withdrew the drawer from the laboratory and carried it downstairs into the open air, where the sunlight dried the substance out even quicker. Before withdrawing from the scene, I tipped the nitrogen tri-iodide onto the concrete flagged floor and waited. Dr Tom Paterson, who was always at hand to assist me on these occasions, and I were most disappointed when the dried material would not explode when we subjected it to extreme shocks from a distance.

This was not the only incident that caused us to send for the 'Michelin man' suit. One of my research students reached for a rather old tin containing sodamide one day and removed the lid. There was a flash, and he dropped the tin, which was so hot it welded itself to the vinyl-tiled floor. We looked up the usual books that detail the potential hazards of chemicals and discovered to our horror that old sodamide can generate an explosive chemical. Fortunately, sodamide dissolves in water for ease of disposal, so I shovelled the mess off the floor and carefully added it to a large bucket of water.

As members of staff in charge of a practical class we would try to visit all the students in the laboratory to check what they were doing and to help them if they were in trouble. On talking to one first year student I soon realised that he was not carrying out his allotted experiment. In fact I discovered that he was trying to synthesise LSD (lysergic acid diethylamide, 'acid', made famous by the Beatle's lyric Lucy in the Sky with Diamonds). I was tempted to offer him a PhD degree on the spot if he was able to succeed. It is not an easy synthesis to attempt fortunately, even for a chemist experienced in the art of organic synthesis.

We had regular fires in the metal waste disposal bins, which were kept under each student bench. These were usually caused by small amounts of air-sensitive and water-sensitive chemicals, such as metal hydrides, being incorrectly disposed of in the bins in which used filter papers were also disposed of.

The problem was that, in the evenings, our cleaners emptied these bins, and the mixed contents ended up in a large store room in the basement of our building, where larger waste disposal bins were kept, awaiting the next call of a Salford City Council bin wagon. One of these bin wagons was driving away from our department one day when its contents caught fire. The quick-acting driver tipped the contents out onto the ground and drove away from the burning pile of rubbish, which was extinguished by firemen. Fortunately, Salford Fire Station was opposite the university at that time.

But there was worse to come. When George Gamlen, a chemist from ICI, was appointed to a Chair of Inorganic

Chemistry at Salford and became our Head of Department, he decided to play safe and have our Tower Building independently inspected by a Safety Officer from the University of Bradford. This inspection was carried out in collaboration with our University Safety Officer, Dr Alan Craig. They started on the top floor of our building and worked their way down to the basement. The last point of call was our large bin store. It had two large metal doors with a bar that dropped across the doors in such a way that it could be padlocked to prevent access to the store. As elsewhere in the building, this room had a suspended fire-proof tiled ceiling, with the services out of sight above the tiles.

Undergraduate and postgraduate students disposed of large quantities of chromatography grade alumina, which was a very fine powder when dry, like flour in its appearance and behaviour. It got everywhere, including on top of the tiles of these 'false ceilings'. Imagine the scene and the seriousness of the situation when the three men conducting the safety check opened the metal doors of this bin store and stepped inside just as there was a soft explosion, which lifted the ceiling tiles, causing a deposit of the white alumina powder to descend on each man. They stepped out into the open looking like ghosts.

I was called to investigate what might have happened whilst the fire brigade was attending the scene. I noticed that as firemen swept up the rubbish on the deck outside the bin store, there were flashes of light when the powder and general rubbish came into contact with any water. That incident was probably caused by inappropriate disposal of a metal hydride, probably lithium aluminium hydride, in the general laboratory rubbish, which reacts with water to produce hydrogen gas, potentially explosive in the right proportions with air and in the presence of a spark.

I never saw the resulting safety report, but we moved the department completely into the Cockcroft Building a few years later, by which time it had shrunk in size as the number of undergraduate students fell and after the dozen or so biochemists started their own department in the Peel Building. The Tower Building was demolished later (not on grounds of safety).

It was also my duty to monitor the use of poisons, such as sodium cyanide, often used by chemists, which are required by legislation to be locked away in a restricted access poisons cupboard. I had to sign a permission form for one of our chemists to withdraw a poison from this cupboard and agree the amount that could be weighed out. All this data was recorded in a poisons book. Despite all these precautions, one of our academic staff members managed to access enough sodium cyanide to take his own life, albeit before I was appointed as the department's Safety Officer.

My experience as Safety Officer in a large Department of Chemistry brought me one or two special assignments. I carried out a provisional investigation into the cause of a fire at the Co-operative Wholesale Society's coffin factory in Manchester, which supplied coffins for funerals across the country. It was relatively easy to confirm the probable cause of the fire since the Greater Manchester Fire Brigade had done some provisional work, which was available for me to examine.

I also investigated a more tragic event at a small family dyeworks in Yorkshire, where a man died as a result of being engulfed in a deflagration (a ball of flame that caused light physical damage to the plant). My first port of call was to meet the works chemist, who was an elderly man. I wanted to have a copy of the procedure that the deceased had followed, and generally discuss whether they had had any other incidents in preparing a brown wool dye. The works chemist was very honest. He admitted that this was not the first time that batches of the brown dye obtained at the end of the process had caught fire in this way. It wasn't the last man they had lost either; another death had occurred on the same plant a few months later.

I was not surprised when I started to research the chemical reactions involved. At the top of the two-storey plant they carried out what is known in chemistry as a diazotisation reaction. The starting material was picramic acid. In fact, the diazotisation of picramic acid, 2-amino-4,6-dinitrophenol, was the first reaction of its kind that the discoverer of these reactions, Peter Griess, carried out in the nineteenth century. The second chemical reaction, which was carried out by letting the product from the first reaction flow by gravity into a reactor on the first floor of the plant, was a 'coupling reaction' with *meta*-phenylenediamine. The resulting brown dye was filtered off on the ground floor of the plant and dried on metal trays stacked on trolleys in large steam ovens.

I discovered that they had used steel trays but changed to drying the wet product on aluminium trays just a few years before my investigation. It was standard procedure to withdraw the trays from the ovens during the drying process in order to break up the lumps of partially-dried product with a metal scraper, similar to a wallpaper stripper, to speed up the drying process. It was at this stage that the deceased was engulfed in flames. He died in hospital the following day from his burns and I was provided with the post-mortem report.

It didn't take much research to discover that the chemical product of the first reaction had the short name diazodinitrophenol, or DDNP, in the chemical literature. This was used dry by the Americans during World War II as the initiatory explosive to set off the less sensitive explosive TNT (2,4,6-trinitrotoluene). My conclusion was that the second reaction, the 'coupling reaction', had been incomplete and that there was residual, shock sensitive DDNP in the drying product, which deflagrated when it came into contact with the metal scraper.

The works chemist who I interviewed was almost old enough to have known Peter Griess. He had produced procedures for the workmen on the plant to follow that contained very old-fashioned names for chemicals, 'dense oil of vitriol' for example for fuming sulphuric acid.

To thoroughly conduct my research in order to establish the likely cause of this tragedy, I ordered several books on explosives from the National Lending Library at Boston Spa, near Wetherby in Yorkshire, using the Inter-Library Loan Service. I often wonder whether today such an activity would attract the interest of those involved in prevention of terrorism.

A young woman who wanted to study for an MSc degree joined my research group with a poor Joint Honours Degree. Her research project involved the preparation of benzyl azide as a starting material, which is quite safe to handle at ambient temperatures but potentially explosive if heated strongly or detonated by striking it with a heavy metal object such as a hammer. The literature recommends that it be distilled under reduced pressure in order to purify it but I told her that under no circumstances should she attempt to do that. I told her she should purify the product by a technique called column chromatography, which can be carried out at ambient temperature.

Unfortunately, contrary to my instructions, she tried to distil it under reduced pressure. Clearly she hadn't reduced the pressure sufficiently in the distillation flask containing the impure benzyl azide before she applied a Bunsen burner – and directly to the flask instead of through a surrounding water bath. Inevitably, under these conditions, there was an explosion in the fume-cupboard. The shatter-proof front of the fume-cupboard had not been pulled down and she was not wearing her cotton laboratory coat. Even worse, her top was made of nylon and her hair had been treated with a highly inflammable product. Her clothes and hair caught fire and she was injured, mainly as a result of molten nylon burning her shoulders.

This was one of the worst experiences I had in my career as a chemist. Litigation followed and a settlement was eventually made out of court. Our defence was that there had been contributory negligence.

During my time in Salford there were three remarkable external incidents that affected the university. The first occurred when an old candle factory caught fire just across the River Irwell from the university. The molten wax flowed on fire out of the factory through the surrounding streets. It was a very spectacular fire.

On the evening of Saturday 30 September 1982 I was sitting at home in Bolton, ten miles from the university, when I heard dull thuds coming from the east. Later, news bulletins informed us that there had been huge explosions on the premises of a haulage company, again very close to the university, which had thrown 50 gallon drums a distance of up to a quarter of a mile. They landed, for example, scattered across an adjacent housing estate. One landed on a car at the

Poet's Corner public house and wrecked the car. The explosions broke windows in the sides of university buildings that faced the haulage business.

My friend Cllr Morrell Atkinson was on the Greater Manchester County Council at that time and served on the committee responsible for the fire brigade. He invited me to accompany him to the factory on the Sunday morning to view the damage and give him any advice I could. Lorries carrying considerable quantities of chemicals, including titanium dioxide (a whitening agent used, for example, in papermaking and in toothpaste) and organic solvents, had been parked in the premises next to others carrying foodstuffs. The haulage company was prosecuted for storing chemicals without a proper licence.

By far the largest explosion that affected us at the University of Salford occurred in 1996, when the IRA bombed the Arndale Centre in Manchester. That blast blew in quite a lot of windows at the university and shook all our buildings. I was amazed when I saw the scale of the damage a few days later and grateful that nobody had been killed on that terrible day.

# CHAPTER SEVEN

# OPPORTUNITIES TO TRAVEL

∽

My academic career gave me the opportunity to travel. My earliest recollection of attending a conference from Salford was when I presented some of Roger Dickinson's work at a conference in a hotel overlooking the beautiful half-moon-shaped bay at Kinsale near Cork in the Irish Republic in 1969. The Salford polychloroaromatic compounds research group visited Barcelona in the autumn of 1973, to attend a conference organised by Professor Manuel Ballester, one of the few other chemists actively working in our field at that time.

Barcelona was a very different place in those days from the city that tourists know today. Then it was under the iron rule of fascist dictator General Franco and people were oppressed by large numbers of police and military who kept order on its streets. The port was a hive of activity. I returned many years later and was surprised by all the changes that had taken place, especially on the waterfront. However, I did manage to find the restaurant, Los Caracoles, where we had dined in 1973 in the old Baroque quarter of the city, just off the Ramblas.

After that, I presented papers at conferences in Heidelberg, Hamburg and Kühlungsborn (then in the DDR) in Germany, Ystad in Sweden, the University of Waterloo in Canada, Bratislava and Cingov in Czechoslovakia, and Toledo in Spain, and at conferences held in various venues across the UK (24 papers presented at international conferences altogether including several plenary presentations).

Every visit brought with it special memories. I saw a wonderful Salvador Dali exhibition in the castle at Heidelberg in October 1981, experienced the Reeperbahn in Hamburg, visited Toronto, the Niagara Falls and the Mennonite towns around Waterloo in Canada in 1985, got lost in the maze of streets in the old city of Toledo, and searched for beer with an alcoholic strength greater than water at a conference on the Swedish Riviera at Ystad.

To attend a conference in September 1992 in the Slovakian ski resort of Cingov, Eileen and I decided to travel by car and call off on the way to see our friends in Vienna. That was the longest journey I ever made by car (over 3,000 miles). We were the hosts of Dr Peter Kutschy at the Safarik's University in Kosice, a Slovakian city situated almost at the Ukrainian border.

Peter, who had worked with me at Salford, booked us into Hotel Centrum in Kosice. It cost us £15 for a double room and £1.40 for two breakfasts. I remember looking down from our hotel room onto the square below, where I had parked my bright red Montego car. A crowd of young people stood admiring it; a red car from the UK had probably never been seen in Kosice before. When I collected it the following morning I noticed that the front bonnet badge had been cleanly removed as a souvenir. It cost me £15 to replace it when I returned home.

Vienna is a city I came to know well and love. In 1984, I took a train from Vienna to Graz, the second largest town in Austria, but nobody told me about this journey before I undertook it. I discovered that the Semmering Railway was built by British engineers in Victorian times. Today it is listed by UNESCO as a World Heritage Site. The railway runs through the tops of the mountains, across 16 viaducts and through 14 tunnels, with stupendous views of the Semmering Pass below. From Vienna travellers should sit on the left and vice versa.

The symbol of Graz is the Uhrturm clock tower on top of the Schlossberg. The Ottoman Turks invaded Europe through the Semmering Pass, which was the scene of a lot of fighting, so it is not surprising that the Landeszeughaus in Graz is the largest armoury in the world. This collection of Baroque weapons is stunning. In one of the old buildings in Graz, I cannot remember which, visitors will find two independent staircases constructed as a double helix, such that one of two climbers can climb in a clockwise direction and the other in an anti-clockwise direction.

I first crossed the 'Iron Curtain' to attend a conference in Bratislava in 1987 and experienced the difficulties that its citizens were facing. The border checkpoint was not far from Vienna. It was heavily guarded and several of the guards held Alsatian dogs to deter escape, but this checkpoint was not like those I experienced gaining access to the DDR.

There were few goods to be purchased in the shops of Bratislava and the quality of the meat in the restaurants was appalling. I also saw evidence of the disaster that trying to re-house a large population of Romas in high-rise flats was causing. On the other hand, I was very impressed by the magnificence of the castle in Bratislava, where I attended a reception.

The British Council funded a long-lasting link between the University of Salford and the Karl Marx University of Leipzig, and I made two visits to the DDR using this scheme. My hosts in Leipzig were Professors Manfred Weissenfels and Klaus Schulze, with whom I maintained a contact.

On my first visit, in 1981, I was briefed by Mr R. J. Wildash, the Cultural Attaché at the British Embassy in Berlin. I felt the oppression of the people of the DDR under the iron fist of the Russian presence. I stayed in Leipzig for four weeks with a widow in her house, which was close to the university. Walking to the university and back each day I always felt I was being followed, and I probably was. People were terrified of the civilian police and especially of the Stasi. They couldn't enter into a conversation with me about politics; even in a car travelling in a remote part of the countryside it was difficult to engage them.

I had some weird experiences in Leipzig. One evening I was told by my landlady that I was invited to a party in an upstairs flat where, as I discovered, a forensic pathologist lived. He had invited several guests, who all spoke perfect English. English tunes were played on the piano - they sang the lyrics perfectly - and English drinks were served. I wondered where all the Johnny Walker whisky and bottles of Guinness came from. Those present were most interested in the trial of Peter Sutcliffe, the Yorkshire Ripper, which had just ended at that time. Nothing felt right during my stay in that flat. Was it bugged, I asked myself, and, if so, why? It was easy to become paranoid in the DDR.

As I was about to leave, I was shown a rack of very old chemical reagent bottles and asked to choose one to take home as a souvenir of the evening. When I pointed out that removing one bottle from this otherwise wonderful display of bottles would ruin the display, the forensic pathologist insisted that I take one anyway, and I have kept it until this day. I chose the only one without a stopper.

Many of the chemicals that were available in the West from companies such as Aldrich and Sigma were unavailable commercially to the chemists of the East. They had to begin their synthetic procedures with the most elementary of chemical building blocks. The laboratories were poorly equipped too, with an absence of the instruments and glassware we took for granted. The academic staff complained that, whilst they were provided with more than an adequate number of technicians, the technicians were lazy and that it took them far too long to carry out simple tasks. Nobody was afraid of being sacked in the DDR; everybody had a job, and was paid a basic salary.

On another occasion a very young technician from the Chemistry Department at Leipzig, where I was based, was instructed to convey me to Halle to present a lecture. I can't remember how, but he received a parking ticket, which required him to visit a local police station. I offered to accompany him so that I could explain that he was helping me, a visitor, but he refused my assistance and trembled as he entered the police station. He never explained to me what had happened in there.

As I approached Halle to present a lecture at the university there, where Professor Werner Schroth was my host, the sun disappeared as we travelled into the city under a cloud of chemical gases, orange mainly in colour. The River Elbe was heavily polluted by chemical and other discharges in the DDR at that time.

Professor Siegfried Hauptmann was one of the best-known organic chemists in the DDR then; his textbook on organic chemistry was used in all their universities (Hans and Judith Suschitzky translated it into English later). They invited me round to dinner one evening. All went well until we sat down for a drink afterwards and began a conversation, whereupon Mrs Hauptmann broke down and became quite hysterical.

I discovered that Professor Hauptmann had been the Vice-Chancellor, or Rector, of the University of Leipzig but had taken a fall from grace. The reason was that their son had gone off on a holiday to Czechoslovakia and fled to the West. She pleaded with me to attempt to make contact with him, but it seemed an impossible job and I declined politely to help. However it made me realise just how oppressed those people felt in the DDR, especially those leading an academic life.

I presented a lecture at the University of Dresden, where Professor Karl Gewald was my host. Hans Suschitzky warned me immediately prior to my first visit to the DDR that should I go to Dresden, capital city of the Free State of Saxony, I was likely to meet with a very rough reception from its inhabitants. Manfred Weissenfels later took me to the top of a hill where his father had resided during the war years. Together with his father, Manfred had witnessed the great fire storm of 13-15 February 1945, which killed 25,000 people; many died through a shortage of oxygen in the Elbe basin. The whole of the Baroque centre of old Dresden was destroyed. I witnessed the part of Dresden which had taken the heaviest pounding from Allied bombing raids; it had been grassed over as a park.

## SCIENCE AND POLITICS: AN UNLIKELY MIXTURE

On my first visit to Dresden they were painstakingly rebuilding the famous old buildings which had been destroyed by the raids, using the original stones wherever possible. The Semper Opera House was in the process of being rebuilt, but Dresden Frauenkirche was a pile of stones at the time of that visit. I was astonished by the Zwinger Palace and by the Saxon jewels in the Green Vault of Dresden Castle; it seemed that at least one set of jewels had been made for every Saxon king or queen and their entire family. This is the richest collection of valuables that can be seen anywhere in Europe.

The first time I visited the DDR I entered through Checkpoint Charlie, about which I had heard and read so much. I passed the three Allied checkpoints and entered some very shabby huts with corrugated tin roofs. It was sweltering in there. I was expecting to be searched thoroughly, but as an official visitor, I had the right visa. It was just as well, because I entered carrying several copies of *Jonathan Livingstone Seagull*, a story by Richard Bach, then a cult book with our university students. It was first published in 1970. I gave all my copies away in the DDR. Goodness knows what the readers thought as they read their books (I hope they did).

I wasn't even asked to open my suitcase on the east side of Checkpoint Charlie. It was my first glimpse of the wall and no-man's land, where so many people died trying to escape from the East. The sand between the wall and the electrified fence was raked every night so that footsteps could be detected, and the East German guards often put dogs in to deter people trying to escape. There were tall watchtowers at regular intervals along the wall, which had an overhanging rounded top to prevent people from climbing over it. Sadly, most of the wall has been destroyed and those lengths of it that have survived in the Berlin of today do not give a feel for what it was really like and the terror it brought to some people's lives.

On the DDR side of the checkpoint a car had been pulled to pieces by the guards to ensure that nobody was hidden inside it trying to escape to the West. On the other side of this famous checkpoint I was met by a young member of the academic staff from Leipzig, Dr Horst Wilde, and the first thing we did was to have a drink in the nearest bar. As we walked away from that bar I saw that all the windows in the buildings along the wall that faced the West had been bricked up to prevent people escaping.

On my second visit to the DDR in 1988 I spent a few days in East Berlin with Professor Jurgen Liebscher at the Humboldt University. I was very happy to be in East Berlin, since I was able to visit the very laboratory where Emil Fischer had carried out his pioneering work on indoles and sugars. Jurgen's wife was a singer with the Comic Opera in Berlin, and I was privileged to receive a ticket to see one of its productions. We dined for the outrageous sum of £5, including drinks, in a café on Unter-den-Linden, where Hitler had been a frequent guest. On this visit to East Berlin I was able to view the Brandenburg Gate from the East, where the wall divided the East from the West, and see the nearby boarded-up Reichstag building, which I visited again many years later after the re-unification of Germany. I also spent a day in the Pergamon Museum, where the Hanging Gardens of Babylon are on display, or what remains of them.

I travelled into the DDR on this second occasion using the U-Bahn system which ran from West to East Berlin and emerged at the check point at Friedrichstrasse Station. At first

I joined the wrong queue. It was the queue of older people returning from West Berlin. The East German authorities encouraged their elderly population to travel to the West in the hope that they would stay. The DDR lost many of its younger generation in the flight to the West that occurred when they started to construct the Berlin Wall on 13 August 1961.

Between the last U-Bahn Station in West Berlin and Friedrichstrasse U-Bahn Station the underground trains slowed down as they passed through two U-Bahn stations which had been closed after the war; they were dark spooky places, covered in dirt and cobwebs. But in the eerie glow of some low-wattage bulbs I could see the armed East German guards waiting in the dark to shoot anybody who attempted to board the trains as they passed through those ghost stations on their way to West Berlin.

On my second visit to the DDR the mood felt different; there was hope in the air and a lowered military presence. On my first visit people had tried to receive West German TV, but the East German authorities blocked the signals, so few people were able to tell what was going on in the West. More people were receiving Western programmes on my second visit and more people had TV sets. I have always been convinced that satellites, beaming images all over the world, have changed the geopolitics of our world more than anything else. That was 1988 and the wall began to be demolished on 9 November 1989. Eileen and I heard the news at a conference in Toledo.

As I emerged from my first visit to the DDR I immediately wrote down the greatest differences that I saw when I arrived back in West Berlin. The gaudy appearance of the neon light advertising, deliberately shining on the East Germans in an attempt to show that there was a world that they were missing out on, was immediately obvious. In the East the colours of the only cars, the Trabants (which East Germans waited up to seven years to purchase, even when they had enough money to buy one), were drab, brown or black. In West Berlin I was hit by the bright colours of the cars, blue, red, yellow, etc. It was very quiet in the East, with little traffic on the roads, even in East Berlin. When I entered the West again I was hit by a wall of sound. The prices of goods were much lower in East Berlin too but there wasn't much to buy.

In October 1988 my colleagues from the Karl Marx University in Leipzig organised a conference on heterocyclic chemistry at Ostseebad Kühlungsborn, and Dr Jurgen Liebscher and I travelled to it in his car. After a brief visit to Leipzig I left East Berlin from Schönefeld Airport with Hans Suschitzky, who had also been invited to present a paper at that conference.

In the early part of 1988, I spent a month at the National Chemical Laboratory in Poona (Pune) and travelled to Aurangabad, Hyderabad and Bombay (today Mumbai) to give lectures. I arrived at the International Airport (Sahara) in Bombay, which was identical inside to most international airports. As I stepped outside the terminal building I was surrounded by porters and taxi drivers who wanted my trade; it was intimidating. Fortunately, the British Council arranged for a driver to pick me up and transfer me to the nearby domestic airport, and he spotted me in the middle of this crowd and rescued me. The domestic airport at that time was quite different from the international airport. I caught a flight to Poona. Before I boarded an Indian Airlines aeroplane, I was asked to identify my luggage on the tarmac at the side of the aeroplane before they loaded it in the hold.

My host in Poona was Dr Ayyanger, who was one of the chemists called in by the Indian Government to investigate the tragic accident at Bhopal, where thousands of citizens were killed by a leakage of methyl isocyanate from a chemical plant. It was interesting to get an account of the accident before people back home knew much about it.

On 7 January 1988, Congress Party Leader and Prime Minister Rajiv Gandhi opened the Indian Scientific Congress 75th Platinum Jubilee celebration at the University of Poona. This was held in the largest marquee I have ever seen. I was told that 8,000 people attended that ceremony. Rajiv Ghandi was made an Honorary Member of the Indian Academy of Science, but then he upset all of India by going to sleep on the platform. Dr Ayyanger managed to get me a ticket for a seat on the second row during these proceedings.

From Poona to Aurangabad, also in the State of Maharashtra, is a distance of about 280 miles. I travelled to Aurangabad on an Ashoka Leyland bus with wooden seats on 13 January 1988. When it came to a narrow bridge blocked by two wagons that had collided, the bus driver drove down into a dry river bed, where he picked his way through lots of large boulders and climbed back up to the road at the other side of the bridge.

A political demonstration blocked the road just beyond Ahmednagor until it was cleared by the police. When we stopped for a tea break I asked the owner of the very primitive café where his toilets were. He opened his hands outside and said "It's open", which seemed pretty obvious to me. He was open. But what he meant was that the toilets were the big outdoors. That was quite a journey.

On arrival at the bus terminus in Aurangabad I was picked up by one of the academic staff from the university, Dr

Shingare, who drove me off at speed on a moped. I sat on the pillion seat with a suitcase in one hand and a holdall in the other as he set off in a cloud of dust to introduce me to his family. When I got off the moped I was convinced that my arms had stretched. Back on the moped again and I was driven to a Nath Industries seed factory, where I was introduced to Dr Gopal, Dr Ayyangar's brother-in-law, who would take me back to Poona by car a few days later. He was keen to show me another part of Nath Industries, 40 miles away in Paithan, where they turned the sugar cane left over after extraction of sugar into corrugated brown paper for packaging.

Before I left I had to see the Paithan Dam, built ten years before my visit. At the bottom of the dam I could see lots of lights. We descended into beautifully laid-out water gardens with fountains and waterfalls, all illuminated by electricity supplied by the dam - *son et lumière* Indian style. India is full of surprises. Coachloads of people were arriving to see this spectacular sight as we left.

Words cannot describe the guest room that I was allocated at the University of Aurangabad. I don't think the bed sheets had ever been washed and there was a large toad occupying the wash basin in a very dirty bathroom. The place stank of mothballs. What a day that was.

But my visit to Aurangabad was worthwhile after all. I was taken on a journey to the magnificent Daultabad fort, near Aurangabad, by a taxi driver who is one of the few who has made me close my eyes. He weaved his way all over the road and drove like a lunatic, at breakneck speed. He asked me before we started our journey if I liked fast driving. I replied with "I like safe driving". I noticed that his car had travelled a total of 189,000 kilometres since new.

The upper Deccan plateau is where the Hindu and Muslim cultures clashed. Daultabad fort was built by the invading Moguls and is heavily fortified. At the main entrance there are two enormous doors carrying long spikes to prevent elephants from battering them down. Inside, unwanted visitors had to cross snake pits and several moats and journey through dark tunnels into which hot liquids were poured. It is uphill all the way to the central keep, which was very difficult to capture on its small hill.

The city of Aurangabad, Bibi Ka Maqbara, a replica of the Taj at Agra built by Auranzeb for his wife, the Ajanta Caves (70 miles from Aurangabad), the Ellora Caves and Temple and the Daultabad fort were some of India's best-kept secrets in January 1988. Judging by what is on the internet today, the position has changed. Aurangabad, now one of India's fastest growing cities, has become a tourist attraction.

I hope the toilets at the cafés where the tourist buses stop have improved since my visit. On the way to the Ajanta Caves I visited a toilet where a man threw a bucket of water in as the last occupant stepped out, then shoved me in, but only after I had crossed his palm with a few rupees. It was so dark inside that it took me a while for my eyes to find a small hole in one corner of the 'toilet' for me to take a pee in.

The Ajanta Caves are stunning. All 29 of them were carved high up on cliffs in a canyon, between 5BC and 5AD, and they were made accessible on foot only a few years before I visited them. Originally, the Buddhists, who carved them out of solid rock, accessed them by rope ladders from the river below. There are 12 main caves in various stages of completion, carved from the top downwards, that are worth visiting. The Ellora Temple and its caves are equally stunning. Today, these are UNESCO World Heritage Sites.

On the 17 January 1988 I caught an Indian Airlines flight arriving from Ahmadabad in Gujarat State and passing through Poona en route to Hyderabad, India's 5th largest city, where I was a guest of Professor Rama Rao, Director of the Regional Research Laboratory (RRL). I was accommodated in the almost new guest house at the Centre for Cellular and Molecular Biology. It was luxurious, so much so that I wasted some time attempting to count the light bulbs. Because the Nizams who ruled Hyderabad loved pearls, the city became the pearl centre of the world. The Charminar District of Hyderabad is where they can be purchased.

Whilst staying in Hyderabad I was able to see the famous Salar Jung Museum and visit the Annual Industrial Fair to which traders travel from all over South East Asia. I met many of the chemists who worked in the RRL, who were doing cutting edge research; most of them had worked with leading chemists all over the world. I travelled back to Poona by air, where I spent a few more days before returning to Bombay.

The train, the Deccan Queen from Poona to Bombay, travelled through the Western Ghats, then down from the Deccan Plateau on a wide gauge track, which gave the railway carriages a 'roomy' appearance, to the Bombay plateau. I was amused that they posted my name on the outside of the first-class carriage in which I travelled. The fellow who collected our breakfast details never wrote anything down and came back with exactly what his several customers had ordered. As the train chugged its way down the steep incline to the plateau below, monkeys climbed in through the open windows and rummaged through the carriages looking for food. Two engines take these trains up to and down from the Deccan plateau.

As I stepped off the train at the splendid Victoria Terminus in Bombay (it's now the Chhatrapati Shivaji Terminus) my bags were taken off me and I saw them disappearing on the top of a uniformed man's head down the long platform. It took me a few minutes to realise that porters meet the first-class passengers and that this was all part of the service.

In Bombay I met the British Council officials who had organised my programme in India, gave two more lectures and saw the sights of Bombay before returning to Europe from Sahara Airport on a Sabena Airlines flight, which allowed me to disembark airside at Abu Dhabi airport for 45 minutes. I have never seen so much gold in one place as I saw at the airport terminal there.

This month in India was arduous, but it was one of the most exhilarating experiences of my life.

In June and July 1991, at the invitation of Professors Paolo Zanirato and Pierro Spagnolo, I was a Visiting Professor for a month at the University of Bologna, one of the largest and oldest universities in the world. At that time Bologna was run by a communist administration. My lasting memory of the city, apart from visits to dozens of churches, was the wonderfully preserved wooden-panelled medical lecture theatre, with its steeply tiered seating arranged 'in the round' and the slab in the centre for demonstrations to be performed for the students.

Professor Spagnolo was appointed at Italy's smallest university – the University of Potenza – shortly after my visit and I spent two weeks as a Visiting Professor there in June 1993.

In March/April 1990 and March/April 1992, I made two equally arduous but extremely interesting visits to the University of Dar-es-Salaam in Tanzania, staying first at the Bahari Beach Hotel then at the State-owned Kunduchi Beach

Hotel, accompanied by Eileen. The road from Dar to the Bahari Beach Hotel and the nearby Kunduchi Beach Hotel was almost impassable at that time, full of deep potholes the depth of which were difficult to estimate when full of water. Fortunately, the British Council loaned us a Land Rover for the duration of each visit. A University of Salford colleague, Dr Basil Wakefield, was already out in Tanzania when we visited the country for the first time, and our visits overlapped by one week.

The Bahari Beach Hotel, where we stayed for a month, was the hotel KLM Royal Dutch Airlines used and they had a spare pilot, Henk, permanently on-site as a security measure. KLM had their own armed guards at this hotel because one of their female crew had had her finger cut off by a man who wanted to steal a ring. KLM also regularly took samples of the drinking water and water from the swimming pool, as well as samples of the food kept in the kitchen, to ensure that their air crews did not go down sick. The samples were transported to Amsterdam for microbiological testing.

We became quite friendly with Henk and joined the KLM crews at several of their weekly barbecues. Henk had a Swedish friend who was a surgeon in one of the Dar hospitals. Just a few days before we arrived in Tanzania on our first visit, she was called to the hospital by Henk, who had found two of his German friends in a very bad way in a villa close to the hotel. They had been visited by two burglars, one carrying an ancient shotgun. In the belief that it was too old to be of any assistance to the burglars, the Germans had tackled the burglars. They were wrong. Fortunately Henk was able to transport the seriously injured men to the Dar hospital where he had told the Swedish surgeon by telephone to be ready to operate immediately he arrived with them. She operated and saved both men's lives. The Germans were in Tanzania building a railway line.

The State-owned Kunduchi Beach Hotel, where we stayed for two weeks, was inferior to the Bahari Beach Hotel, which was owned by an international consortium of businessmen, but it had a more impressive beach. The swimming pool at the Kunduchi was hardly fit to swim in when we stayed there.

In their briefing session the British Council staff warned us of the dangers we might face in Tanzania. One of the tricks played on those travelling in vehicles was to put a rope or wire across a road, tied from one tree or post to another. The temptation would be to stop, but that meant trouble, so we were told to drive the Land Rover straight at the rope/wire in the hope that it would break. Another trick played by the local 'bandits' was to lay a large snake or a man across a road to stop a vehicle. We never experienced such an event, thank goodness. We always tried to get back to the Bahari Beach Hotel before darkness fell if we were not accompanied.

An African oil painting was a rare sight in the early 1990s, but an artist called Tinga Tinga (Edward Saidi Tingtinga) had made quite a reputation for himself in the Oyster Bay area of Dar-es-Salaam. He came to Dar as a construction worker and felt that he could make more money selling paintings to tourists. Self-taught, he developed an instantly recognisable style of oil painting on board and started a co-operative, which allowed him to pass on his skills to a group of young followers. Tragically, one day in 1972 the police mistook Tinga Tinga for another man when he was running away from a fracas in a Dar street, and they shot him dead.

At the Village Museum in Dar we came across some of

these young men and bought four of their paintings. They cost £1.50 each. Today, Tinga Tinga paintings, especially the originals, are selling on the internet for a lot more than that.

The Makonde tribe live along the East African coast, from the Mozambique border with Tanzania to Kenya, and have developed an ebony wood-carving industry. Eileen and I were lucky enough to be able to bring some examples of their art home with us. I was unaware until I visited Tanzania that ebony is the almost fossilised internal trunk of a tree (there are several species of the genus Diospyros) which looks white from the outside. It is used to make musical instruments such as clarinets and, of course, the black keys of pianos. There was a danger when we were in Tanzania that the tree would become extinct. Today, when the trees are used for wood carving in Tanzania, several trees must be planted for every one cut down. For a while it became illegal to export ebony from Tanzania.

At the bar in the Bahari Beach Hotel we met a retired man called Misha, who had arrived in East Africa from Eastern Europe and made a fortune trading precious stones. When he realised that we were interested in the Makonde tribe and their wood carvings he invited Eileen and me to his beach villa to see his vast collection of Makonde art. Misha had collected Makonda wood carvings from the days when the tribe realised there was money to be made out of tourism. I hope that his collection, which he kept in a large shed as well as in his villa, is in good hands today and that it has been kept together.

The other tribe in Tanzania (as well as Kenya) which is known for its art work, especially the jewellery made from coloured glass beads, is the elegant-looking Maasai tribe. Our first meeting with the Maasai tribe was when we went up country on safari to the Mikuma National Park game reserve near Morogoro. A group of Maasai youths, each dressed in traditional costume, were standing at the roadside waving their long spears at us. Much to our concern our driver stopped, engaged them in conversation and invited them to climb into the back of his personnel carrier to sit with us. They had smiles on their faces but it was, nevertheless, a daunting experience.

In former times young Maasai males were sent out of their own village to kill a lion or be killed. This was their initiation as adult Maasai warriors. By the early 1990s, the tradition had changed and they were expected to exist in the wilderness for several weeks, obviously by killing animals for food, until they returned as adults to their tribe. Our driver agreed to give the young Maasai warriors a lift back to their village.

As we advanced up the drive to the Mikuma National Park wildlife lodge, we came face to face with a very angry African bull elephant, advancing towards us with its ears flapping furiously. Even our driver was alarmed by this sight. Fortunately, as he put the vehicle in reverse gear and backed very slowly away from the elephant, it decided to take a different direction.

The game lodge was very comfortable and sited on a small hill above a lake, where the game came to feed. A guide was recruited for £5, and he showed us round the following day. It is essential to hire guides on these game reserves because they track the rarer game on a day-to-day basis, and are in contact with their colleagues, who also track it. In this way we were able to see lions in the wild as well as the more ubiquitous zebras, giraffes, elephants, etc.

I picked up one tip on this trip. Older male lions, when they are thrown out of their pack, hide in bushes at the side of roads waiting for their next meal. I heard that it was not uncommon for lorry drivers to 'disappear' when they get out of their broken-down vehicles. It's better to travel with a colleague who can use a gun.

Tanzania was a place of extremes in the early 1990s. At least one in five children died before the age of five. Malaria was, and still is, a very serious problem in this part of Africa. Early in the evening, as we drove out of Dar, we would find prostitutes completely surrounding the main roundabouts touting for business. In the villages we saw a lot of poverty, but we were amazed to see children setting out for or returning from school immaculately dressed in their brightly-coloured school uniforms.

In Dar there was an American-style ice-cream parlour, 'Dar Sno-Cream Parlours Ltd', which seemed completely out of place. And, there were some excellent restaurants, obviously built to cater for the various ex-patriot communities. We usually visited the Kilimanjaro Hotel when we were in Dar.

We journeyed too to Bagamoyo, north of Dar-es-Salaam, where David Livingstone's body was laid out in the Old Church awaiting a high tide so that he could be transported to Zanzibar. Bagamoyo was one of the main east African trading ports long before the deep harbour port of Dar-es-Salaam was established.

A very modern hovercraft transported us to the exotic spice island of Zanzibar from the harbour of Dar-es-Salaam during our second trip to Tanzania. As we stepped off the hovercraft we were greeted by an Asian man with a broad smile on his face, who offered to be our driver for the visit at a rate of only £5 a day. We accepted, and he took us to the Narrow Street Hotel in the old city of Stone Town in a very old Austin car, which he told us was 30 years old. It didn't appear to have any springs. All the spares to keep these old cars running were made locally.

The Narrow Street Hotel had a magnificent large brass studded wooden door, a feature of the old houses of Zanzibar, but no available running water. The owner brought us up some buckets to our room at the top of the hotel. Eileen wasn't impressed; she likes her comforts. The following morning we were awoken at about 8 am by a loudspeaker on the top of a mosque immediately next to our bedroom, calling people to prayers. Our driver returned and showed us the sights of Zanzibar, David Livingstone's house, the slave market, the spice fields and so on.

Formerly Zanzibar was an overseas territory of Oman, but it gained independence in 1858. The island became a British Protectorate in 1890 and remained so until independence from the British in 1963. On 12 January 1964, the African majority on these islands began a revolution that led to the overthrow of the Sultan of Zanzibar and, today, Zanzibar and its neighbouring islands are ruled by Tanzania.

I enjoyed teaching my Tanzanian chemistry students; they were friendly and very willing to listen and learn. Most chemicals were imported into Tanzania in the early 1990s; there wasn't even a decent soap manufacturing industry, so there was a great future for them. We were surprised to meet an importer and distributor of chemicals, Jim Harvey, who came from Bolton. I kept in touch with Jim and his African wife Martha for several years after returning to Britain.

The laboratories and lecture theatres at the university 'on the hill' were of a reasonable standard but my students complained about their accommodation. Student strikes were not uncommon; when they happened the Government closed down the University.

I realised that research in the organic laboratories was a little different from at home. It was impossible, for example, to use ether, because it boiled at the ambient temperature of the laboratories, which lacked good air conditioning. Most of the organic chemists were extracting chemicals from natural products at that time, to determine their structures. For many years staff at the University of Salford accepted chemical samples from Dar to run their spectra on instruments that Dar couldn't afford to buy. We also examined their MSc and PhD theses, which I found to be of an acceptable standard.

In order for me to pay the Bahari Beach Hotel for my stay in Tanzania the British Council asked me to visit the university's Finance Department. On my first visit I didn't take a suitcase or briefcase with me. "What are you going to carry the money in?" asked a member of staff, who was surprised that I was not accompanied. One of them went to a large safe and produced bundles of shilling notes tied together with

Eileen on a Zanzibar beach with George and Edith Mhehe.

string. It was a one-foot cube of paper money. In Tanzania such an amount of money would have kept a family for several years. They wrapped it up in newspaper for me and I quickly left and transported it to the hotel, where the staff locked it away in their safe.

Whilst I was working in the daytime at the university, my wife entertained herself back at the Bahari Beach Hotel by reading or sunbathing. One day she was approached by a smartly-dressed man who claimed to be a lecturer from the university. He also claimed to know me, but must have acquired my name from someone, probably one of the hotel staff. His story was that he had run out of petrol and he wanted to borrow some money. Of course, he was the perfect con man, and Eileen was taken in by him. Fortunately, the amount of money that she gave him was quite a small amount, about £12, but it must have been worth a fortune to him.

In the bar at the Bahari Beach Hotel on 3 April 1990 we also met Mark, a young Englishman from Mozambique who was helping his father to run a wildlife enterprise that involved cruising on rivers to look at the abundant crocodile and other wildlife. The only way to get to their camp was to fly in. It turned out that he was engaged back in England to one of my daughter's best friends, Andrea Long. As they say, it's a small world.

Sadly, after my second visit to the University of Dar-es-Salaam, the Head of the Department of Chemistry, Dr George Mhehe, was tragically killed, along with his lovely wife Edith and their driver, in a road traffic accident. Their vehicle was hit head-on by an unlit lorry on a dark African night (not uncommon, as we discovered). The roads were so full of potholes in the early 1990s that vehicles never kept to one side of a road for very long. They left two orphaned children. We collected a considerable sum of money in Salford and sent it out for a Trust Fund to be established for their children's education.

I have always wanted to return to Tanzania to see how the country has progressed since the time of our visits. I have heard from those that have been there since that considerable progress is being made. The roads are much better than they were, and there appear to be more hotels to accommodate visitors in Dar-es-Salaam.

# CHAPTER EIGHT

# THE MAGIC OF CHEMISTRY

∽

Even before Michael Faraday started to present his Friday Evening Discourses and Christmas Lectures in 1826 at the Royal Institution in Albemarle Street, just off Piccadilly in London, there was a strong interest from the general public in scientific experiments. Humphrey Davy, who was Faraday's predecessor at the Royal Institution, attracted so many people to his lectures that Albemarle Street became blocked with horses and carriages. As a consequence it became the first street in the world to be designated a one-way street. Every Christmas the Royal Institution Christmas Lectures are broadcast on television.

Not long after I arrived in Salford the local representative of the Royal Institute of Chemistry (RIC; not to be confused with the Royal Institution), Dr Malcolm Spencer, proposed that I put a lecture together for the Manchester Christmas Lecture. Organic Chemistry at Work was presented at 6.30 pm on Friday 6 December 1968 as a two-hour demonstration lecture at the University of Manchester Institute of Science and Technology (UMIST) in their Sackville Street building. So many people turned up to this lecture that there was standing room only and many people had to be turned away. Thereafter the Manchester section of the RIC started to issue tickets for all their Christmas Lectures, 10% more tickets than seats in order to ensure a full lecture theatre.

My colleague at Salford Dr Chris Cook, who came to Salford from the Department of Colour Chemistry at the University of Leeds, helped me in the early days to put the lecture together and assisted in the first presentations.

The Manchester Local Section of the Royal Society of Chemistry (RSC) (I was on the committee for several years) invited me several times to present my lecture as their Christmas Lecture at the University of Manchester, Stockport College and in Bolton, where two performances are given in the day. Sadly, the Stockport venue is no longer used.

Dr Colin Chambers, who was a chemistry teacher at Bolton School before he retired, and I started Christmas Lectures at Bolton Technical College on Manchester Road in January 1975. John Salthouse presented Son-et-Luminaire there and the Reverend Ronald Lancaster presented his famous Fireworks demonstration lecture in the same hall. We covered the demonstration tables in paper, which Ron soon set on fire. Fortunately, I had a fire extinguisher on hand just in case.

In December 1981 we moved to the Octagon Theatre in Bolton, where I presented The Magic of Chemistry 'in the round'. We used that venue for four years, then transferred to the Albert Hall in Bolton Town Hall in December 1985, where two performances were presented to audiences of 600 schoolchildren, who travelled from all over the North West, until 2008. The RSC's Bolton Christmas Lecture was presented in Farnworth Little Theatre in 2010, a much smaller venue than the Albert Hall. Bolton School started to host the Bolton Christmas Lectures in 2011.

After the first few performances, I gave my demonstration lecture the more attractive title of 'The Magic of Chemistry'. I presented it over 360 times at venues all over Britain and abroad, in Denmark (Arhus, Copenhagen and twice in Odense in 1987), Sweden (in Lund in 1987), Eire (twice in Dublin, in 1985 and 1991), and Italy (seven performances in Naples in 1993). I estimate that I travelled in my car over 3,000 miles each year to present The Magic of Chemistry. It became one of the best-known lectures of its kind in Britain.

I presented it at the Bolton Festival in August 1990, at the Edinburgh International Science Festival in 1993 and in the famous Faraday Lecture Theatre at the Royal Institution in 1992 to launch the RSC's Chemistry Week. The Magic of Chemistry was one of three 'headline presentations' at 'SciTech95', an annual science fair held in Derby; the other two lectures were given by David Bellamy and Johnny Ball (who started his career as a stand-up comedian in Bolton's working men's clubs; he lived in Daubhill, Bolton).

My lecture changed as the years went by. I always tried to include some up-to-date technology to provide some added interest for the audience. I illustrated The Magic of Chemistry with music and over 200 slides, which were 'phase dissolved' from three carefully mounted projectors onto a central screen. The availability of PowerPoint today makes such presentations a lot easier. 'Polymers' and 'colour' were the two broad themes that ran through my lecture. Below is a brief outline of the contents of The Magic of Chemistry.

On the day before each presentation or tour I spent half a

day weighing out exact quantities of the different chemicals, making sure all the equipment and glassware was clean and in good working order and collecting the projectors and other audio-video equipment, before I loaded my car with everything carefully packed into several wooden crates. On arrival at the venue I needed a further three hours to set out the demonstrations and arrange all my equipment, and at the end I needed at least another hour to pack everything away again. I estimate that each of the over 360 performances needed two whole days of my time.

I often opened The Magic of Chemistry by exploding balloons filled with a hydrogen or a hydrogen-oxygen mixture and suspended by thin cotton thread from a string line tied between two retort stands in a darkened room. Exploding the first one with a lit wax taper tied to the end of a bamboo cane set the second one of a line of three balloons off, followed by the third.

This attention-grabbing start was followed by a discussion about the difference between addition and condensation polymers. Addition polymerisation was demonstrated with ball and stick molecular models. I mentioned the main addition polymers and talked in detail about polytetrafluoroethylene (PTFE - Fluon or Teflon), discovered by Roy Plunkett in 1938, which played an important role in the development of enriched uranium for manufacture of the atom bomb (the Manhattan Project), and explained using space-filling molecular models why it has non-stick properties that make it so useful in our kitchens.

I wrote to Roy Plunkett to pose a few questions to him on his discovery and in his response, dated 20 January 1984, he said he was keen not to be associated with the Manhattan

Project. Shortly after his important discovery in the DuPont laboratories he left to start work on producing tetraethyl lead, which was developed as an additive to improve the performance of aircraft fuel.

John Charnley, who pioneered artificial hip operations in the late 1950s and early 1960s at Wrightington Hospital in Lancashire, initially chose PTFE to make sockets that would allow a stainless steel ball to rotate freely within them. Unfortunately, he discovered that his first 100 patients who received PTFE sockets needed to have a second operation to replace them with a high-density polyethylene socket. Later, other hip joints, using different materials, were provided by different companies. Shortly after I was elected to Parliament in 1997, I visited the workshop where John Charnley had carried out his pioneering work. All his equipment was still there as he had left it, and I suggested to the hospital that they should prepare a museum for the public to visit.

I moved on to show how polystyrene beads can be 'blown' into the light material – expanded polystyrene - used in packaging and insulation of our houses. I demonstrated the manufacture of polymethylmethacrylate (Perspex or Plexiglass) and explained how the two strengths that cast and extruded Perspex can exhibit depend on the lengths of their polymer chains. I visited the mill at Darwen which was chosen to manufacture Perspex during World War II. One of its first uses was to manufacture cockpit covers for Spitfire and Hurricane aeroplanes. Darwen was chosen to manufacture Perspex because it is covered in cloud more than most areas of the country, which prevented the Luftwaffe from bombing the Perspex plant.

The next topic for discussion was condensation polymerisation, and I carried out the nylon rope trick to make nylon-66, one of six nylons then in commercial production. I explained how commercial nylons are 'melt spun' into fibres of different diameters (the denier) in 'spinnerets', and I showed the audience a huge nylon 'cheese' on which was wound 4,000 miles of continuous unstretched nylon-66 thread. Finally, I explained why this form of nylon has to be stretched before it can be sold commercially.

The second condensation polymer I made in my lecture was polyurethane. When commercial toluene di-isocyanate was mixed with a commercial polyhydric alcohol in a beaker in the right proportions, a mushroom-like shape set on top of the beaker.

The second part of my lecture began with an explanation of the electromagnetic spectrum, the so-called 'visible' part of the spectrum which we can detect with our eyes, being a small band roughly in the middle. I illustrated colour blindness (Daltonism, after John Dalton, who was colour blind) by use of slides. Then I discussed the primary and secondary colours and showed how different colours can be produced using these basic colours. Thus, for example, by overlaying magenta, yellow and cyan images on an overhead projector a recognisable image is produced. I explained that this is the basis of digital photography. Digital electronic printers contain a roll carrying these secondary colours, which are heat transferred onto the 'photographic' paper to produce the recognisable image.

When Japanese technologists were developing digital cameras they had a major problem, which was solved by chemists working at Blackley, Manchester, for ICI's Colours and Fine Chemicals business. None of the available dyes that the Japanese had to hand withstood the high temperatures (up to 400°C) required for this transfer process. The Manchester chemists, led by Peter Gregory, were able to develop the necessary dyes, and I was able to borrow their prototype printers to demonstrate this process to the general public before it became as widely known as it is today.

Hewlett Packard developed the first inkjet printers, but the available dyestuffs blocked the very tiny nipples of their jets. The Manchester ICI chemists, led by Nigel Hughes, chemically modified some very water-soluble food dyes so that they could be used in these early printers without them blocking the jets or resulting in inks that smeared on wet paper. Suitable coloured dyes followed later.

My next experiment, the 'sunset experiment', demonstrated the Tyndall effect, namely that colloidal materials have colours different from their elemental form. Thus, flowers of sulfur are yellow. However, it is possible to show blue sulfur to an audience by passing a beam of light through a large beaker containing a solution of sodium thiosulfate to which a few drops of concentrated hydrochloric acid are added. Only short, or blue, wavelength light is scattered off the colloidal (almost invisible) particles of sulfur that form, and the non-scattered light can be collected on a white screen. As the particles of sulfur grow in size in the beaker, their colour changes and an effect is seen on the screen rather like a sunset. At sunset in the Bay of Naples it is the particles of dust that blow off the crater of Vesuvius that provide some of the best sunsets in the world by light scattering.

Next, I demonstrated how fireworks are given their colours by setting fire to alcohol containing various metal salts in several porcelain evaporating basins.

I moved on to discuss dyestuffs, first those naturally occurring, such as indigo, Tyrian purple and cochineal, which is extracted from a gland in female cactus lice. In Lanzarote these are reared on cacti grown in rows in fields. I described how William Perkin discovered the first synthetic dye, mauveine, in 1856.

I demonstrated how a reduced form of a dye (such as indigo) can be applied to cloth and then fixed on the cloth through an oxidation reaction (the reverse of reduction) by taking out of my pocket a yellow handkerchief which I plunged into a bath containing an aqueous solution of a reducing agent (sodium hydroxide plus sodium dithionite), whereupon it became blue. On taking it out of the bath, washing it in water and waving it about in air, the yellow colour of the handkerchief was restored. These are 'vat dyes'.

I showed the audience how easy it is to produce colours by mixing various aqueous solutions of chemicals and to eliminate some of the colours by pouring in aqueous solutions of other chemicals. Oxidation of glucose in a moderately warm aqueous alkaline solution in the presence of indigo carmine produces some interesting colour changes, which can be repeated if the mixture is poured vigorously from a height into a second glass beaker in such a way that more oxygen is dissolved into the solution. Using 'tricks' such as the iodine clock reaction these colours can be made to appear at timed intervals, depending on the concentration of the solutions.

An experiment which always amazed people was the 'triple dyeing experiment'. A hot dye bath was made up ahead of the presentation, which contained three different dyes, one that dyes only cotton, one that dyes only wool and one that dyes only polyester. When an apparently white piece of material was dipped into this dye bath and removed after a few minutes, a flag was observed, such as the Union flag, after washing the excess dyes off with water. The trick was to sew the three different materials together in the right way. I usually made a tricolour flag in this way, although I have produced a red dragon on a white background in Wales.

Pointing at female cacti lice on cacti in Lanzarote.

A typical layout of experiments at the beginning of a performance of
The Magic of Chemistry.

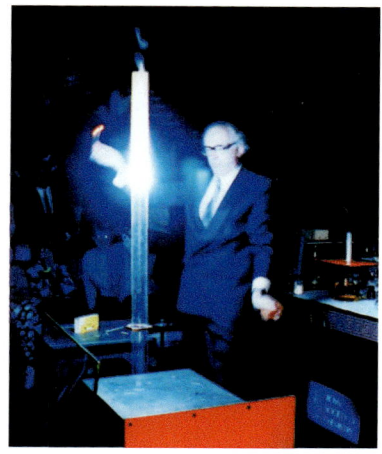

Explosion of a nitric oxide-carbon disulfide mixture in the Faraday Lecture Theatre, Royal Institution.

There are several organisms which exist in nature that emit bioluminescent light under the right conditions. Some fungi on dead trees exhibit this phenomenon when the weather conditions are just right, as do fireflies in the tropics, glow worms in the hedgerows and the automobile bug, which emits red light from its rear end and white light from its front end (hard to believe but true).

At this point in the lecture I showed part of a BBC Horizon film, *Trials of Life*, in which David Attenborough talks about the more exotic examples of bioluminescence. My favourite example is the Bermuda fire worm ('Whirlygigs') which emits a bluish-green light into the sea in a bay off the island of Bermuda when it is mating. To see this phenomenon the observer should go to the bay 55 minutes after sunset on the third, fourth or fifth day after any full lunar moon!

In the early presentations of my lecture I demonstrated the same phenomenon, except that chemists call it chemiluminescence, by oxidising solutions of a chemical called luminol in a dark room. This effect can be short lived, so I graduated to making bis(aryl)oxalates in my laboratory and oxidising them in dimethyl phthalate with hydrogen peroxide in the presence of various dyes, which produces a range of bright and long-lasting coloured lights.

I discovered through my contacts that the American Cyanamid company were about to commercialise this reaction, and I believe I was the first person in the UK to import their Cyalume light sticks, which I bent to mix the chemical solutions and threw out into my audiences. Of course, most people in Britain today are aware of these light sticks; no pop concert would be complete without them.

Throughout my lecture I exploded homemade fireworks, let off magnesium flash boxes or woke up my audience in a number of other ways. My finale was to apply a lit wax taper to the top of a long glass tube filled with a mixture of nitric oxide gas and carbon disulfide vapour. A blue light appears at the top of the tube which accelerates down to the bottom of the tube whilst emitting a sharp whistling sound. This experiment, which is sometimes called the 'barking dog experiment', is best carried out with all the lights out.

Theatrical Pyrotechnics provided me with materials for my special effects. Malcolm Armstrong, the owner of this company, gave a lecture entitled 'Fireworks' when I was treading the boards, as did the Reverend Ronald Lancaster, the Manager of Kimbolton Fireworks. Malcolm made Salisbury Plain look like an authentic battleground for army training exercises and provided special effects for film and television, for example for the James Bond films. Ron Lancaster began his career as a chemistry teacher at Kimbolton School in Cambridgeshire, where he started to make fireworks under licence for school displays. His well-known book, *Fireworks: Principles and Practice* is now in its 4th edition.

Over the years I received so many requests for the 'recipes' of my experiments that I persuaded British Drug Houses (BDH) in Poole to publish *The Magic of Chemistry* as a booklet, in 1985. It has been out of print for some time now, although there are copies of it in the depository libraries of the UK. Reference is made to my lecture in *Encyclopaedia Britannica's Yearbook of Science and the Future* in a chapter by George B. Kauffman entitled Lecture Theater, published in 1995.

In March 1993, I received an invitation from Professor Paolo Manzelli at the University of Florence to open the First European Chemistry Week on Sunday 28 November. This was also the launch of one of the largest annual science fairs in the world, which is held at Mostra d'Ottremare, a large conference site in Naples, Italy. Altogether, the organisers wanted me to give ten lectures during the week, but I agreed to present my lecture six times. 'FuturoRemoto1993' was the eighth of these annual science fairs. Since my first presentation in Naples would be my 300th performance of The Magic of Chemistry at the end of my 25th year, I agreed to visit Italy.

Fortunately, in June and July 1993 I was invited to be a Visiting Professor at the University of Potenza - Italy's most southern university at that time. Eileen and I enjoyed a holiday in Sorrento after that, which gave me an opportunity to travel to Naples to discuss the logistics of my 'FuturoRemoto93' performances with the organisers at della'Fondazione IDIS there. They suggested that retired Professor Gioacchino Cozzolino (he insisted on me calling him Gioco) would help me to bring the lecture together. I agreed to send lists of the chemicals and equipment I required. This was the first time The Magic of Chemistry had been on tour without me being able to take my chemicals and equipment by car. Air France refused to transport any of my chemicals other than the dyestuffs.

DuPont Fibres in Gloucester transported a nylon-66 'cheese', carrying a 4,000 mile continuous thread of unstretched nylon, to Naples, and ICI Italia provided the ingredients I required to make polyurethane mushrooms. We were unable to acquire any Cyalume light sticks in Italy, but at the last minute, Luminasa (Europe) Ltd were able to import some chemiluminescent bangles from Japan.

I arrived in Naples one week before the first presentation of my lecture to bring everything together. Chemicals had to be weighed out in multiple amounts and solutions made up in order to save time. Gioco transported me to a glassblower so that I could obtain several long tubes for demonstration of the nitric oxide-carbon disulfide 'explosion'. Much to my surprise the glassblower worked in a store surrounded by drums of solvents and other chemicals for sale, which was on the ground floor of a high-rise block of flats.

Finally we visited the conference site, where we chose the largest hall in which to present the lectures. A demonstration bench was constructed on a stage, and we provided wooden blocks to elevate some of the demonstrations so that they could be seen in the long, narrow hall. A large screen was assembled overhead and the lighting and audio video equipment was set up. I was told that Mussolini had spoken several times in this hall.

I was almost ready. However, the lecture was being translated into Italian, and I was provided with two university students, Massimo Iossa and Gabaella De Lucia, to help me with that. I provided them with a script each which I had prepared in advance but, as rehearsals progressed, we found that the scripts required modification. To get to this stage had been a remarkable achievement for all concerned. It had been a logistical nightmare for me.

10,000 'flyers' were distributed across the large city of Naples, and huge posters appeared announcing a 'conferenza-spettacolo'. The box office was inundated with requests for the free tickets. To meet an overwhelming demand I agreed to present one more lecture, seven altogether.

At that time Italy didn't have a tradition of presenting demonstration lectures. The Magic of Chemistry proved to be a huge success in Naples. I was kept busy signing over 100 posters during the week and responding to over 40 requests, mainly from teachers, for more information about my experiments. I pointed out to the students who I talked to that 'Na-Po-Li' (the symbols for sodium, polonium and lithium) was a very chemical name, which seemed to amuse them.

I was accompanied in Italy by Moira Donnelly (Public Affairs Officer), Imelda Topping and Dr John Monaghan, representing the RSC, who had a stand in 'del Bar di Chimica' on the main conference site. My lectures in Naples were sponsored by the RSC as well as by the Sezione Campania of the Società Chimica Italiana. At the end of this event we took a few days off and enjoyed the autumn sunshine of Italy by visiting the island of Capri amongst other places. I was exhausted.

Later, when I received suggestions of tours with The Magic of Chemistry in Bangladesh and Australia, I politely rejected them. I was invited back to Naples to present more lectures, but I was heavily involved in national politics by the time I received the second request.

Moira Donnelly introduced me to the idea of 'chemical busking'. Dr Tom McC. Paterson (University of Salford) and I set up a roped-off stage at a crossroads in a large new shopping mall in Telford on 11 November 1994. We performed our various experiments on this stage for the best part of a day to see if we could stop the shoppers in their tracks and interest them in our chemistry. We used a vacant shop nearby to prepare all our experiments and keep our chemicals away from the people. In Telford this experiment was hugely successful, so we decided to repeat this event in the smaller One Stop Shopping Mall at Perry Barr, Birmingham, where it was less successful. Jeff Rooker (now Baron Rooker), then the local Member of Parliament, was kind enough to come and talk to us, which helped with the local publicity.

Ann Hubbard, winner of the 1994 Salter's Prize for Chemistry Teacher of the Year, and I launched the RSC's 'Huddersfield Experiment' in November 1995, by giving a combined performance before a capacity audience of over 1,000 dignitaries and members of the general public in Huddersfield Town Hall. Because our lecture attracted more demands for tickets than there were places available, we gave two more performances to close the 'Huddersfield Experiment' a year later.

I had planned to end our performances with a display of indoor fireworks but I could not persuade Standard Fireworks, the famous Huddersfield firework company, to work with us, much to the disappointment of the audiences. Our posters were printed on a background of fireworks.

During the year of the 'Huddersfield Experiment' buses toured Huddersfield with The Magic of Chemistry posted on their sides. This was an attempt by the Royal Society of Chemistry (RSC) to raise the profile of chemistry by measuring the impact of bombarding one community with events connected to chemistry throughout an entire year.

## SCIENCE AND POLITICS: AN UNLIKELY MIXTURE

The Huddersfield Experiment: I am on the extreme right with Ann Hubbard, Barry Sheerman MP (second from the left), the Mayor of Huddersfield (centre) and others.

When I was selected as a Prospective Parliamentary Candidate on 10 November 1994, Dr Stephen Benn, the Parliamentary Liaison Officer at the RSC, came to me with an interesting proposition, namely that I entertain Members of Parliament with the more exciting parts of The Magic of Chemistry in the Houses of Parliament following my election to Parliament, which occurred on 1 May 1997.

On 5 November 1997, I dressed as Guy Fawkes and Dr Paterson, who was taking over my role as a demonstration lecturer, dressed as Robert Catesby, and we performed several experiments in the Jubilee Room, just off Westminster Hall. I believe we were the first people to legally explode gunpowder in the Houses of Parliament. The room was packed with media people and Members of Parliament. Right up to my retirement from Parliament in 2010 my Parliamentary colleagues reminded me of that day. Tom's father was a pyrotechnologist who had passed his skills on to his son, and Tom could make explodable gunpowder.

Donald Anderson (Member of Parliament for Swansea East, now Lord Anderson) and Dr Michael Clark (Member of Parliament for Rayleigh, now retired) hosted this event on behalf of the RSC (they were Parliamentary Advisers to the RSC) and the invitation cards carried an invitation 'to attend a unique Live Demonstration of Explosive Chemical Energy in Action' to herald the Royal Society of Chemistry's Chemistry Week, 14-21 November 1997.

As Tom and I came out of the St Stephen's entrance to the Houses of Parliament on that day, carrying a mock barrel of gunpowder, we were met by a barrage of press and television

With Dr Paterson on 5 November 1997 - facing the press outside the Palace of Westminster.

# SCIENCE AND POLITICS: AN UNLIKELY MIXTURE

Eileen Iddon, Donald Anderson MP, Dr Paterson, me, Dr Stephen Benn, Michael Clark MP and Sadia Choudhry outside the Palace of Westminster.

With Dr Paterson on 5 November 1997 outside the Palace of Westminster, accompanied by Sadia Choudhry.

cameras. I never received that kind of publicity again in all 13 years of my time in Parliament. We were even interviewed on the *Today* programme by John Humphreys.

Stephen pointed out to me that there was a close connection between the Gunpowder Plot and Salford. The Yorkshire Roman Catholic conspirators tried to engage their Lancashire counterparts in the plot. Robert Catesby and Guy Fawkes are reported by the author William Harrison Ainsworth in his book *Guy Fawkes: The Gunpowder Treason*, published in 1841, to have visited Ordsall Hall (conspirator John Percy was the owner at the time), which is less than a mile from the University of Salford. I should have realised this connection since I had visited the hall several times. It stands in Guy Fawkes Street!

The logistics behind taking chemicals into the Houses of Parliament, especially explosives such as gunpowder, were daunting, but we overcame them. I applied for and was granted a 'Certificate to Acquire and Keep Explosives' by Greater Manchester Police, and the Health and Safety Executive issued me with a 'Recipient Competent Authority Transfer Document', which complied with the requirements of the 'Placing on the Market and Supervision of Transfers of Explosives Regulations 1993'. I approached the Serjeant at Arms in the House of Commons, the Speaker of the House of Commons, then Betty Boothroyd (Member of Parliament for West Bromwich), and the Fire and Safety Officers of the Houses of Parliament for their permissions also and, much to my surprise, these were granted. At this time the IRA were still very active in Britain.

I supplied lists to all concerned of the chemicals and apparatus that I would be transporting in my car to the Jubilee

Room for my presentation along with a list of the experiments that we were to perform. I agreed to offer my car for inspection on arrival at 8.30 am in New Palace Yard. When I arrived and wound my window down to explain to the policeman the procedure that had been agreed, namely that he should check the contents of my boot against the lists provided, he responded in an Irish accent with "That'll be all right sir, you're an MP".

I regularly took The Magic of Chemistry on tour, especially at Christmas time. In December 1974, I travelled to Cornwall, before the M5 had been extended from Bristol to Exeter, to present a lecture at the Mining College in Redruth. This presentation was followed by another in Plymouth and two more at the University of Exeter. I repeated this arduous tour in 1982 and again in 1986 and 1990. However, the longest UK tour was a four-day trip to present the lecture in Aberdeen, Thurso and Inverness, a round trip of 1,075 miles. On this journey, in December 1993, I experienced blizzard conditions in the Cairngorms and ice, fog, driving rain and high winds as well. It was the first time schoolchildren in Thurso had seen a Christmas lecture or any demonstration lecture live.

One Christmas I gave a lecture in Aberdeen in the morning and needed to travel in the afternoon to Aberystwyth for a dinner in the evening and a presentation the following day at the university. In driving rain on a very dark evening I travelled along the shores of Lake Bala (goodness knows why I chose to drive through central Wales) only to be met by a queue of traffic in Bala village.

When I got to the head of the queue I saw that a policeman needed to interview me, so I wound down the window and said "Good evening officer". His first question was "Where have you travelled from, sir?"

"Aberdeen, officer" I responded.

"And where are you travelling too?" asked the policeman.

"I'm going to Aberystwyth."

"What is the registration number of your vehicle?" asked the policeman.

"I am afraid I can't tell you?" I responded, and I proceeded to explain that I had only had the car two days - it was a new car.

I expected after this conversation that the policeman would want to inspect my car, but he didn't. Then, I foolishly asked him why he was interviewing me, and he pointed to a burned-out building in the village. "See that building over there? Well that was the shop of an estate agent who sold houses to English people, and the Welsh Nationalists fire bombed it last night", he explained to me. If he had opened the boot of my car, I would have been marched down to the village cop shop for a far more serious interview than the one I had endured.

I had several mishaps during the 29 years I presented The Magic of Chemistry. The most memorable was in Oxford, where I was invited to present my lecture in the lecture theatre in which Thomas Huxley famously defended Darwin's theory of natural selection in a debate with Samuel Wilberforce, the Bishop of Oxford, in 1860 and where, in 1894, wireless telegraphy was demonstrated for the first time.

As I raised the lit wax taper to light the first of three hydrogen-oxygen-filled balloons, my newly-recruited assistant turned the lights off completely, as instructed, but too soon. I lit the first balloon and, at the same time, burned through the cotton thread that suspended it from my string line. As the other balloons exploded, the first one was propelled down the long narrow lecture theatre over the heads of my audience,

Presenting The Magic of Chemistry at the Royal Institution – Professor Charles Rees, President of the RSC, hosted this event and can be seen sitting on the front row (right of gangway).

Presenting The Magic of Chemistry in Rumworth Labour Club, Bolton.

getting lower and lower as it approached the back row of seats. Fortunately, it was extinguished at that exact point and fell in the gangway at the rear of the lecture theatre. There were shouts of "encore!" as my panic started to fade. I couldn't believe my luck.

Comedians say that audiences differ hugely from one part of the country to another. I agree. I presented my lecture at the University of Glasgow in a very old medical lecture theatre. The seats were arranged to rise steeply to the ceiling, so that the students had a good view of the body on the marble slab below. All I could see were half of the faces of most of my audience – 'whatsits'. They heckled throughout my performance; I heckled back (I was a politician too by this time). It was a difficult but well-humoured audience to handle and a good time was had by all present. They rewarded me by presenting me with a bottle of whisky at the end.

Before I started a journey to present lectures in Great Yarmouth and King's Lynn in November 1980 I decided to telephone the organiser and discuss the venues with him. He described the venue in Great Yarmouth as a 'theatre in the round'. Since I had played in the round before at the Octagon Theatre in Bolton, I wasn't too worried until I arrived at the Hippodrome in Great Yarmouth. It is a circus ring with an enormous seating capacity.

This was probably the most difficult venue in which I ever presented my lecture, and to the largest audience I ever had - about 1,000 young people sitting in only half of the circus ring. I had to suspend an enormous screen from the roof of the ring in order to show my slides, and I arranged tables across the ring so that all the audience were close to some of the demonstrations. When I threw my Cyalume light sticks into the audience they were flying over my head for the rest of the performance. I was exhausted at the end.

The stage manager apologised that the dressing room was not free for me to use. David Essex, who was admired by our eldest daughter, played the venue the evening before and his band left the dressing room in quite a mess.

With Dr Tom Paterson presenting The Magic of Chemistry in the Science Museum, Kensington - November 1997.

Tom Paterson and I gave the final two presentations of The Magic of Chemistry at the Science Museum in Kensington on 14 November 1997. After that I gave my 'kit' away and retired. After I retired from Parliament colleagues from the Open University and the School of Chemistry at the University of Manchester suggested that I 'tread the boards' again. They offered me insurance, laboratory space, chemicals and apparatus, but what they could not give me was the physical and mental energy it takes to undertake these performances time and time again. I only wish I possessed that energy now.

When I started to present demonstrations to the general public, I had a feeling that many older chemists were not in favour of what I was doing. They probably thought I was trivialising science. I am pleased to say that that is an attitude long since abandoned, even by the 'old school'.

Likewise, television producers were also frowned upon for trying to introduce science on television as 'entertainment'. Raymond Baxter made a breakthrough when he presented *Eye on Research* from 1958 to 1961. In 1957, Patrick Moore began his highly popular programme *The Sky at Night* (the 700th performance was in March 2011), and David Attenborough started up the *Horizon* programmes in 1964. In 1965, *Tomorrow's World* was presented by Raymond Baxter and James Burke, and it attracted over ten million viewers. A revolution occurred in 1966 when music played out the programme and it was broadcast back-to-back with *Top of the Pops*.

The Royal Institution Christmas Lectures were broadcast for the first time in 1966 and, in 1971, the Open University started to broadcast science programmes on BBC2, at some very unusual hours. Jacob Bronowski, Jonathan Miller, David Attenborough, Magnus Pyke, Heinz Wolfe, Johnny Ball, Adam

## SCIENCE AND POLITICS: AN UNLIKELY MIXTURE

In the Green Room at Pebble Mill with Bob Syme (extreme left) and Raymond Baxter (extreme right).

Hart-Davis, Robert Winston, and more recently, Brian Cox and Jim Al-Khalili have all made their contributions to popularising science on television (and radio), as have many others.

As I became a well-known person who could demonstrate chemical experiments, television researchers became aware of what I was capable of. I received an invitation in 1984 from the producers of *The Adventures of Sherlock Holmes*, a 13-part series that was produced at the Granada TV studios in Manchester. Jeremy Brett starred in the role of Sherlock Holmes and David Burke was a memorable Dr Watson.

My job was to set up the Victorian chemistry set in Baker Street, and I showed Jeremy how to conduct the various experiments that the script required. We made some pretty colours, distilled liquids in the old retort, changed the colour of litmus paper and filled the room with smoke. I had to hang around on the Baker Street set for long periods, but the upside of this job was that a woman who carried money in the pocket of her apron paid me as I walked off the set on several occasions.

On March 24th 1994, I appeared during 'SET7 Week' (seven days of Science, Engineering and Technology in the UK – the first National Week of SET) on a special programme, broadcast from Pebble Mill in Birmingham. Alan Titchmarsh presented the programme, which was a celebration of an anniversary of the BBC TV programme *Tomorrow's World*. Raymond Baxter, the first ever presenter of *Tomorrow's World*, was interviewed, as were Kate Bellingham, the monocled President of the Inventor's Club, Bob Syme and Professor Steve Jones.

A rehearsal was held prior to the programme being recorded before a live audience, in order to get the timings and the camera angles right. As the live recording of the programme began, the all-women pop group who kicked it off made mistakes, and their part of the programme had to be recorded again. By this time my experiments had been prepared and the solutions of chemicals had been heated to the right temperatures.

When my turn to be interviewed by Alan came, the triple dyeing experiment worked perfectly. I was able to produce chemiluminescence in boiling tubes while the audience waved their light sticks round in the dark, I managed to change my pocket handkerchief from its yellow to a blue colour in the reducing bath and change it back to yellow after washing it and waving it in the air, but the temperature sensitive oxidation of glucose failed to give the desired colour changes. I believe this was the first time that members of the general public were made aware of the commercial availability of Cyalume light sticks in Britain.

## SCIENCE AND POLITICS: AN UNLIKELY MIXTURE

Wearing a red coat (see text) while presenting The Magic of Chemistry in a primary school.

When I came off the stage, Professor Steve Jones, a well-known academic geneticist, said to Alan Titchmarsh during his interview, which followed mine, "See, any fool can do experiments", a remark that didn't go down well with me. Light-heartedly, I reminded him of it on several occasions when I met him after that, usually at the 'Annual Scientists Meet the Media Event' at the Royal Society.

My colleagues at the University of Salford emphasised that I should wear a cotton laboratory coat and safety glasses on television, so as not to give science teachers the wrong impression about health and safety requirements, especially as I was the department's Safety Officer at that time. When I watched a replay of the programme in the comfort of my own home, I was horrified by my appearance as a stereotypical dotty professor. A few days later I went to Aults, a well-known men's outfitters in Bolton, and bought a red coat identical to the one I had seen my singer friend Gary Ryan wear on television, when he won a round of *Stars in Their Eyes* singing Neil Diamond songs. I didn't wear a white coat again to present my lecture after my Pebble Mill appearance.

I salute all those brave men and women who perform demonstrations today before live audiences. I am reminded of an experience that the late Dr John Salthouse, a lecturer at the University of Manchester, had when he presented his Son-et-Lumière demonstration lecture. John's lecture can be described as "look what happens when I mix this with that". It was full of flashes and bangs, some quite loud.

An elderly gentleman arrived to take his seat for the lecture extremely early and insisted on talking to John while he was preparing his demonstrations (this can result in trouble, as I found out myself on one or two occasions). John thought that the gentleman had been very friendly until a summons arrived several weeks later. The elderly gentleman claimed that John had caused him to go deaf! After that experience, John warned his audiences in advance of any loud noises, which spoiled the fun for most of his audiences.

# PHOTOGRAPHS AND ILLUSTRATIONS

~

I thank the people or organisations listed below for their kind permission to publish photographs. Every attempt has been made to contact copyright holders but this was not always possible. The author is happy to be contacted by copyright holders who feel that their photographs have not been acknowledged and apologises for any unintended omissions in this respect. Many of the photographs are from the author's own archives or from family collections.

The photograph of Violet Stazicker in the introductory pages was taken at Phil Waine's Studio, 56 Friargate, Preston.

The photograph of the author in the introductory pages appears with permission of the Parliamentary Labour Party.

**CHAPTER 1**

P. 4 top: Photograph by Monk Photo, Fishergate, Preston.

P. 11: Photographs by Henry Melling, 135a Church Street, Preston.

P. 19 top: Photograph taken at Phil Waine's Studio, 56 Friargate, Preston, 22 November 1941.

P. 20 top left: Photograph by Theo J. Gidden, 18 London Street, Southport.

P. 30 bottom: Photograph by Francis Turner, Leyland.

## CHAPTER 3

P. 116: Copyright English Heritage (Aerofilms Collection).

P. 121 top and bottom: *Hull Daily Mail.*

P. 128 bottom: University of Hull.

P. 131 bottom: Photograph by Donald I. Innes, 13 The Square, Hessle.

P. 135 top left: *Hull Daily Mail.*

P. 135 bottom left: Photograph by Herbert H. Ballard, Hague Studios, 82 Chanterlands Avenue, Hull.

P. 149: University of Hull.

## CHAPTER 4

P. 172: Photograph by the *Yorkshire Post.*

P. 175 top left: Family of the late Professor Hans Suschitzky.

## CHAPTER 5

P. 210 bottom: Family of the late Professor Hans Suschitzky.

P. 218: University of Salford.

P. 219: University of Salford.

## CHAPTER 8

P. 269: The Royal Society of Chemistry.

P. 275: The Royal Society of Chemistry.

P. 276 bottom: The Royal Society of Chemistry, Andrew Wiard.

P. 277: Photographs by Dr Stephen Benn.

P. 281 top: The Royal Society of Chemistry.

P. 287: *Bolton Evening News.*

# INDEX

Aberdeen, 279, 280
Aberystwyth, 279, 280
Abu Dhabi, 250
Academic Staffing Committee, University of Salford, 220
Acetylene bicycle lamps, 54
Addition polymerisation, 263
Adler, Larry, 100
Ahmadabad, India, 249
Ahmednagor, 246
Ainsdale County Secondary School, Southport, 84
Ainsworth, William Harrison, 278
Airey, Mrs., teacher, 33, 34
Air raids, 28
Air-sensitive chemicals, 189
Ajanta Caves, India, 248
Albermarle Street, London, 260
Albert Hall, Bolton, 261
Aldermaston March, 119
Alderney, 198
Al-Khalili, Jim, 285
Alty's brickworks, 32
Alumina powder, 230
American Cyanamide, 270
Anderson, Donald, 276, 277
Annual safety inspections, 225
Antibiotic drugs, 43
Applied Chemistry Degrees, 182
Armstrong, Malcolm, 270
Arndale Centre, IRA bomb, 235
Artificial hip joints, 264
Ashby, Dr. John, 189
Ashcroft, Martin, 25, 59, 64, 70, 79, 89
Ashcroft, Philip, 16
Ashurst Beacon, 54
Ashworth, John, 177, 179, 218
Aspey, Harold, 88, 105

Aspro-Nicholas, 143
AstraZeneca, 43
Atkinson, Cllr. Morrell, 235
Attenborough, David, 269, 284
Aughton, Mrs., teacher, 34, 35
Aurangabad, Bibi Ka Maqbara, 248
Aurangabad, Daultabad Fort, 247, 248
Aurangabad, India, 214, 245, 246
Auschwitz, 213
Austria, 146, 212, 213
Automobile Association, 41
Automobile bug, 269
Ayres, Joyce, 123, 134, 145, 150, 155
Ayyangar, Dr. N. R., 246, 247
Azides, 205, 233, 234
Azo-dyes, 43

Babylon, Hanging Gardens of, 243
Bach, Richard, 242
Baden Baden, 147
Bagamoyo, Tanzania, 255
Bakelite, 46
Baker Street, 285
Bala, 279
Baldwin, Prof. Roy, 128, 133
Ball, David, 9
Ball, Johnny, 262, 284
Ball, Marjory, 155
Ballester, Prof. Manuel, 236
Ballroom dancing, 61, 108, 109, 117, 122
Bamford, Penny and Wendy, 141
Bank Bridge, Tarleton, 96
Bank Hall, Bretherton, 95, 96, 126
Banks, 70
Banks, Riverside nightclub, 122, 123
Baptism Certificate, 19
Barcelona, 236

Barclays Bank, 188
'Barking Dog' experiment, 270
Barnes, Dr. Austin, 191
Barnsley, 150
Barron, Bert, 99
Barron, David, 26, 65, 70, 98, 99, 130, 140, 155
Barron, Philip, 16, 30
Barrow Bridge, Bolton, 36
Battersea Park, 76
Baxter, Raymond, 284-286
The Beatles, 129, 229
Becconsall Boatyard, 3, 49, 52
Becconsall Church, 3, 6, 24, 28, 31
Becher, Prof. Jan, 214
Beeching, 32
Begtrup, Prof. Mikael, 214
Belfast sinks, 38, 39
Bellamy, David, 166, 262
Belle Vue, Manchester, 93
Bellingham, Kate, 286
Benger's Laboratories, Holmes Chapel, 188
Benn★, Dr. Stephen, 275, 277, 278
Benn, Tony, 174, 175
Bentine, Michael, 86, 87
Bentley, Derek, 95
Benzo[$b$]thiophenes, 142, 188-190, 205
Benzo[$b$]thiophene 'rock', 189
Benzyl azide, explosion, 233, 234
Bergman, Prof. Jan, 215, 217
Berlin, 214, 239, 243, 244
Berlin, British Embassy, 239
Berlin, Pergamon Museum, 243
Berlin Wall, 244
Bermuda fire worms, 269
Berwick-on-Tweed, 171
Best, George, 208
Beverley Arms, 129
Beverley Minster, 129
Beverley, Race Course, 129
Bevin boys, 29, 40
Bhopal, India, 246
Biggles, 49
*Billy Cotton Band Show*, 87, 225

Bioluminescence, 199, 269
Biphenyls, 148
Biros, 58
Black, James W., 204
*Blackadder*, 87
*Black and White Minstrel Show*, 87
Black market, 42
Blackpool, 49, 60, 93, 189, 190
*Blackpool Belle*, 109
Blackpool illuminations, 94, 95
Blackpool Tower and Circus, 60, 61, 94
Bladons Store, Hull, 144
*Blankety Blank*, 87
Blundell, James, 25
Blyton, Enid, 49
Bodmer, Sir Walter, 178
Bologna, 214
Bolton RSC Christmas Lectures, 261, 262
Bolton Festival, 262
Bolton School, 262
Bolton Technical College, 261
Bolton Wanderers FC, 9
Bombay, India, 214, 245, 249, 250
Bombay, Sahara International Airport, 245, 250
Bombay, Victoria Terminus, 249
Bonfire night, 52, 53
Bonnington, Chris, 219
Bookbinding, 79
Boothroyd, Betty, Speaker of the House of Commons, 278
Boothstown, 192, 193, 197, 199, 200
Bootle Hospital, 196
Bosworth, Stuart, 218
Bourne-Arton, Anthony, 173
Bowden, Keith, 137, 138, 149
Braddock, Bessie, 27
Brady, Ian, 164
Brandenburg Gate, Berlin (DDR), 243
Bratislava, 237, 238
Bratislava Castle, 239
Bretherton, 32, 54, 79, 96
Brett, Jeremy, 285
Brewis, Derek McHardy, 122, 129, 131, 135, 137, 140, 141, 145

Bridgewater Canal, Worsley, 193, 200
Bridgewater Hotel, Worsley, 199
Bridlington, 152
British Council, 208, 239, 245, 250-252, 257
British Drug Houses (BDH), 148, 270
British Library, 179
Brixton, 198
Broadbent, Howard, 109
Bromine chemistry, 192
4-Bromomethyltetrafluoropyridine, 168
Bronowski, Jacob, 284
Brown Cow public house, Salford, 208
BSc, Special Hons. Degree in Chemistry, 115, 133, 134, 149
Buchan, Ogilvy Angus Milne, 163-165
Buckley, Alan, 122, 137, 145
Budget cuts for universities (1981), 178
Bullock, Ken (the glass), 186
Bullying at school, 84
Burke, David, 285
Burke, James, 284
Burscough Bridge, 42, 89, 101
Bush television sets, 88
Butchering, 55, 56
Byron, Gloria, midwife, 197

Cairoli, Charlie, clown, 61
Calico Printers Association, 136, 137
Campaign for Nuclear Disarmament (CND), 118, 119
Camp coffee, 55
Camp Hall, Cottingham, 114, 115, 123
Canada, 137, 213, 237
Cancer drugs, 143, 152
Candle factory fire, 234
Cannock, 107
Capodimonte, 31
Carbenes, 205
Cardiff, 206, 207
Carmichael, Ian, 85
Carr, David, 210
Carr House, Much Hoole, 110
Carr Wood, Tarleton, 26, 27
Carry On films, 85
Cars, 61-64

Castle, Barbara, 155, 219
Castleford, 154
Catapults 54
Catesby, Robert, 275, 276, 278
Cat's eyes, 63, 64
Cavern Club, 130
Cave's Chemist Shop, Southport, 81, 82
Chadwick, Elizabeth (great grandmother), 11
Chadwick family, 10-12, 15, 89
Chambers, Dr. Colin, 261
Chambers, Prof. Richard D., 160-162, 169, 174, 176
Chancellors, University of Salford, 178
Changabang, 219
Channel Islands, 198
Chapman, Prof. Norman Bellamy, 112, 128, 131, 132, 135, 137, 142, 149, 150, 214
Charnley, John, 264
Chartered Chemist status, 220
Checkpoint Charlie, 242
Chemical Abstracts, 200
Chemical busking, Perry Barr, 274
Chemical busking, Telford, 273
Chemical Society, 132, 202
Chemical Society, Journals, 162, 166, 170
Chemiluminescence, 269
Chemistry sets, 80, 81
Chemistry Week, 276
Cherbourg, 198
Cheshire salt, 2
Children's toys and games of the 1940s and 1950s, 45-47
Chorley FC, 9
Choudhry, Sadia, 277
Christ Church Boys' Secondary School, Southport, 65, 67, 70-72, 74, 75, 79, 80, 83-85, 106, 124, 126, 127
Christ Church School, toilets, 80
Christmas, 47, 48
Churchill, Winston, 17
Churchtown, Southport, 80
Ciba-Geigy, Trafford Park, 186
Cimetidine, 204
Cingov, Czechoslovakia, 237
Civil Defence Programmes, 138
Claremont Hotel, Southport, 70

# SCIENCE AND POLITICS: AN UNLIKELY MIXTURE

Clark, Dr. Dave, 160, 169
Clark, Dr. Jim, 207
Clark, Michael, 276, 277
Clarke, Dr. Ken, 128, 137, 142, 145, 149
Cleminson Hall, Hull, 115
Clothes horse, 39
Coates, Prof. Geoffrey, 166, 176
Cobalt-60 source, 187
Cochineal, 267
Cockcroft Building, University of Salford, 187, 226, 227, 231
Colburn, Nikki, 210
Colleges of Advanced Technology (CATS), 176, 179
Collins, Cannon, 119
Colloquia, 169 (Durham), 183 (Salford)
Colour blindness, 265
Colours, primary and secondary, 265
Combine harvesting, 100, 101
Comedy in the 1950s and 1960s, 85–88
Comic Opera, Berlin (DDR), 243
Condensation polymers, 265
Condensed milk, 55
Conscription, 115
Constantine, Prof. Tom, 179
Control of Subtances Hazardous to Health (COSHH) Regulations, 225
Convocation Lectures, 219
Cook, Dr. Chris, 261
Co-operative Bank, 188
Co-operative Wholesale Society, coffin factory fire, 231
Copenhagen, 214
Corless, Mr., teacher, 34, 35
Cornwall, tour of, 279
Coronation Street, 153
Cottingham, 114, 115, 122, 132, 134
Cottingham Road (number 102), 139, 145
County Hall, Preston, 65
Cowboys, 26, 45, 49, 50
Cox, Prof. Brian, 285
Cozzolino, Prof. Gioacchino, 271
Craig, Dr. Alan, 224, 225, 230
Crerand, Pat, 208
Cricket, 77, 79, 88, 199
Croft, Dr. (Tarleton GP), 44

Crompton, Samuel, 222
Crossens, 25
Crossley, Duncan, teacher, 106
Croston, 32, 54, 79, 96, 220, 221
Croston Coffee Day, 58
Crumpsall Hospital, 136
Cunard Line, 28
Cunningham, 167 (Dr. Jack), 167 (Baron) (Lord Felling)
Cyalume light sticks, 270, 272, 282, 286
Cycling, 54
Cytokinins, 204, 205
Czechoslovakia, 208, 212, 213, 237, 241

*Dad's Army*, 87
Dali, Salvador, 237
Dalton, John, 265
Daltonism, 265
*Dam Busters March*, 84
Dan Dare (*Eagle* comic), 80
Danish Ministry of Education, 214
Dar-es-Salaam, 214, 215, 255
Dar-es-Salaam, Bahari Beach Hotel, 250, 252, 253, 257, 258
Dar-es-Salaam, Kilimanjaro Hotel, 255
Dar-es-Salaam, Kunduchi Beach Hotel, 250, 252
Dar-es-Salaam, Oyster Bay, 252
Dar-es-Salaam, Sno-Cream Parlours Ltd., 255
Dar-es-Saalam, Village Museum, 252
Darlington, 171, 173
Darwen, 264
Darwin's Theory of Natural Selection, 280
Davies, Roy, 211
Davy, Humphrey, 260
Day trips, 93
DDNP (diazodinitrophenol), 233
DDR (East Gemany), tours of, 237, 239, 240, 242
DDT, 191
Deafness, 194
Deccan Plateau, India, 248, 249
Deccan Queen, 249
Deflagrations, 230–232
Delaney, Joe, 186
Delaney, Sheila, 186
Delph Tea Gardens, Parbold, 54

# SCIENCE AND POLITICS: AN UNLIKELY MIXTURE

Denmark, tour of, 208, 214, 262
Derby, Science Fair, 262
Derwent Patent Abstracts, 201
Desert Rats, 31
Dialdrin, 191
Diamant, Rudi, 180
Diamond, Harry, 129, 131
Diamond, Neil, 287
Diazotisation, 232
*Dick Barton, Special Agent*, 86
Dickinson, Roger, 188-190, 236
Dick Kerr's Works, Preston, 94
Didsbury, 187
Dinky Toys, 46, 69
Diseases of the 1940s, 43, 44
*Dixon of Dock Green*, 87
Dixon, Reginald, 61
*Doctor Zhivago*, 85
Dolly blue, 39
Donnegan, Lonnie, 130
Donnelly, Moira, 273
Dow Chemicals, USA, 191
Drakesmith, Fred, 162
Dresden, 214
Dresden, fire storm of 1945, 241, 242
Dresden, Frauenkirche, 242
Dresden, Semper Opera House, 242
Dresden, Zwinger Palace, 242
Dryburn Hospital, Durham, 171, 173
Dubbin Mixer, 88
Dublin, 262
Duke of Hamilton, Holsworthy, Devon, 213
Duncan, William, 204
Dunkirk, 30, 31
DuPont Fibres, 272
Durant, Graham J., 204
Durham Castle, 159
Durham, Cathedral, 159
Durham, City, 99, 159
Durham, City Register Office, 165
Durham, County Hotel, 174, 175
Durham Gaol, 159, 164
Durham, Miners' Gala, 174, 175
Durham, railway station, 159, 163

Durham, Student Labour Club, 173
Dust explosions, 225

*Eagle* comic, 80
Ealing comedies (Boulting Brothers), 85
East Lancashire Road (A580), accidents on, 192, 193
Ebony, 253
Edinburgh International Science Festival, 262
Egestad, Borge, 216, 217
El Alamein, 31
Elderberry wine, 58
Electromagnetic spectrum, 265
Eleven-plus examination, 64-68
Ellora Caves and Temple, India, 248
Elsevier, 203
Embley, Ethel, 110
Emett, Rowland, 76
Emmett, John C., 204
Emyln Hall, Walkden, 200
Enediynes, 192
English Channel, 198, 199
Essex, David, 282
European Chemistry Week, 271
Evans, Timothy John, 95
Excel Bowling Alley, Walkden, 199
Experiments at home, 81, 83
Explosions, 142, 161, 162, 167, 168
Explosives, 131
Express Instrument Hire, Tarleton, 1

Faraday, Michael, 260
Farnworth, 193
Farnworth Constituency Labour Party, 200
Farnworth Little Theatre, 262
Fawkes, Guy, 52, 275, 276, 278
*Fawlty Towers*, 87
Fazackerley, George, 11, 17
Feast, Dr. Jim, 159, 160
Fellowship of the RSC, 220
Female cactus lice, 267, 268
Ferens Hall, 114-120, 135
Ferens Hall, photograph, 117
Ferguson Fawsitt Arms, Walkington, 152
Ferguson, Sarah, Duchess of York, 178

Ferry boat parties, 155
Festival of Britain, 75
Films of the 1950s and 1960s, 49, 85
Finney, Tom, 18, 77
Fireflies, 199
Fireworks, 53, 261, 266, 270
Fireworks safety, 206, 207
First day covers, stamps, 189
Firwood Fold, 222
Fischer, Prof. Emil, 142, 243
Fitton, Dr. Alan, 205
Flamborough Head, 132, 133, 152
Flame retardants, 192
Fletcher, Edward, 173
Fluoroquinolines and fluoroisoquinolines, 176
Fog, 63, 132, 192, 279
Della'Fondazione IDIS, 271
Foot, Michael, 27, 119, 174
Ford, Henry, 63
Formby, George, 87, 101
Forse, Rev. L. N., 17, 64, 128
Foxcroft, Annabelle, 172
France, 146
Franco, General, 236
Freemasons, 99
Free radicals, 167
Fresher's Ball, 117, 122
Fresher's initiations, 116, 117
Freud, Prof. Sigmund, 212
Friedrichstrasse Station (DDR), 243, 244
Funeral, of mother, 125
FuturoRemoto 1993, 271
Fylde Coast, 93

Gallagher, Peter, 210
Gamlen, Prof. George, 191, 229
*Gandhi*, 85
Gandhi, Rajiv, Prime Minister of India, 246
Ganellin, Dr. Robin, 204
Garrick Theatre (see Southport)
Gas cylinder, safety, 200, 226
Gas masks, 28
GCE examiner, 201
GCE A-Level examinations, 108, 111

GCE O-Level examinations, 83
GCE OA-Level examinations, 107
GCE Scholarship Level examinations, 108, 111
General knowledge quizzes, 145, 152, 153
Germany, 146
Gewald, Prof. Karl, 241
'Ginny Greenteeth', 57
Glandular fever, 110, 151
Glover, Mary, 64
Glow Worms, 269
Glyndwr University, 208
Godparents, 17
Goole, 154, 155
*Goon Show*, 86
Gopal, Dr., 247
Gosling, Chas, 115
Graduates of the Royal Institute of Chemistry (GRIC), Part I & II, 181, 182, 188
Graduation, 134 and 135 (BSc), 144 (PhD), 216 and 218 (DSc)
Granada TV, 208
Gray, Dr. George, 147, 148, 156
Graz, Austria, 214, 238
Graz, Landeszeughaus, 238
Graz, Uhrturm Clock Tower, 238
Great Universal Stores, 92
Great Yarmouth Hippodrome, 282
Greater Manchester County Council, 235
Greater Manchester Fire and Rescue Service, 231
Greater Manchester Police, 278
Green Goddess, 24
Greenwood, Walter, 177
Gregory, Peter, 266
Gregson's Well public house, Liverpool, 130
Greiss, Peter, 232, 233
Grey College, Durham, 162-164
Grey Hound public house (Boothstown), 199
Grimmett, Prof. Ross, 209
Gronowitz, Prof. Salo, 189, 218
Grundy, Alan, 194
Guide House, Lytham, 24
Guide Road, Hesketh Bank, 24, 58
Guinness, Alec, 85
Gujarat State, India, 249
Gunpowder Plot, 278

Guy Fawkes Street, Salford, 278
Guy, Peter, produce merchant, 102

Haley, Bill, 50, 52
Hall, Martin, 178
Halle, 214, 240
Hamburg, 237
*Hancock's Half Hour*, 87
Hanky Park, Salford, 177
Harlowe, Michael, 178
Harris, Martin, 178
Harris, Rolf, 197
Hart-Davis, Adam, 284, 285
Harvest time, 100, 101
Harvey, Dave, 145
Harvey, Jim and Martha, 256
Haszeldine, Professor Ron, 158, 159, 161, 169, 183
Hathaway, Dr. Brian, 139
Haulage company explosion, Salford, 234, 235
Hauptmann, Prof. Siegfried, 241
*Have a Go*, 86
Haworth Arms, Hull, 148
Headingley Methodist Church, Leeds, 171
Health and Safety Executive, 278
Heathrow Airport, 97, 98
Heeler dogs, 101
Heidelberg, 208, 214, 237
Hemming, Graham, 144
Heptafluoroquinoline and heptafluoroisoquinoline, 167
Herbal Drinks, 86
Herm, 198
Hesketh Arms, 10
Hesketh Bank, 3, 9, 10, 24, 25, 31, 32, 35, 58, 79, 93, 108, 109, 114
Hesketh family, 12, 16
Hessle, 154
Heyes, Henry, 17, 20
Heyes, Milly, 18, 20
Hill, R. H., 73-75, 77
Hindley, Myra, 164
His Masters Voice (HMV) gramophone, 16, 100
Hitler, Adolf, 243
Hofmo, Gunvor, 213

Holgate, Sid, Master of Grey College, Durham, 163
Holloway, Stanley, 60
Holmes Chapel, 188
Holmes, Sherlock, 285
Holsworthy, Devon, 213
Holt, Geoff, 119
Home, Evelyn, 139
Home Guard, 29, 30
Honeyburne, Rev. J. H., 72
Honeymoon, 171
Hope Hospital, Salford, 194, 196, 197
*Horizon*, 269, 284
Horlock, John, 177
Hornby, Frank, 68, 69
Hornby Dublo railway sets, 46, 69
Hornsea, 152
Horrocks, Rev. Jeremiah, 110
Howard, Jean, 108
Howard's Farm, 2, 5, 39, 101
Howarth, Gerald, 107
Hoyle, Prof. Sir Fred, 119
Hubai University, Wuhan, China, 208
Hubbard, Ann, 274, 275
Huddersfield, 181
Huddersfield Experiment, 274, 275
Huddersfield Town FC, 9
Hughes, Bert, 142
Hughes, Edward D., 132
Hughes, Nigel, 266
Hull, see Kingston-upon-Hull
Hull, Bill (family funeral director), 38
Humber Bridge, 155
Humber ferries, 155
Humboldt University, Berlin, 243
Humphreys, John, 278
Hundred End, 25
Husband, Prof. Tom, 177, 218
Hutchinson, Prof., 165, 166
Hutton Grammar School, 64, 67
Huxley, Thomas, 280
Hyderabad, Centre for Cellular and Molecular Biology, 249
Hyderabad, India, 214, 245, 249
Hyderabad, Nizams, 249

# SCIENCE AND POLITICS: AN UNLIKELY MIXTURE

Hyderabad, Regional Research Laboratory, 249
Hyderabad, Salar Jung Museum, 249

ICI Colours and Fine Chemicals, 266
ICI Dyestuffs, 43, 135, 136, 158
ICI Pharmaceuticals, 43, 204
ICI Plant Protection, 191
Iddon, Ada (aunt) 8, 22, 48, 126, 127
Iddon, Alice (aunt), 2-4, 8, 21
Iddon, Alice (grandmother), 1-4, 7, 8, 31, 127
Iddon, Arnold (cousin), 32
Iddon, Bessie, 22, 126
Iddon, Betty (aunt), 2-4
Iddon, Celia (cousin), 21
Iddon, Charlotte, 10
Iddon, Don (journalist), 9
Iddon, Eileen (second wife), 86, 97, 175, 212, 237, 244, 251, 256-258, 271, 277
Iddon, Ellen (aunt), 2-4, 29, 31
Iddon, Frank (cousin), 7, 22, 29, 40, 41, 55, 126
Iddon, Graham (brother) 7, 15, 21, 41, 51, 59, 66, 91, 97, 100, 101, 118, 124, 126, 134, 187, 199, 220, 221
Iddon, Harry (cousin), 7, 21, 109
Iddon Henry (uncle), 2-4, 7, 32
Iddon, Jack (father), 1, 2, 4, 7, 8, 10, 11, 15, 16, 27, 30, 35, 45, 86, 97, 101, 105, 111, 118, 124, 127, 128, 134, 199, 221
Iddon, Jack (cricketer), 9
Iddon, James (uncle), 2, 3
Iddon, Jane Ellen (aunt), 8, 58
Iddon (Mayor), Janie (cousin), 22
Iddon, Private John, 3, 6
Iddon, John (nephew) 10, 221
Iddon, Lily May, 68
Iddon, Lucy Jayne, 10
Iddon, Merrilyn (first wife), 172, 173, 187, 188, 192, 197, 199, 200
Iddon, Miriam (aunt), 2, 3
Iddon, Pamela Mary (sister-in-law), 97, 220
Iddon, Richard (grandfather), 1-4, 7
Iddon, Richard (uncle), 2-4, 7-9, 16, 17, 22, 40, 94, 104, 126-128
Iddon, Robert (uncle), 2-4, 7, 22
Iddon, Ronnie (cousin), 21
Iddon, Sally Jane (daughter), 172, 173, 187, 195 (photographs), 197, 222, 282

Iddon, Sheena Helen (daughter), 48, 173, 195 (photographs), 197, 222
Iddon, Violet (mother), 11, 15, 18, 45, 65, 70, 86, 91, 92, 97, 105, 124-126
Iddon, Wilf (cousin), 32
Iddon, William (uncle), 2-4, 7
Imidazoles, 192, 204, 209
Imperial College, London, 218
Independent Order of Rechabites, 88
India, tour of, 245
Indian Academy of Science, 246
Indian Airlines, 245, 249
Indigo carmine, 267
Indoles, 142, 188, 206
Ingold, Prof. Sir Chistopher, 132
Innsbrück, 146, 214
Inn Valley, Austria, 146, 147
International conferences, 209
Inverewe Gardens, 171
Inverness, 279
Iraq, 187
Irish Republican Army (IRA), 235, 278
Isle of Man, 98, 99, 213
*ITMA*, 86
Ithon, 10

Jackson, Dave, 122, 129, 131, 135
Jacques, Hattie, 85
*Jake the Peg*, 197
James Bond films, 270
James, John, 143
James, Sid, 85
Jealotts Hill, ICI, 191
Jenkins, Roy, SDP, 200
Jesuits, 24
Johnson, Betty Iddon (cousin), 22, 29
Johnson, Ellen (aunt), 8, 29, 31, 127
Johnson, Enoch, 22
Johnson, Percy Lunt (uncle), 3, 29
Johnson, Richard Lunt (cousin), 29-31
Joint Honours Degrees, 224, 233
*Jonathan Livingstone Seagull*, 242
Jones, Prof. Sir Ewart R. H., 220
Jones, Mr. R. E., teacher, 76, 81, 83
Jones, Ron and Jen, 95, 96, 98

Jones, Prof. Steve, 286, 287
Joule House, Salford, 185
Joule, James Prescott, 185
Joules, 185, 186

Kaiserslautern, 214
Karl Marx University, Leipzig, 239-241, 244
Kassenally, Prof. A. S., 119
Kauffman, George B., 271
Kenya, 253
Khan, Irene Zubaida, 178, 223
Kilner, Dr. Mel, 170
Kimbolton Fireworks, 270
Kimbolton School, 270
King George VI, 17
King of Gwent 10
Kings Arms Hotel, Berwick-upon-Tweed, 171
Kings Arms public house, York, 144
Kings College, London, 111, 112
King's Liverpool Regiment, 3
Kings Lynn, 282
Kingston-upon-Hull, Central Police Station, 154
Kingston-upon-Hull, City Hall, 134, 135, 144, 154
Kingston-upon-Hull, College of Further Education, 154
Kingston-upon-Hull, docks, 154
Kingston-upon-Hull, New Theatre, 144
Kingston-upon-Hull, old city, 155
Kingston-upon-Hull, Paragon Station, 114
Kingston-upon-Hull, public houses, 155
Kingston-upon-Hull, Queen's dock, 154
Kingston-upon-Hull, Queens Gardens, 154
Kingston-upon-Hull, Royal Infirmary, 151
Kingston-upon-Hull, telephones, 119, 120
Kinsale, Cork, 236
Klee, Kenneth, 26, 89
KLM Royal Dutch Airlines, 251
Kosice, Slovakia, 214, 237
Kuhlungsborn, 237
Kutschy, Dr. Peter, 237

Lab. trips, 152
Lachrymators, 169
Lake District, 89, 93
Lancashire County Council, 3, 65
Lancashire County Council, Education Committee, 65, 66
Lancashire County Cricket Club, 9, 199
*Lancashire Evening Post*, 105
Lancashire Fire and Rescue Service, 24
Lancaster, Rev. Ronald, 261, 270
Lanzarote, 267, 268
Larkhill Place, Salford, 185
*Last of the Summer Wine*, 87
Lathom, 101
*Lawrence of Arabia*, 85
Lawton, Tommy, 77
Laxey, 98, 99
Leaches, 49
Lead pipes, 38
Leeds, 171, 188
Leeds and Liverpool Canal, 16, 26, 30, 31, 42, 51
Lego bricks, 46
Leipzig, 214, 239
Lewis, Terry, 200
Lever Bros., Port Sunlight soap, 39
Leyland, 9, 25
Leyland FC, 9
Liebscher, Prof. Jurgen, 245
Lingard family, 10, 220
Linz, 214
Liquid crystals, 148
Little Holland, 24, 25
Liverpool, 3, 10, 17, 24, 27, 28, 41, 77, 94, 95, 99, 130, 131, 185, 196, 215
Liverpool, dock road, 27
Liverpool, dock road overhead railway, 28
Liverpool, Lime Street Station, 27
Livingstone, David, 255, 256
Llandaff Cathedral, 10
Llansannan, 89, 91
Lofthouse, Nat, 77
London, seeing the sites, 97, 98
London School of Economics, 179
Long, Andrea, 258
Long Service Award, 218
Looe, Cornwall, 145
Lord Hesketh 16
Lord Lilford, 17, 96, 104, 105, 126

# SCIENCE AND POLITICS: AN UNLIKELY MIXTURE

Lord Nelson public house, Croston, 220
Los Caracoles Restaurant, Barcelona, 236
Lostock Hall, 17, 18
*Love on the Dole*, 177
Lowe's Farm, Lathom, 101
Lowry, L. S., 182, 183, 185
Lowry Centre, Salford, 185
LSD, 229
Luftwaffe, 28
Luminaso (Europe) Ltd., 272
Luminol, 269
Lund, Sweden, 214, 262
Lytham, 24, 92-94
Lythgoe, Prof. Brian, 151

Maass, Dr. Douglas, 180, 201
Maasai tribe, Tanzania, 253, 254
Magic of Chemistry, 260
Magic of Chemistry, summary, 262
Magnesium flash boxes, 270
Magnetic Resonance Imaging (MRI), 160
Maharashtra State, India, 246
Maier family, 213
Maier, Ruth (the Anne Frank of Norway), 213
Makonda tribe, Tanzania, 253
Manchester, 9, 24, 185, 187, 188, 191, 193, 209
Manchester docks, Salford, 185
Manchester, RSC Christmas Lectures, 202, 260
Manchester Ship Canal, 185
Manchester United FC, 9, 185, 208
Manchester, Victoria railway station, 181
Manhattan Project, 263
Manzelli, Prof. Paolo, 271
Market gardening, 102-105
Marriage, to Merrilyn Muncaster, 171
Martin Mere, 24, 25
Martin-Smith, Prof. Mike, 143, 144
Martland, Alan, 89
Martland, Joe, 89, 90
Masonic Hall, Salford, 181
Mathews, Stanley, 77
Matriculation, 112
Mauveine, 267
Mawdesley, 9, 54, 79

Maxwell Building, 180, 208
Maxwell, Robert, 180, 203
Mayor family (Tarleton boatyard), 26
Maypole dancing, 36
McIntyre, A. C. W., 84
McNamara, Kevin, 155
Meccano sets, 46, 68
Media City, Salford, 185
Mee, Ann, 64
Melling, Hugh, 49
Melling, Jack, 56
Melling, Joan, 26, 60
Melling, Stephen, 25, 44, 50, 53, 59, 65, 70, 88, 89
Melling's Mill, 27, 48, 49, 51
Mennonite towns, Canada, 237
Merck, 148
Mere Brow, 70, 75, 86
Mere Brow, Methodist Chapel, 75, 86
Mersey Sound, 129
Metal hydride fires, 229, 230
Meth-Cohn, Dr. Otto, 189, 190, 205, 211, 216
Methyl isocyanate (Bhopal), 246
4-Methyltetrafluoropyridine, 168
Metronidazole, 204
Mhehe, George and Edith, 257, 258
*Michael Parkinson Show*, 87
Michlemore, Cliff, 207
Mikuma National Park, Tanzania, 253, 254
Miller, Alice (grandmother), 1
Miller, Jonathan, 284
Milligan, Spike, 86
Millionaires Row (Leigh Road), Boothstown, 200
Mince pies, 47, 48
Mines Rescue Station, Boothstown, 193
Mississippi river boat, 120
The Moguls, 248
Monaghan, Dr. John, 273
Monastral Blue, 136
Monroe, Marilyn, 151
Montgomery, Field Marshal Viscount, 31
*Monty Python*, 87
Moore, Patrick, 284
Morogoro, Tanzania, 254
Morrell, Mr, 106

Morris, John, 187
Morris Mini, first car, 188
Morris, Ronnie, 187
Mosley Common Colliery, 193
Mostra d'Ottremare, 271
Mozambique, 253, 258
*Mr Bean*, 87
*Much Binding in the Marsh*, 86
Much Hoole, 94, 95, 110
Muncaster, Cyril, 172
Muncaster, Evelyn, 172
Muncaster, Merrilyn (first wife), 171, 172
Munich, 146, 147
Munich, conference, 174, 176
Musgrave, Prof. William Kenneth Rogerson, 160-162, 167, 169, 174, 176
*Music While You Work*, 86
Myers, Ruth, 60
Myth and Magic in Modern Medicine, 153, 154

Naples, 31, 262, 266, 271-273
Naples, science fair, 271-273
Naples War Cemetery, 31
Nath Industries, India, 247
National Chemical Laboratory, Poona, 245
National Geographical Magazine, 79
National Grid, 178
National Health Service, 42-44
National Lending Library, Boston Spa, 233
National Trust, 16
Natural product chemistry, 151
Naylor, Lance, 129, 131
Naze Mount, Lytham, 24
Nazis, 213
Needler Hall, Hull, 115, 117
Neidlein, Prof. Richard, 214
Neville's Cross, Durham, 171, 173
New Holland, Lincolnshire, 155
New Inn, Durham, 165
New Palace Yard, 279
Newland Park, Hull, 144, 145, 151
New York Hotel (Hull), Cabaret Club, 129-131
New Zealand, 209
Niagara Falls, 237

Nicholas Research Institute, 143
Nicotine, insecticide, 103
Nigeria, 119, 209
Nissen huts, 115
Nitrenes, 205
Nitrogen tri-iodide, 228
*para*-Nitroso-*NN*-dimethyaniline, 150
Nobel Laureates, 215, 216
Noble, John, 185
*Noel Edmunds Show*, 207
North East Wales Institute (NEWI), 208
North Yorkshire Moors, 140, 141
Nuclear chemistry, 134, 187
Nuclear Magnetic Resonance Spectroscopy (NMR), 160
Nylons, 234, 265

Octagon Theatre, 261, 282
Odense, 214
Okafor, Benedict Ekigwe, 119, 120
Old school house, 1, 2, 4
Ollis, Prof. David, 218, 219
Oman, 256
*One Foot in the Grave*, 88
*Open All Hours*, 87
Open University, 284
Opiates, 203
Ordsall Hall, Salford, 278
Organochlorine pesticides, 191
Orme, Stan, award of Hon. DSc, 216, 218
Ormskirk, 17, 42, 107
Ormskirk Grammar School, 64
Orville-Thomas, Prof. W. J., 191, 205, 206
Oslo, 213
Ostseebad Kuhlungsborn, 245
Overseas students, 119
Owen, Dr. David, SDP, 200
Oxford University, 280
Oxidation of glucose, 267

Paderborn, 214
Paithan Dam, India, 247
Palace Green, Durham, 159, 163, 165
Palmer, Dr. Frank, 131

# SCIENCE AND POLITICS: AN UNLIKELY MIXTURE

Pancreatic cancer, 154
P&O Line, 28
Paneth, Prof. Friedrich, 167
Paragon Square, 121
Paragon Station, Hull, 114
Parbold Hill, 54
Parfitt, Dr. Bob, 143
Paris, 214
Parker, Dr. R. E., 220
Parker-Ashley, Noel, 144
Parkinson, Thomas, 29
Parkinson, Thomas Alan, 26, 29, 59, 64, 67, 70
Parkinson, Molly, 29
Parsons, Mike, 204
Paternoster lifts, 183, 226
Paterson, Dr. Tom McC., 228, 273, 275-277, 283, 284
*Pathe News*, 50
Payne, John, 123, 145
Pearson, Mr. W. P., 76, 84
Pebble Mill Studios, Birmingham, 286, 287
Peel Building, 182-184, 187, 231
Peel Park, 182
Peer reviewers, 202
Pentachloropyridine, 161, 167, 190, 191
Pentafluoropyridine, 162, 168
Percy, John, 278
Pergamon Press, 203
Perkin, William, 267
Perspex, 264
Pfizer, Kent, 189
PhD examination, mine, 143
PhD examinations, others, 215, 216
meta-Phenylenediamine, 232
*Philatelic Bulletin*, 189
Philips, Leslie, 85
Phillips, Prof. Glynn, 191, 205-208
Phoenix, Pat, 153
Photolysis, 205
Pianolos, 100
Pickervance, Bill, 44, 60, 92
Pickervance, Derrick, 26, 34, 44, 45, 60, 61, 64, 77
Pickervance, Doris, 18, 44, 60
Pickervance, Muriel, 44, 60, 91

Pickles, Wilfred and Mabel, 86
Picramic Acid, 232
Pierrepoint, Albert, 95
Pinder, Dr. Roger, 145, 171, 172
Plunkett, Roy, 263
Plymouth Argyle FC, 9
Polybromoheterocyclic compounds, 192, 204
Polybromoimidazoles, 192, 204
Polychloroheterocyclic compounds, 190
Polychloro-organic compounds, 190, 191
Polystyrene, 264
Polyurethane, 265
Pontefract, 154, 190
Poona, 214, 245, 246, 249
Porton Down, 169
Postdoctoral collaborations, 208
Postgraduate demonstrators, 148-150
Potenza, Italy, 214, 215, 250, 271
Presley, Elvis, 129
Preston, 3, 9, 10 17, 18, 23-25, 31, 41, 65, 70, 94, 95
Preston Guild, 76
Preston North End FC, 9, 18, 88
Price, Dr. Dennis, 192
HRH Prince Philip, Duke of Edinburgh, 178, 183
Procter, Prof. Gary, 211
Promotions of colleagues, 220
PTFE (Teflon), 263, 264
Publications, 209, 212
Punch and Judy shows, 85
Punting, 164
Puppet shows, 197
Purines, 205
Pye, Tommy, wrestler, 199
Pyke, Magnus, 219, 220, 284
Pyrazoles, polybromo, 192
Pyrimidines, 205

Queen Elizabeth II, Coronation, 75
Queen Elizabeth II, stamps, 189
Queen Mother's visit to Hull, 121
Quinn, Joe, 145

Radiation damage, 205, 206
Radiation sterilisation, 206

Radio in the 1950s and 1960s, 86-88
Radioactive materials, 187
Radio Caroline, 86
*Radio Fun* (comic), 49
Radio Luxembourg, 86
Rag days, photographs, 121, 123
Rag days, 120, 121,123
Raleigh bicycles, 54
Ramage, Prof. George, 180-182, 188, 190
Ramblas, Barcelona, 236
Rao, Prof. Rama, 249
Reader, promotion to (1986), 218
Reading FC, 9
Reckitt and Colman, Hull, 203
Red Lion public house, Walkden, 193
Reeperbahn, Hamburg, 237
Rees, Prof. Charles, 218, 219, 281
*Restoration*, 96
*Reveille*, 109
Ribble buses, 70, 110, 124
Ribble estuary, 24
Ribble marshes, 58, 93, 94
Richard, Cliff, 155
Ring-opening reactions, 189, 192
River Astland, 24, 25
River Danube, 212
River Douglas, 3, 25, 26, 31, 49, 51, 52, 96
River Elbe (DDR), 241
River Humber 152, 155
River Inn, 146
River Irwell, 182, 185
River Mersey, 185
River Mosel (Moselle), 146
River Rhine, 146
River Ribble, 24, 25, 31, 93
River Thames, 155
River Weir, Durham, 159, 164, 171, 174, 175
Rix, Brian, 85
Roberts, Gwilym Edffrwd, teacher, 106, 107, 113
Roberts, Prof. J. D., 160
Roberts, Prof. Stan, 211
Rochdale FC, 9
Rock and Roll, 50
*Rocking Horse Winner* (film), 45

Rodgers and Hammerstein musicals, 85
Rodgers, Bill, SDP, 200
Rodgers, Michael, 122, 129, 137, 139, 141, 142, 144, 145, 152
Rodgers, Shirley, 144
Rogan, Dr. P. J., 42, 43
Roman Catholics, 24, 99, 123, 278
Rommel, 31
Rooker, Jeff, 274
Roper, John, 200
Roscoe, Prof. Henry Enfield, 81, 209
Rose, Frank, 43
Rose and Crown public house, Much Hoole, 94, 95
Rose hips, 58
Ross, Bill, 144, 145
Rothwell, Dame Nancy, 9
*Round the Horn*, 86
Rover 90 car, 63
Royal Ballet Company, 144
Royal Engineers, 143 Field Park Squadron, 30
Royal Institute of Chemistry, 181, 201, 260, 261
Royal Institute of Technology, Stockholm, 215
Royal Institution, 260, 262, 281
Royal Institution Christmas Lectures, 260, 284
Royal National Life Boat Institute, 93
Royal Oak Hotel, Chorley, 155
Royal Signals Establishment, 148
Royal Society, 208, 287
Royal Society of Chemistry (RSC), 132, 160, 166, 202, 220, 261, 273-276
*RSC News*, 208
Rufford, 10-12, 14, 16, 24, 25, 42, 54, 79
Rufford Boy Scouts, 89, 90
Rufford Hospital, 12
Rufford New Hall, 12
Rufford Old Hall, 15-17, 24
Rumworth Labour Club, 281
Runcorn, ICI, 191
Rupert Bear, 49
Ryan, Gary, 287

Sabena Airlines, 250
Safarik's University, Kosice, 237
Safety Officer, 224 (Chapter 6)
Safety talks, 224, 225

Sailing, 197
Saint Andrew's C. of E. Primary School, Boothstown, 197
Saint Mary the Virgin Church, Rufford, 10, 11, 13, 15, 16
Saint Mary's Church, Tarleton, 3, 5, 45, 86
Saint Mary's College, Durham, 163, 165, 166
Saint Michael's and All Angel's Church, Croston, 220, 221
Saint Trinian's films, 85
Salford Art Gallery and Museum, 182, 185
Salford City Council, 185
Salford City Council, bin wagon, 229
Salford Fire Station, 229, 230
Salford Quays, 185
Salford, Royal College of Advanced Technology, 176, 177, 180, 213
Salthouse, John ('Son-et-Luminaire'), 261, 288
Salvation Army, 48
Salzburg, 147
Samphire (sampi), 94
Sark, 198
Satellite TV, 244
Sauter, Prof. Fritz, 214
Saxon jewels, Green Vault, Dresden, 242
Saxony, 241
Scarborough, 99, 122, 140
Scheinmann, Dr. Feodore, 183, 207
Schonefeld Airport, Berlin (DDR), 245
Schroth, Prof. Werner, 240
Schulze, Prof. Klaus, 239
Science Museum, Kensington, 283, 284
Science Research Council (SRC), 134, 137, 148 and 188 (studentships), 208
Scientific publishing, 202, 203
Scotland, 171
Scrowston, Dr. Mike, 149, 151-154, 205
Scrowston, Shirley, 153, 154
SDP, 179, 200
Secombe, Harry, 86
Sellers, Peter, 86
Semmering Railway, Austria, 238
Senate, University of Salford, 220

Senior Demonstrator, appointment as, 158, 160
Senior Lecturer, promotion to (1978), 218
Serotonin, 140-142
Shaw, Lt. Colonel B. D., 131
Shaw, Percy, 64
Sheerman, Barry, 275
Shingare, Dr., 247
Shorter, Dr. John, 137
Showman's Guild, 60
Shrove Tuesday, 53
Sicily 31
Silcock's Fair, 58, 59
Sinatra, Frank, 63
Skinner, Dennis, 174
Slinger's Farm, 58, 93, 94
Smalley, Dr. Bob, 205, 211
SmithKline & French, Welwyn Garden City, 204
Snell, Mr., 74, 79
Societa Chimica Italiana, Sezione Campania, 273
Society of Registration Officers, 10
Sodamide, 228, 229
Sodium cyanide, 231
Soil sterilisation, 102
Sollom, 10
Sommerville, Dr. Tony, 224
'Son-et-Luminaire', 261, 288
Soper, Donald, 98
Southport, 17, 18, 22, 25, 31, 41, 49, 53, 54, 65, 66, 70, 88, 95, 97, 101, 108-110, 125, 141
Southport, Atkinson Art Gallery, 80
Southport, bus station, 82, 85
Southport and District Cricket League, 79
Southport, Education Committee, 77
Southport fairground, 96
Southport, Floral Hall, 81, 109, 122
Southport, Garrick Theatre, 82, 85, 101
Southport Infirmary, 125
Southport, Municipal Gardens, toilets, 78, 80
Southport, Prince of Wales Hotel, 85
Southport, Promenade Hospital, 124
Southport, Swan fish and chip shop, 86
Southport Technical College, 83, 106-108, 110, 111, 151
Southport, Town Hall, 71, 80
Southport, Victoria Baths, 77, 78, 82

*Southport Visiter*, 81
Spagnolo, Prof. Pierro, 214, 250
Spencer, Prof. John, 191
Spencer, Malcolm, 201, 260
Spinnerets, 265
Spinners folk group, 130, 131
Sport, 76-79, 88, 170, 171, 197
Spurn Point, 154
Stanmore, 96, 97
Stamp collecting, 189
Stapedectomy operation, 196
Starkie estate, Bolton, 222
*Stars in Their Eyes*, 287
Stasi (DDR), 239
Stazicker, Elizabeth (grandmother), 12, 14, 15
Stazicker, Margaret (aunt), 11-13, 100, 221
Stazicker, Violet (mother), 10, 11, 13
Stazicker, William Hugh (great grandfather), 11
Stechworth Drive, 192, 194, 197, 222
Steele, Tommy, 88
Stockholm, 214-216
Stockport College – RSC Christmas Lectures, 261
Story, Tony, 167
Strathclyde, 145
Stretched purines, 205
Strickland, Roy, 84
Student Chemical Society, Hull, 117, 127, 129, 139, 140, 145
Student Chemical Society, Salford, 207, 216 (tie)
Student pranks, 137-139
Sulfur, blue, 201, 266
Sulphonamides, 43
Sunday Night at the London Palladium, 87
Sunday school, 36
Suschitzky, Prof. Hans, 175, 176, 190, 191, 205, 206, 209-213, 223, 241, 245
Suschitzky, John and Wendy, 212
Suschitzky, Judith, 210-213, 223, 241
Sutton, Dave, 9
Swedish Riviera, 237
Swedish Royal Academy, 215, 216
Syme, Bob (Inventors' Club), 285, 286

Tagamet, 204
Tanner, Elsie, 153
Tanzania, 250-252, 255, 258
Tarleton, baby clinic, 23, 67
Tarleton, boatyard (home of the Mayor family), 26, 31
Tarleton, Bowling Club, 18, 126-128
Tarleton, cinema, 49, 50
Tarleton, Co-operative store, 39, 40
Tarleton, County Council Secondary School, 65
Tarleton FC, 9
Tarleton, Fire Station, 24, 28, 67
Tarleton, Holy Trinity Church, 17, 32, 33, 36, 37, 50, 53
Tarleton, Holy Trinity C of E Primary School, 32-36
Tarleton, Methodist Chapel, 36, 88
Tarleton, Morris Dancers, 60
Tarleton, Parish Council, 118
Tate and Lyle, Liverpool, 27
Tatlow, Prof. John C., 161
Tattershall Castle (Humber ferry boat), 155
Taxanes, anticancer drugs, 152
Taylor, Joan, 73, 75
Taylor, Mollie, 86
Taylor, Wilf, 73, 75, 80, 84-86
'Teach Yourself' series of books, 83
Technical University of Vienna, 214
Teenage years, 70 (Chapter 2)
Teflon (PTFE), 196, 263, 264
Temperance, 88
Temporary Lecturer, appointment as, 161
Terylene, discovery of, 136, 137
Tetrabromothiophene, 192
Tetraethyl-lead, 264
Thatcher, Margaret, 174, 179
The Magic of Chemistry, 153, 202, 219, 260 (Chapter 8)
*The Sky at Night*, 284
The Twist, 129
*The Two Ronnies*, 87
Theatrical Pyrotechnics, 270
Thiazoles, polybromo, 192
Thiophene, 190, 216
Thiophene derivatives, 192
*Thirty Nine Steps*, 86
Thomas, Terry, 85

Thompson, Alice (aunt), 8, 11, 17, 21
Thompson, John Thomas (uncle), 3, 21
Thompson, Richard (cousin), 7, 21, 31
Thompson, William Charles, 67, 74, 84
Thurso, 279
Thwaite Hall, Hull, 115
Tinga Tinga paintings, 252, 253
Tingtinga, Edward Saidi, 252
*Tit-Bits*, 109
Titchmarsh, Alan, 286, 287
TNT (trinitrotoluene), 142, 233
*Today* programme, 278
Toledo, Spain, 237, 244
*Tomorrow's World*, 284, 286
*Tonight* programme, 207
Tonsils, removal of, 151
*Top of the Pops*, 87
Topping, Imelda, 273
Tootle Cottage, 12, 14
Tootle Lane, 12, 14
Toronto, Canada, 237
Tower Building, University of Salford, 180, 182, 183-187, 189, 226, 230, 231
Trabant cars, 245
Trafford MB Council, 68
Trafford Centre, 186
Trafford Park, 186
Travel, 236 (Chapter 7)
Treherne, Jim, 115
1,2,3-Triazoles, polybromo, 192
Tumarkin, Mr. A., ENT consultant, 196
Tunis, 31
TV programmes in the 1950s and 1960s, 87, 88
Tyndall effect, 266
Tyrian Purple, 267

UCP Restaurant, Blackpool, 60
Underground canals, 193, 194
Underhill, Alan, 139
University College, London, 111, 132, 204
University of Aurangabad, 247
University of Birmingham, 161
University of Bologna, 214, 215, 250
University of Bradford, 230
University of Cardiff, 205-207

University of Copenhagen, 214
University of Dar-es-Salaam, 215, 250, 256, 258
University of Dresden, 241
University of Dunedin, 209
University of Durham, 144, 158 (Chapter 4), 159, 165, 179, 191
University of Essex, 138
University of Glasgow, 282
University of Heidelberg, 214
University of Halle (DDR), 240
University of Hull, 54, 109, 111, 112, 114 (Chapter 3), 158, 170, 188, 202, 214, 216, 218
University of Hull, aerial photograph, 116
University of Hull, photograph of postgraduates, 149
University of Hull, photograph of undergraduates, 128
University of Keele, 176
University of Lancaster, 176
University of Leeds, 151, 261
University of Liverpool, 215
University of London, 213
University of Lund, 189, 216, 218
University of Manchester, 9, 202, 209, 261, 284
University of Manchester Institute of Science and Technology, 158, 162, 183, 186, 202, 228, 260
University of Nottingham, 131
University of Poona, 246
University of Potenza, Italy, 250, 271
University of Salford, 43, 139, 177 (Chapter 5), 220, 224, 235, 239, 251, 257, 278, 287
University of Salford, Library, 179, 180
University of Sheffield, 218
University of Strathclyde, 143
University of Vienna, 212
University of Waterloo, Canada, 237
University of West Indies, 163
University of Wyoming, 167
Unter-den-Linden, Berlin (DDR), 243
*Up Pompeii* 87
Uranium enrichment, 263
Urban Splash, 96

*Val Doonican Show*, 87
Vat dyes, 267
Vauxhall Insignia car, 63

Vice-Chancellors, University of Salford, 177, 178
Vickery, Alan, 129, 131
Victoria University, Manchester (Owens College), 209
Venkatasamy, Vijayanathan, 119
Venus, transit of, 110
Vesuvius, 266
Vienna, 213, 214, 237, 238
Viney, Dave, 129, 131
Visiting Professorships, 215
Vold, Jan Erik, 213

Wakefield, Dr. Basil, 180, 190, 192, 210, 251
Wales, 9, 10, 89-91, 93, 198, 208
Wales, Gillian, 123
Walker, Jennifer, 172
Walking Days, 58
Walkington, 152-154
War Museum of the North, 185
Warton, 93, 94
Waterhouse, Elizabeth, 172
Wayne, Phil, 23
Webster's furniture store, Tarleton, 37, 58
Weissenfels, Prof. Manfred, 239, 241
Welsh harps, 165
Welsh nationalists, 280
Welsh 'taffia', 206
Wembley, 88, 97, 98
West, Robert, 12
Westbury Hotel, London, 97
Wester Ross, 171
Western Ghats, India, 249
West Ham College of Technology, 213
West Ham FC, 88
West Lancashire Plain, 1 (Chapter 1), 17, 54, 68, 221
Westminster Hall, Jubilee Room, 275, 279
*West Side Story*, 85
*What's My Line?*, 87
Wheeler, Jimmy, 85
Whitehall Farces, 85
Whitworth, Clifford, 177
Wikipedia, 9
Wilberforce, Samuel, 280

Wilberforce, William, 155
Wildash, R.J., 239
Wilde, Dr. Horst, 243
Williams, Kenneth, 85
Williams, Shirley, SDP, 200
Wills, 199
Windsor, Barbara, 85
Winston, Lord Robert, 285
Withernsea, 152
Woburn Avenue, 222
Wolfe, Heinz, 284
*Woman* magazine, 139
Womens Institute, 153, 154
World Heritage Sites, 238, 248
Worsley, Bridgewater Canal, 193, 200
Worsley, Bridgewater Hotel, 199
Worsley, Labour Party Branch, 200
Worsley, Old Hall, 197
Worsley, the Delph, 193
Wray Castle, 89, 91
Wrexham, 208
Wrigley's chewing gum, 97
Wyman, Mick, 79
Wynn-Jones, Prof. Evan, 191

Yale University, 208
Ye Olde White Harte public house, Hull, 155
Yorkshire Ripper (Peter Sutcliffe), 239
Yorkshire Tar Distillers, 154, 190
Ystad, Sweden, 237

Zalin, Mr. H., ENT consultant, 196, 197
Zanirato, Prof. Paolo, 214, 250
Zanzibar, 255, 256
Zanzibar, Narrow Street Hotel, 255, 256
Zanzibar, slave market, 256
Zanzibar, Stone Town, 255
Zanzibar, Sultan of, 256

\* In 2014 Dr. Stephen Michael Wedgwood Benn became the 3rd Viscount Stansgate when his father Tony Wedgwood Benn died.